Creating Young Writers

Using the Six Traits to Enrich Writing Process in Primary Classrooms

Vicki Spandel

DIRECTOR AND LEAD TRAINER AT WRITE TRAITS
WITH A FOREWORD BY BARRY LANE

PEARSON

Boston ■ New York ■ San Francisco
Mexico City ■ Montreal ■ Toronto ■ London ■ Madrid ■ Munich ■ Paris
Hong Kong ■ Singapore ■ Tokyo ■ Cape Town ■ Sydney

This book is lovingly dedicated to all those teachers—
primary students included—
who are making magic happen in their classrooms.

SERIES EDITOR: *Aurora Martínez Ramos*
EDITORIAL ASSISTANT: *Erin Beatty*
SENIOR MARKETING MANAGER: *Elizabeth Fogarty*
PRODUCTION ADMINISTRATOR: *Michelle Limoges*
EDITORIAL PRODUCTION SERVICE: *Modern Graphics, Inc.*

ELECTRONIC COMPOSITION: *Modern Graphics, Inc.*
COMPOSITION AND PREPRESS BUYER: *Linda Cox*
MANUFACTURING BUYER: *Andrew Turso*
INTERIOR DESIGNER: *Karen Mason*
COVER DESIGNER: *Joel Gendron*

For related titles and support materials, visit our online catalog at www.ablongman.com.

LIBRARY OF CONGRESS CATALOGING-IN-PUBLICATION DATA

Spandel, Vicki.
    Creating young writers : using the six traits to enrich writing process in primary classrooms / Vicki Spandel.
        p. cm.
    Includes bibliographical references and index.
    ISBN 0-205-37953-2
        1. English language—Composition and exercises—Study and teaching (Primary)   2. Language arts (Primary)   I. Title.

LB1528.S67 2003
372.62'3—dc21

2003051719

Printed in the United States of America

10   9   8   [CIN]   07   06   05   04

Contents

Foreword

The word *assessment* stems from the Latin verb *assidere*, to "sit beside." When we assess anything, we sit beside it and describe it. The best tools for assessing help us describe something with such insight that we come to share a common language and common understanding that drives both teaching and learning.

In our everyday life we assess things all the time. When I take my car to the auto mechanic to get the noisy muffler fixed, I listen for that pinging sound on the way home—and that's one way I assess the work. When my daughter insists she *did* in fact clean her room, I may offer a brief assessment based on the unmatched socks behind her door. Assessment can even help people reflect on how they managed to get themselves into their present situation. Consider Louise, for instance . . .

When it comes to writing, the six traits offer us a sensible, thoughtful, helpful way to talk about words on the page. The forerunner to this book—*Creating Writers*—is not only the bible of six-trait writing, but reflects Vicki Spandel's unique ability to teach assessment in a way that drives and even inspires instruction. Her dozens of student samples and her close observations of master teachers light the way for other teachers to begin linking trait-based instruction to writing process and making the teaching of writing both joyful and effective.

With *Creating Young Writers*, Vicki's work now reaches primary classrooms. But why should we bother with assessment at primary levels? Isn't it enough that young students are writing? Must we rip their work off the refrigerator door and slice it apart? Well, the truth is that when it's done right, assessment celebrates writing, helping young writers value what they have done and repeat their success in later works. In *Creating Young Writers*, Vicki shows teachers how to look at any piece of writing and focus on the power and strengths within. The shared language of the craft she creates with terms like *organization*, *leads*, *fluency*, *detail*, and many others offers students and teachers both increased understanding of how writing works and a sense of control over that writing. Knowing the craft helps keep the ball in their court. It builds confidence—one of the best foundations for skill.

> *What we value is what we assess; therefore, what we assess should be what we value.*
>
> **—Grant Wiggins**

> *Life is a restaurant described by two elderly patrons. One says, "The food is terrible," the other, "And such small portions."*
>
> **—Woody Allen**

Years later, Louise wondered if she'd used the right rubric that night she decided to marry Neil.

From *Revisers Toolbox*, by Barry Lane, Discover Writing Press, 1998. Used with permission.

It's probably no surprise to those who know me that my favorite of the six traits is voice, the personal expression in a piece of writing, or—as a second grader once described it to me—"My tongue on the page!" Once a young writer recognizes the sound of his or her own voice, it's much easier to recognize the kind of impersonal voice that so often obscures meaning in a piece of writing. On a good day, a teacher may even overhear a student writer say, "You know, I like this story, but the first part doesn't sound like me. I don't hear my voice!" This kind of self-assessment (which applies to any of the six traits) will go much further than any grade or comment because it is fueled by the writer's own perception.

In my work teaching writing across the United States, I have seen first-hand the desire of young writers to be taken seriously, to be treated as young artists in the studio—not just students completing assignments. In *Creating Young Writers*, Vicki showcases the work of these young writers/artists, and encourages teachers to work alongside their students, in a writing workshop that features process, sharing, modeling, literature, writers' language, and positive feedback. The kind of atmosphere, in short, where assessment and instruction truly do sit side by side, each supporting the other.

In this book, you will find numerous samples of fiction and nonfiction books to help you and your students learn from master authors. In addition, you'll find practical writing lessons that combine traits with writing process, and numerous authentic student samples that show ideas, voice, fluency, and other features of strong writing emerging in the work of our very youngest writers. At a time in America where mandated testing has tempted too many of our veteran and first-year teachers to turn to formulaic writing instruction for quick answers, *Creating Young Writers* comes as a precious antidote: real writing instruction that can motivate students and boost test scores without deadening spirits.

Vicki Spandel is a writer who teaches writing. If you read her book carefully and follow its philosophy, you are likely to find yourself immersed in the world of writing, creating along with your students and going further as a writing teacher than you ever dreamed you could. As the title suggests, you will create a class of writers, and one important member of that class will be you.

Barry Lane

Preface

Danielle (Grade 1) reviews her work. Photo and caption courtesy of Tyler (Grade 4).

*S*ince *Creating Writers* first made its debut in 1990, primary teachers have been asking for a version just their own—and so this book fulfills a promise I made to my publisher and to those many teachers almost 14 years ago. The original teacher team (from Beaverton, Oregon) with whom I worked in developing the six-trait model in 1984 had not thought of teaching trait-based writing to primary students—nor had I at that time. Primary teachers, though, are among the most innovative and resourceful people in the entire world. They knew from the beginning what it took me somewhat longer (visiting primary classrooms and working with primary students) to discover—that primary students are not only strong writers but that they also learn writer's language faster than the rest of us.

Six-trait writing started as a model for assessment but quickly became much more. All this happened largely through the efforts of my mentor teacher, Ronda Woodruff, who taught fourth grade at the time (and who, in reality, taught everyone who was ever lucky enough to meet her). As a rater for our district (and then our state) writing assessment, Ronda said, "You know, I sit here reading these papers, and it's like a light bulb is going on—I am learning to be a better writer. If this is happening to me, as an adult, why couldn't it happen with my students?" She gave it a try with her fourth graders—and the results stunned us all. We saw students learn to think and speak like writers. We heard them in response groups talking about fluency, voice, leads, details, and other features of strong writing. We saw improvements in their revisions and in their drafts—and perhaps most striking of all, we saw students learning to like writing more than ever. Motivation went up. They *loved* analyzing the writing of others—other students, teachers, professional writers. They took what they learned as assessors and used it to strengthen their own writing. Literally, they took control of their writing process.

Had Ronda taught primary students herself, she would have used trait-based writing to do so, I have no doubt. Since she didn't, that leap was for others to make, but make it they did. Primary teachers across the country have searched for ways to bring a trait-based approach into their writing process and into writers' workshops. What they have found is that primary writers quickly pick up writer's language and quickly look at the books shared in their classrooms (at all writing, really) in a whole new way.

Because trait-based writing is based on acquisition of language and an understanding of how writers work, it does not replace, but only enhances, writing process. This means that teachers who incorporate the six traits into their curriculum do not need to change *any* of the good things they are already doing—reading aloud, providing time for writing, modeling writing and revision, teaching and modeling conventions, providing time for sharing, conferring with students, and so on. It is simply that now they have the richness of a common language for talking about voice, let's say, or development of details, or organizing information, or writing fluent sentences. And this common vocabulary helps everyone to see the strengths in beginning writers' work and to talk about it in a way that gives young writers confidence and understanding.

Why the need for a new book? Because beginning writers write a little differently and learn a little differently. Their writing may, at first, look like scribbles or collages of letters and letter-like shapes, and it often incorporates art as well as text. Conventional letter shapes, words, or sentences gradually appear, but even before that begins to happen, we need to recognize these young writers *as writers*. The truth is, they are writing in their heads from the very beginning. They are thinking of ideas and expressing them orally with remarkable voice and (often) memorable word choice and fluency. In time, given encouragement and opportunity to write, their capacity for conceptualizing their world and putting their own voice on those interpretations is captured on paper. They learn to write by trying it out, by writing often, by copying what they see in the environment, by listening to good literature read well, and by imitating what they hear and see—as well as, of course, turning their imaginative spirits loose. In giving them a language with which to respond to the writing of others (e.g., listening for details or voice), we smooth the path for them a bit.

For those teachers who have read and used *Creating Writers* or who know the six traits well, this book provides an extension and complement to the work you are already doing. It includes rubrics designed to capture the strengths teachers see in their young students' work, strengths that have not often been reflected in more advanced writing rubrics. It also includes many ideas for teaching trait-based writing to students within the context of a larger writing process framework. The book emphasizes

✔ Time for writing
✔ Modeling by the teacher
✔ Use of good literature to illustrate specific traits—but also to simply show our love for books
✔ Use of writer's language as a tool for helping students (and ourselves) to talk about the writing we do and the writing we love
✔ Independence—helping students to find or choose personally important topics, revise and edit their own work (once they are ready), and recognize their personal growth as writers
✔ Use of portfolios that give us a picture of student performance over time
✔ Assessment of very young writers at the classroom level

If the six traits of writing are new to you, skim through the book, and you are likely to feel right at home within a short time. These six traits—ideas, organization, voice, word choice, sentence fluency, and conventions—are familiar to anyone who writes or anyone who teaches writing. They are simply the basic qualities that make writing work. So, as a teacher, you can be sure that you are working with these traits—or some of them—as you talk about writing with your students, write comments on their papers, read to them, or model writing for them. You may call them by slightly different names, but you are using them all the same. So, within these pages, you likely will find some old friends and some ideas for making them an even better fit within your classroom.

Perhaps the writing samples I have included here will remind you of your own students' work (or your own children's work), and as you explore them, you will hear echoes of the voice, the ideas, the words, and the rhythm of the students who write with and learn with you. I hope you enjoy the journey as much as I have.

A WORD ABOUT THE PHOTOS

The photographs that appear in this book are the result of an amazing and conscientious photojournalism project conducted *by students themselves*, who set out to document writers at work. They wanted to show writers reading, drafting, revising, sharing, editing, getting ready to publish—and sometimes just exploring the world for ideas. The students who worked on this effort include those in Mrs. Arlene Moore's transitional first grade class (from Lincoln Elementary School, Mt. Vernon, Washington), who chose the subjects for the photos and created their own captions, and fourth graders from Ms. Jennifer Wallace's class (at Clyde Hill Elementary, Bellevue, Washington), who observed and documented the work of primary students through their photographs and who also created the captions to accompany what they observed. Through this project, each class gained—I hope!—increased insights into how writers go about their craft. I am infinitely grateful to these young photojournalists for their time and creativity and to the wonderful teachers who helped me to make this project a reality. Thank you from my heart.

ACKNOWLEDGMENTS

So many people have contributed to the making of this book that it would be impossible to thank them all individually, but I wish to mention some whose work and inspiration have paved the way for me.

First of all, my deepest thanks to each of the student writers who contributed personal text and/or artwork to this project. Your work was magnificent and gave me hours of pleasure. Thank you, everyone—including those whose work does not appear here. In the end, it was impossible to include every piece (we would have needed four books to do it), and choosing was extremely difficult. But in the choosing I learned more about writing than I could have learned in any other way, and so every young writer whose work passed through my hands became my teacher.

Very special thanks go to the highly talented Ms. Naomi Brautigan (grade 3), whose remarkable artwork graces the cover of this book. Thank you, Naomi, for sharing your wonderful vision with us. It is an honor to have your work embrace this book. Thanks also to Naomi's mother, Beth Olshansky, for so generously sharing her daughter's work as well as numerous ideas from her program Image-Making Within the Writing Process (housed at the Laboratory for Interactive Learning at the University of New Hampshire, www.picturewriting.org). I hope the emphasis on student art within this text does justice to your inspirational ideas.

Thanks also to the many teachers and parents who granted me the extraordinary privilege of publishing their students' work. What a rare and special gift.

I am infinitely grateful to Penny Clare (a colleague of Beth's), who taught me so very much about the use of writing in creating ideas, expanding thinking, expressing thoughts, and complementing one's work. Because of you, Penny, I will never look at young writers' work the same way again.

In addition, thanks to *all* the teachers who allowed me to visit classrooms and to work with their students and who shared their insights about the many ways there are to "make magic" within a primary writing environment. Special thanks to the incomparable Arlene Moore, my friend and colleague—and one of the best teachers I've ever had; the extraordinarily talented Lois Burdett, who continues to amaze and entertain us all; Minnie Huchinson, who spent so much time educating me about strong primary classroom environments; and Sammie Garnett, who (though she does not seem to appear in this book) is really behind every line. I also wish to acknowledge my appreciation to Ginnie Hoover, Linda Laws, Kim Gregory, Tommy Thomason and his wife Debby, Julie Ahrens, Jenny Wallace, Nancy Livingston, Merideth Croft, and the many other teachers who shared teaching ideas and helped me collect the samples of student work without which this book would not have been possible.

I also wish to acknowledge my many colleagues and friends at Great Source Education Group, Wilmington, Massachusetts, who have been so supportive of my work and who will find this book, I hope, a wonderful complement to their extraordinary resources. I am lucky to work in an environment that nurtures imagination, staffed by tireless and creative teachers. Thank you for encouraging me in so many ways.

Special thanks to Ann Marland, who always helps me behind the scenes in too many ways to describe and who makes sure that I get enough caffeine to meet the deadlines. And to May Fan, who is not only the best doctor around (she actually takes time to talk with you) but who also cares enough about education to hear my request for help—and to answer with the writings of her creative and very witty children.

My deepest appreciation to the many people who have been my mentors since the whole six-trait wild ride began: Carol Meyer, former evaluation and assessment specialist for the Beaverton, Oregon School District (It's still going, Carol!); the Analytical Writing Assessment Model Committee, whose genius launched it all; Rick Stiggins, the guru of classroom assessment who has taught me enough to fill many college textbooks and classes; Donna Flood, who always believed because that's who and how she is; Barry Lane, whose humor has kept me going through the years and who dares to write the way he speaks; Ronda Woodruff, who allowed me to teach alongside her and who can never be replaced; Margery Stricker Durham, who remains my favorite teacher—the toughest by far, the most interesting, and the best—and who may not escape this book, even though she's in Montana; Sneed B. Collard, who writes the best nonfiction books I've ever toted around; Tommy Thomason, who laughs when I tell him he writes skinny books but who does a masterful job of condensing; Donald Graves, who said bravely and truthfully that writing without voice was merely writing "to whom it may concern" and whose words have helped me keep this vibrant trait of voice alive in teachers' hearts and minds; and Jeff Hicks and Fred Wolff (along with all the other remarkable trainers at Write Traits), who care enough about six-trait writing to miss meals, sleep, and planes and who make it all come alive for teachers.

I also appreciate comments made by the reviewers of the manuscript: Wendy A. Ellis, Arkansas Department of Education; Dennis O'Connor, University of Northern Iowa; and Gladys Ross Yarbrough, Georgia State University.

There are simply no words to thank my family, so I won't even try. I'll just say thanks Jerry, Nikki, Mike, and Chris. I am so very lucky to have you all.

Vicki Spandel

1 Face to Face with the Six Traits

Andrea checks on the pumpkin grass: "Green hair is sticking up out of this pumpkin!"

We can start on the first day of school, establishing the expectation that youngsters will learn to read and write. We don't need to wait until children know all their letters, know their sound-to-symbol relationships, know how to spell all the words they want to use. We don't need to wait until children can read. Young children are writers as soon as they draw or put a symbol on paper and tell us what it says. We should call them writers and treat them as writers from that moment on.

—Marcia S. Freeman
Teaching the Youngest Writers, p. ix

My beliefs about children and writing are based on three assumptions: (1) young children can write, (2) young children want to write, and (3) young children possess the knowledge, interests, and experiences to write about.

—Carol Avery
And With a Light Touch, p. 65

*T*his book begins with the foundational belief that young children can and do write. The drive—the need to communicate with others—is a natural thing, so what we teach is not so much *doing it* as doing it *well*, doing it with *purpose*. How can we do this? By making time for writing, certainly. Time alone, however, will not do the trick—at least not the amount of time given to us. So we must teach our students to look within—within their own writing and within the writing of others. That's where the lessons lie. That's where the truth is.

Have you ever asked yourself what makes good writing work? If so, you are a critical reader—and probably a writer as well. Ever ask this question of your students? If so, you are already a six-trait writing teacher at heart. The six-trait model came about because teachers asked this question of their students and of themselves. This book can show you how to turn the answer to this question into powerful writing instruction.

Third-grade teacher Judy Mazur asked her students one day to complete this sentence: "Good writing has . . . ." According to Judy, her students had "immersed themselves in writing" for the past six months, and she wanted to get their perspectives as readers and critics. Here are their responses:

✔ Punctuation   ✔ Main idea
✔ Voice   ✔ Details
✔ A problem and a solution   ✔ Mysterious ending
✔ Interesting leads   ✔ It's understandable
✔ Good language   ✔ Conclusion
✔ Exciting characters   ✔ Title
✔ Setting   ✔ Sensory images
✔ Author's name and other
  information

Judy's students are already thinking like writers. They may not have known it at the time, but they touched on virtually every one of the traits that teachers themselves have most often identified as vital to writing success: *ideas, organization, voice, word choice, sentence fluency,* and *conventions* (Spandel, 2001, pp. 26, 42–54). We shouldn't be surprised by this. In Judy's class, after all, students read and write all the time. It's natural for them to ask the question, "What makes writing work?" both from a reader's and a writer's point of view. Further, as we can see from this one activity, Judy herself encourages this sort of reflective thinking, which heightens students' awareness. This question about what makes for successful writing, along with the answers students, teachers, and writers have come up with, is the foundation for this book.

 ## WHERE DO THE SIX TRAITS COME FROM?

Traits of good writing have been around as long as writing itself. No one *invented* them anymore than Newton invented gravity. Strong writers—people such as Sandra Cisneros, Eve Bunting, Cynthia Rylant, Roald Dahl, Maurice Sendak, Mem Fox, and Faith Ringgold—all incorporate these traits (qualities) into their writing, even though they have not been to six-trait workshops and certainly do not (so far as anyone knows) write with rubrics in their hands. The point is, the traits are not a novelty; they're simply the essence of what makes writing *work* and so are an inherent part of every piece of writing ever generated and every piece to come. It is impossible to write well without compelling ideas, some sense of structure, strong voice, well-chosen words, fluent sentences, or conventions that give clarity to meaning.

Writers (and readers, for that matter) have long had a sense of what makes writing work; they just have not (for the most part) bothered to write it down. So it is not the traits themselves that are new but the *rubrics that describe them.* It's a little like sketching a new map reflecting geographic features that have been around for ages.

The six traits that are the focus of this book were first described in detail and put into rubric form (see Appendix 1) by a group of seventeen teachers in the Beaverton, Oregon, school district in 1984. These teachers had done a little

FIGURE 1.1

Art and text combine to make meaning (Ryan, 2).

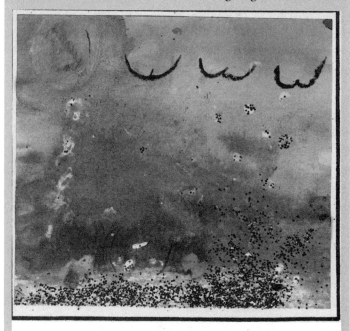

The woods in the forest are dark brown. The leaves are floating in the wind. In the woods a bird is chirping softly in the sky. The snow is fluffy and sparkles like glitter. A piece of ice blue sky is above the forest green. The snow is crunchy when a cat creeps through looking for food. While the snow rests on a tree you can hear the nibbling sounds from a chipmunk nibbling on a nut.

brainstorming of their own, but they wanted to make sure that what was in their heads matched the actual qualities they would find in student writing. To do this, they read hundreds of sample student papers and ranked them into three groups based on their effectiveness: strong, midlevel (or developing), and just beginning (in need of extensive revision). Then they documented their reasons for ranking the papers as they did. Because six prominent features influenced their rankings, their responses were translated into the first draft of what is now known as the *six-trait model of instruction and assessment*. They did not start out looking for six important writing features; it just turned out that way. If they had come up with four key qualities or eight, we would have had a different model.

The most recent version of their original six-trait rubric appears in Appendix 1 of this book. It is intended for use by students in grades 3 on up—right through college. The adapted version for primary writers (grades K through 3) appears in Chapter 8, "Assessing Young Writers." It has been modified to incorporate aspects and nuances of each trait that are characteristic of younger writers' work.

IT'S MEANING—NOT TERMINOLOGY—THAT COUNTS!

One interesting thing about writing traits is that no matter *who* identifies them (from students to professional writers and long-time teachers), common threads continue to emerge. In 1984–1985, for example, I also worked with teachers in the Portland, Oregon, public schools, who—quite independently of Beaverton—came up with their own rubric for assessing student writing. They used the same method Beaverton had used: reading, ranking, and recording. Their six traits were virtually identical. Sometimes, though common themes emerge, the traits or qualities of good writing are called by slightly different names. Yet the thinking behind those different terms is the same.

Earlier, in the 1960s, a writer-researcher named Paul Diederich (1974) had used this same reading-ranking method to answer the question "What makes writing work?" Diederich, in fact, had been the inspiration in both Beaverton and Portland. The teacher-writer team Diederich worked with identified five traits, ranked here in order of apparent influence on their thinking:

✔ Ideas
✔ Mechanics (usage, sentence structure, punctuation, and spelling)

✔ Organization and analysis
✔ Wording and phrasing
✔ Flavor (voice, tone and style, and personal qualities)

Notice that in this list sentence fluency appears as both sentence structure and style. Otherwise, the parallel to Beaverton's six-trait list is striking. In his work on the International Assessment, researcher Alan Purves (1992) and his team of educational reviewers also identified five traits (Spandel, 2001, p. 41):

✔ Content
✔ Organization
✔ Style and tone
✔ Surface features (primarily conventions)
✔ Personal response of the reader

In this set of traits, style encompasses voice, word choice, and fluency; personal response also touches on voice. Again, the match is very strong.

Recently, the state of Texas revised its state rubric to incorporate these key features of writing:

✔ Focus and coherence
✔ Organization
✔ Development of ideas
✔ Voice
✔ Conventions

Again, the links are very strong, despite slight variations in wording. *Focus and coherence* is connected to the traits of *ideas* and *organization* (in the six-trait model). *Organization* connects not only to that trait specifically but also to *word choice* (for it addresses absence of wordiness) and *fluency* (how sentences link together to create a smooth flow of ideas). *Development of ideas*, similarly, connects to *ideas* directly but also to *voice* because it touches on risk taking to promote individual style. *Voice* is virtually the same in both rubrics, emphasizing individual approach and perspective as well as audience awareness. In the Texas rubric, however, *conventions* also encompasses phrasing and fluency—thus connecting that feature to the six-trait model's *sentence fluency* and *word choice*. I use Texas only as an example; *many* state rubrics contain language that strongly reflects the six traits.

In 1984, teacher and writer Donald Murray (1984, pp. 66–67) identified his own list of six traits:

✔ Meaning
✔ Authority
✔ Voice
✔ Development
✔ Design
✔ Clarity

Murray's list is unique in that it is the only one not to include conventions in any form. *Meaning* and *development*, however, could be construed essentially as *ideas*; we could consider *clarity* part of *ideas*, too. *Design*, of course, is *organization*—by another name. And *authority* is a part of *voice*, but it also comes, certainly, from knowledge of the topic—again part of *ideas* in our rubric. *Voice* can be said, in its broadest sense, to encompass *word choice* and *sentence fluency* because it is closely connected to both.

The point is that terms are secondary. It's the concept that counts. No matter what we choose to call these key traits—and no matter whether there are six of them or five (or some other number)—*most* of us are moved by the same things in writing. So as adult readers, suppose that we were to read a piece about the history of mathematics from Charles Seife's *Zero: The Biography of a Dangerous Idea*:

> *A key clue to the nature of Stone Age mathematics was unearthed in the late 1930s, when archaeologist Karl Absolom, sifting through Czechoslovakian dirt, uncovered a 30,000-year-old wolf bone with a series of notches carved in it. . . . A wolf bone was the Stone Age equivalent of a supercomputer. Gog's ancestors couldn't even count up to two, and they certainly didn't need zero. In the very beginning of mathematics, it seems that people could only distinguish between one and many. A caveman owned one spearhead or many spearheads; he had eaten one crushed lizard or many crushed lizards. There was no way to express any quantities other than one or many [Seife, 2000, pp. 6–7].*

Do you like this piece? I do. I find it very engaging, and I'm a little surprised by my own response because my personal knowledge of math is anything but extensive. So I ask myself, "Why? Why do I like this so much?" Well, it's an intriguing idea, expressed clearly and with authority; it has voice; and it has fluency. Perhaps some people would say that it's skillfully punctuated. True. But—score one for Murray—it's the *voice* that really grabs me. It's voice that keeps people who do not normally read math books for pleasure reading *Zero*. This is the power of writing traits: They keep readers reading. But now, what does all this have to do with writing or with young writers?

 ## CREATING A VISION OF SUCCESS

As my friend and colleague Rick Stiggins reiterates consistently, "Students can hit any target that holds still for them" (2001, Chap. 1). What Rick is saying, really, is that no matter what we teach, in order to help our students be successful, we must show them what effective, strong performance looks like. How do we do this? Well, first, we must define it for ourselves. I cannot possibly hope to teach writing well if I do not know good writing when I see it. So I begin by teaching myself. I read—and I write. A lot. From a book such as Charles Seife's *Zero* I learn that informational writing can be compelling and that if it's good it will not put readers to sleep. I also learn that good informational writing is penetrable, that it makes apparently complex ideas easy to grasp. Reading has taught me more by far than most of the college courses I took on writing—and perhaps you feel that way as well. As author Stephen King tells us, "Constant reading will put you into a place (a mind-set, if you like the phrase) where you can write eagerly and without self-consciousness. It also offers you a constantly growing knowledge of what has been done and what hasn't, what is trite and what is fresh, what works and what just lies there dying (or dead) on the page" (2000, p. 150). In *What You Know By Heart*, Katie Wood Ray puts it this way: "Every single text we encounter presents a whole chunk of curriculum, a whole set of things to know about writing" (2002, p. 92).

Next, I must share my vision with students. I have several ways to do this. One is to share with *them* samples of what good writing can look like. And of course, writing comes in many shapes and forms, so I will need numerous examples: picture books, chapter books, poems, recipes, newspaper clippings, some of my own work, and some by other students, too. In addition, I must model writing for them—let them see it in action. This is a critical part of the vision because in modeling I show students both process and product, and with writing this is vital. Writing is not, after all, just about publishing. It's about getting there and making decisions along the way. And finally, I can share rubrics—rubrics that define in writing my vision of successful performance. If my students were eighth graders (or even fifth graders), I could hand rubrics out, and we could review them together. With primary students, I'll need to find some other methods. I will need to use the language of the rubrics when I talk about writing and when I share books. I also will need to use it when I talk about my own writing as I model. When I comment on students' work, I will weave in some trait language: "Alicia, your *voice* comes through loud and clear here" or "Sean, you have written a *full sentence*, and I can read every word!" or "Frances, you have used a *new word* here—*nerve-wracking*—it really helps me picture how you felt in that huge auditorium!"

This is a book about teaching writing traits to *very young writers*—writers who may not even be creating anything like conventional text yet, who are writing with scribbles and lines and pictures and imitations of print. So why share traits with them at this age? Are they even ready? Absolutely.

First, as Judy Mazur's student list shows, young writers are already thinking about writing anyway. Why not tap into that insight? Why not give form and language to what subconsciously, instinctively many already know? Children are inherently good evaluators. Some of the best. They know a good, chewy cookie from a dry imitation. They know a warm, friendly voice from one that's remote or cold. And they know a good piece of writing from one that is listless, voiceless, tired, or just plain confusing. Ask them, and you'll see. In teaching traits, we respect their skill as assessors and offer some guidance to make their senses even more acute.

Second, as Rick Stiggins has pointed out, we do it to create a vision of success for students. If we teach them what to look for in good writing, we increase—exponentially—the chances that they will write well, too. Think of these six elements not so much as traits for judging writing quality but rather as keys to writing well. If we had called them the *six keys to good writing*, people likely would have made the instructional connection immediately. This is where the *true* power of trait-based instruction lies—showing students the *keys* to writing well:

✔ Have a strong, clear idea.
✔ Use details and pictures to paint a picture in your reader's mind.
✔ Write with authority and voice.
✔ Organize your information so that a reader can follow it.
✔ Use words that make sense—and that are lively as well.
✔ Write with fluency and variety—the way good dancers dance.
✔ Make your conventions as strong as you can so that readers can figure out your message.

In short, teach your students to *look within*. Looking within is the essence of good assessment, which is not really about making judgments at all but about building understanding.

It's All About Language

At primary level, teaching traits is *mostly* about teaching language, giving students a writer's vocabulary for thinking, speaking, and working like writers. Remember, you do not need to be writing fluent sentences yourself to know what fluency is. Your ears will tell you. You do not need to write stories filled with voice to know voice when you hear it. The smile on your face, the tears in your eyes, or the chill up your back will tell you. And this knowledge will become a foundation for your own writing so that as you begin to generate stories, poems, essays, or explanations of your own, voice, fluency, and all the rest will slip in as easily as old friends slip into your house for a visit.

A QUICK REVIEW OF THE TRAITS—THROUGH THE EYES OF JUDY'S STUDENTS

If you have read *Creating Writers*, the six traits are already very familiar to you. If you haven't, this very quick review will get you started on forming some definitions in your own mind—definitions I'll help you to expand and refine in the chapters that follow through student examples and teaching ideas.

Take a closer look at the students' list at the beginning of this chapter. Let's see if we can connect that list to the six traits teachers and writers have identified. As we do so, ask yourself two things:

✔ Which of these traits is already evident in some way in *my own students' writing?*
✔ Which of these traits *would I like to teach to my students if I could?*

Connections to Ideas

Judy's students listed *main idea, details, exciting characters*, and *setting*. What do these important elements of writing have in common? They are all part of a larger concept we have come to call *ideas*. Ideas are the heart and soul of good writing, the writer's main message or story line. The main ideas and details are critical to any piece of writing; characters and setting play an important role in a story—one form of writing.

Notice, too, the students' use of the word *understandable*. This is an insightful comment. Pick up any piece of writing, anywhere, written for any purpose at all, and the very first thing that is likely to strike you is whether the writing makes sense. As basic as an element such as *clarity* may sound, it is hardly a given. Just this morning my computer warned me that I had just committed a "sharing violation." A little clarity on that one would have helped.

Judy's students also recognize that good writing has a *main idea* and *details* that create images in a reader's mind. Here's a detailed snapshot from Beverly Cleary's autobiography (*A Girl from Yamhill*) in which Cleary describes an episode with her first grade teacher, Miss Falb:

> *Once I was ordered, without being told why, to the cloakroom, where I huddled, sniffling, among rubbers and lunch bags. For weeks after that, the smell of peanut butter sandwiches made my stomach curl. Once a plump and cheerful girl named Claudine was punished by being sentenced to crouch in the dark cave under Miss Falb's desk with Miss Falb's feet in their ugly black oxfords [Cleary, 1988, p. 78].*

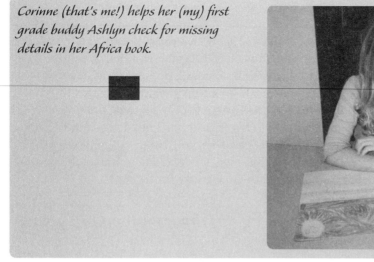

Corinne (that's me!) helps her (my) first grade buddy Ashlyn check for missing details in her Africa book.

Feel yourself cringing just a little? Smell the rubbers and lunch bags? That's clarity—and detail.

Connecting to Organization

Organization is the design and structure of a piece of writing; it holds the information together and also presents it to the reader in a way that is both comprehensible and memorable. A mystery story and a recipe may be organized very differently, but both need structure (what Murray calls *design*).

Judy's students mentioned several essentials of strong organization: an *interesting lead*, *problem and solution* (a type of structure), and a *mysterious ending* (or other good conclusion).

A good lead (beginning) is vital. Once a writer has a message or story in mind, the big question is, "How/where should I begin?" All readers know this well. If the lead is flat, readers get bored and go on to something else. *Jack on the Tracks* (by Jack Gantos) opens this way: "It was dark. Dad was driving and I was riding shotgun" (1999, p. 3). Suppose that Gantos had started his book like this: "In this book, I will explain to you, the reader, how it feels to move to another town." It's not likely that many readers would have gotten to page four. Leo Lionni's much-loved children's book, *Frederick*, opens with this line: "All along the meadow where the cows grazed and the horses ran, there was an old stone wall" (1967, p. 1). You want to know who lives under that wall, don't you? It doesn't take young readers/listeners long to learn that a good lead takes you by the hand.

Organization is also about internal structure, creating a pattern that showcases ideas effectively so that you are not just tossing them at a reader in some hodge-podge manner.

Certainly, as Judy's students noted, a good conclusion is critical. When you find a greeting card with a picture you like and then open it, what are you looking for? The punch line. It's the ending that makes any joke work. When we are disappointed in a book—or a TV show or film—what is it that lets us down? Often it's the ending. We feel our time's been wasted if the ending's not right. But when it works, we know that, too. It's sad when Charlotte (from *Charlotte's*

Web by E. B. White) dies, but it has to be that way. Spiders—even the brainy, compassionate ones—cannot live forever. Though Charlotte was dear to Wilbur, he still lost her. Sometimes, as readers, we resist the truth, but we still value it, and we recognize it when we hear it. Skilled writers know that the way you wrap up a piece of writing determines the final impression you make on a reader and often determines whether the piece as a whole has believability.

Connections to Voice

If I read a book [and] it makes my whole body so cold no fire can warm me, I know that is poetry.

—Emily Dickinson, American poet (1830–1886)

All readers respond to *voice*. Judy's students are no exception. Of all the thousands of definitions put forward for this elusive concept, I still like Donald Murray's best. "Voice," Murray says, "separates writing that is read from writing that is not read" (1984, p. 144). That cuts right to it. Voice is the quality that keeps us tuned in, that makes us feel as if we know the writer. It's a sharing of self. Voice also forms a bond between reader and writer; it creates a sense of trust. Very often I hear voice defined as personality: "It's the personality of the writer on the page." This is true, to an extent. But voice is so much more than personality. It is also confidence (that comes from knowing a topic well), enthusiasm, curiosity, and a passion for honesty that is uncompromising. As Anne LaMott reminds us, "Good writing is about telling the truth" (1995, p. 2).

Young reader-writers are among the greatest judges of voice because they have not learned to feign politeness or interest they do not feel. Read any piece of writing to a group of first graders, and you will know at once from their body language and facial expressions whether they think it has voice (or, sometimes, whether the way you are *reading* it allows the voice to come out). As we shall see from their examples, young writers virtually explode with voice. It is a natural part of who they are. In *Children's Letters to God: The New Collection*, Nan comments on how difficult it must be for God to love everyone in the world because, as she confesses, "There are only 4 people in our family and I can never do it" (Hample and Marshall, 1991).

The Link to Word Choice

Word choice is all about using the right word at the right moment. Good word choice contributes to clarity certainly, but it can also evoke feelings, moods, likes, and dislikes. Judy's students refer to *sensory images* and *good language*. For young writers, *good* language often means *new* language. As a first grader told me with some passion one day, "We're sick of words we already know. We want some new ones."

In his classic, *Amos and Boris*, William Steig tells the story of an unlikely but devoted friendship between the whale Boris and the courageous little mouse Amos. He might have written, "Boris loved how cute and sweet little Amos was. And Amos admired Boris for being so big and strong." Those words make sense, but they don't *sing*. Luckily for us, Steig wrote instead, "Boris admired the delicacy, the quivering daintiness, the light touch, the small voice, the gemlike radiance of the mouse. Amos admired the bulk, the grandeur, the power, the purpose, the rich voice, and the abounding friendliness of the whale" (1977). These words are likely to be "new ones" for many students who hear them. But they will hear and even *feel* the power when you read this magical tale aloud, and soon Steig's words will belong to them, too.

In *The Twits*, mischievous author Roald Dahl, always up for a bit of the grotesque, forces us to look closely at Mr. Twit's moustache, where we are dismayed to find "maggoty green cheese or a moldy old cornflake or even the slimy tail of a tinned sardine" (1980, p. 7). Then comes the killer line: "By sticking out his tongue and curling it sideways to explore the hairy jungle around his mouth, he was always able to find a tasty morsel here and there to nibble on." That's the power of verbs. Looking was bad enough, but Dahl's verbs force us, like it or not, to mentally probe through the moustache for the maggoty cheese.

Connections to Sentence Fluency

Sentence fluency is the rhythm and flow of language—the way it plays to the ear. Poetry, like song lyrics, is the essence of fluency when it is well crafted. Prose, however, can mimic the qualities that make those two forms of writing so captivating. Fluent sentences are varied both in length and in structure. The variety is purposeful: "Helen laughed. *Perhaps* she found my outfit odd. *Small wonder*—since it had previously belonged to a professional rodeo clown." Skillful writers find ways to hook sentences together. They also read their own writing aloud to get the sound and rhythm. Fluency is readily measured by how easy it is to read text aloud and to weave in plenty of expression as you do so. Less fluent writing is sometimes choppy or repetitive: "We ate together. It was fun. We sat on a rock. It was by the lake." Or it may be a series of thoughts linked by endless connectives: "We ate together and so it was fun because we sat on a rock and it was by the lake."

When Judy's students refer to *good language*, they may be dancing around the edges of *fluency*, as well as referring to words they like. After all, the two go together. Further, both *word choice* and *fluency* contribute to *voice*. When the little mouse Amos (of *Amos and Boris*) first sets sail, Steig describes the scene this way: "He was enjoying his trip immensely. It was beautiful weather. Day and night he moved up and down, up and down, on waves as big as mountains, and he was full of wonder, full of enterprise, and full of love for life" (1971). Notice the varied sentence beginnings, the purposeful use of repetition to create rhythm, and the masterful emphasis that goes with the parallel structure—"full of wonder, full of enterprise, and full of love for life." Sometimes we think that students do not notice these little differences on writing. They do, though. I *would* be surprised to hear second graders chatting about the effectiveness of parallel structure, but it would not surprise me at all to have one say (as second grader Marie said to me), "I like the sound of that" (meaning *Amos and Boris*).

"Yes," I said, "he writes with a lot of *fluency*." This simply gives Marie a word for describing what she has noticed anyway.

Connecting to Conventions

The trait of *conventions* includes anything a copy editor would deal with: spelling, punctuation, use of capitals, grammar and usage, and indenting or using other means to indicate paragraphing. These are textual conventions. This trait also can include manipulation of text features (for example, font size or type, bullets, illustrations, graphics) to create effective presentation on the page; these are *visual* conventions.

As the name implies, *conventions* signify what is currently acceptable. Whereas once wehadnospacesbetweenwordsforexample, we now consider such spacing essential to readability. It is all a matter of common usage, though, and conventions are ever changing. Further, conventions as I'll address them in this book begin with the simplest of traditions, such as writing from left to right on the page and making sure that the letter *E* always faces the same way. As students gain conventional skill, they can begin to concern themselves with correct spelling; proper use of capital letters, periods, versus question marks; and so on.

While Judy's students do not cover the whole range of conventions, they certainly touch on this important trait with attention to punctuation and mention of a title, as well as the author's name and other critical information. Although they do not mention spelling, capitalization, and grammar specifically, my hunch is that they are aware of the need for these attention-to-detail features of writing.

Presentation (format, layout) on the page—or visual conventions, if you will—are highly significant to many young writers, especially once they are ready to publish and to think about title pages, book covers, and so on. We should not judge a book by its cover we are told, but we most surely do, as designers are well aware. I am skeptical of anyone who claims *never* to have bought a book solely on the basis of its cover—the illustration, the font, the color, the whole look of it. The covers of Chris Van Allsburg's books invariably hook me. Even if I did not know him to be ingenious, the covers would persuade me to give him a chance. (Which book covers call to you?)

WHERE SHOULD I BEGIN?

Begin with writing, providing opportunities for your students to write often and for many purposes—even if they write only a word, a phrase, or letter string at first. Opportunity is the key. Write with them, and model writing. Create stories and poems, and share them with your students. Do not collect or assess everything; the thought of doing this will inhibit you from encouraging writing. And if you want writing to feel as natural as breathing, you must do it. All the time, every day—to think, to reflect, to recall, to record, and to create.

Begin with talking. Don't be timid about using good writers' language. Talk about the voice you hear in the books you share. Listen together for fluency, and talk about what you find. Use terms such as *detail, lead, conclusion, making connections, audience, word choice,* and *conventions.* In writing as in nearly anything we do, knowing the language of the territory is the first step to power.

Begin with reading, with sharing the books you love. In the case of primary students, the first experience with writing traits often comes from listening to language used well, from conversation, and from the wondrous experience of being read to by someone who truly believes that books are magical. If you can picture yourself, long ago, comfortably curled

FIGURE 1.2

Laura (K): The "joy" of writing.

up somewhere—on a rug or favorite pillow, in a snug chair, or perhaps resting on your elbows at the foot of the bed—and listening to a voice that lifted meaning from the page, remembering how very good that felt, then you already know what it means to teach the traits. It all springs from that treasured time.

Here's the secret: Young students *hear* the traits long, *long* before those traits ever appear in their own writing. When you ask students to describe what they picture as you read and they can do that, you have taught them what details are. You have only to give it a name. When you see students hanging on your words, waiting for you to turn the page, and they ask you to please, *please* keep reading, you have taught the trait of voice. You have only to give it a name. Soon your students will be listening for favorite words and inviting leads and conclusions that ring true—and all the things that you and they teach one another to value in writing. When you name these things, you empower your students to think and to speak like writers. It is a fine gift.

CHAPTER 1 IN A NUTSHELL

- The six traits of good writing are not an invention but simply a way of describing the qualities of good writing that have been with us as long as writing itself.
- What *is* new is the use of *rubrics*—written descriptions that capture what the key qualities of writing look like at various levels of performance.
- Rubrics may use slightly different terminology or language, but in the end, most tend to focus on similar key features, and these features of good writing should be the focus of our instruction.

- Good teaching means creating for students a vision of success. We do this by sharing samples of strong writing (often through literature) and by sharing the language of the rubrics through our comments and the way we talk about writing.
- Teach the traits through writing—simply providing time and opportunity to write—through talking—using the language of the traits yourself—and through reading—remembering that young students hear and recognize the traits in action even before those same traits show up in their personal writing.

EXTENSIONS

1. Brainstorm your own list of the qualities that you think are most important to good writing. As you do this, it is helpful to have some examples in front of

you—favorite books, articles even a sample of your own writing. Compare your list to what Judy's students wrote and to the six traits identified in this chapter. What similarities do you see? What differences?

2. Scrutinize a sample of your own writing. What traits do you think are strongest in your own work? Voice? Ideas? Fluency? Conventions? Do you attend more closely to some features of writing than to others? Why do you think this is?

3. Now look carefully at a favorite book. What are the most noticeable traits of that piece of writing? What made you choose it as a favorite? What does this tell you about the power of the traits?

4. If you are currently teaching, brainstorm a list of favorite traits or characteristics with your students. You can do this just the way teacher Judy Mazur did, by having your students complete the sentence: *Good writing has* . . . . You may find it helpful to read a favorite book or poem, or even several favorite pieces, to get the mental wheels turning before you pose this question. Once you create the list, keep it posted where students can see it, and refer to it as you share other written pieces. Your students may wish to add to the list also.

5. As you can see from the section called "It's Meaning—Not Terminology—That Counts!" people have come up with slightly different (though remarkably similar) lists of key writing traits. How would you explain the slight differences that do exist? Which of the trait lists do you feel most comfortable with? Why do you think that is?

WHAT'S NEXT?

Chapter 2 offers numerous examples of students' writing, helping you identify the key features in young writers' text and art that show development of ideas, organization of information, expression of voice, thoughtful word choice, fluency, and emerging conventions.

SOURCES CITED

Avery, Carol. 2002. *And With a Light Touch*, 2d ed. Portsmouth, NH: Heinemann.

Cleary, Beverly. 1988. *A Girl from Yamhill*. New York: William Morrow.

Dahl, Roald. 1980. *The Twits*. New York: Penguin.

Dickinson, Emily. Quoted in *Largely Literary Designs*. Yellow Springs, Ohio: Division of Antioch Publishing.

Diederich, Paul B. 1974. *Measuring Growth in English*. Urbana, IL: National Council of Teachers of English.

Freeman, Marcia S. 1998. *Teaching the Youngest Writers: A Practical Guide*. Gainesville, FL: Maupin House.

Gantos, Jack. 2001. *Jack on the Tracks*. New York: Farrar, Straus & Giroux.

Hample, Stuart, and Eric Marshall, compilers. 1991. *Children's Letters to God: The New Collection*. New York: Workman.

King, Stephen. 2000. *On Writing: A Memoir of the Craft*. New York: Scribner.

Lionni, Leo. 1967. *Frederick*. New York: Knopf.

Murray, Donald M. 1984. *Write to Learn*. New York: Holt, Rinehart and Winston.

Purves, Alan C. 1992. "Reflections on Research and Assessment in Written Composition," *Research in the Teaching of English 26*(February), pp. 108–122.

Ray, Katie Wood. 2002. *What You Know By Heart*. Portsmouth, NH: Heinemann.

Seife, Charles. 2000. *Zero: The Biography of a Dangerous Idea*. New York: Penguin Putnam.

Spandel, Vicki. 2001. *Creating Writers*, 3d ed. New York: Addison Wesley Longman.

Steig, William. 1971. *Amos and Boris*. New York: Farrar, Straus & Giroux.

Stiggins, Richard J. 2001. *Student-Involved Classroom Assessment*, 3d ed. Upper Saddle River, NJ: Prentice-Hall.

2 Looking Within: Seeing Traits in Children's Writing

Andrew (1): "Moving Day"

Children can write sooner than we ever dreamed possible. Most children come to school knowing a handful of letters, and with these they can write labels and calendars, letters and stories, poems and songs. They will learn to write by writing and by living with a sense of "I am one who writes."

—Lucy McCormick Calkins
The Art of Teaching Writing (1994, p. 83)

Writing is actually a form of thinking. If teachers who want to encourage students to be good thinkers are not using creative writing, they are missing out on the best way to get students to process information, which is especially valuable in learning.

—Bea Johnson
Never Too Early to Write (1999, p. 11)

Although we pay lip service to the idea that a picture is worth a thousand words, we don't really believe it. It's the thousand words that really interest us.

—Tom Newkirk
More Than Stories: The Range of Children's Writing (1989, p. 65)

In order to support our student writers we must know them; teaching writing can't be learned by reading a book or attending a summer course. Those are important tools . . . but the truth is that our student writers teach us how to be teachers of writing, and assessment is the way we learn.

—Kathleen Strickland and James Strickland
Making Assessment Elementary (2000, p. 66)

*J*odie, a September first grader, writes the following note:

HIo! IUS TLVNSTL WEMVDNDNW IHV A DGNMDBN I
HLPMYMOMCK

To the untrained eye (i.e., anyone not used to reading primary children's work), this may look like a jumble of letters without meaning. That's our assessment brain at work, of course. In truth, Jodie is rather an accomplished young writer. She is thinking and writing in full sentences, and combining several ideas into one note. She is even experimenting a bit with conventions, including an exclamation point for emphasis and putting spaces between sections of her note (although not as yet between individual words). To fully appreciate Jodie's accomplishments, we have only to translate her note into more conventional English:

Hello! I used to live in Seattle. We moved, and now I
have a dog named Ben. I help my mom cook.

Now we may look at the same passage and say, "Wow—how did I miss all that?" The traits of writing—the qualities that define good writing—sometimes look rather different in primary-level examples—especially those from very young students. This is why we must teach ourselves what to look for and then remind ourselves how important it is to comment on it. The commenting part is critical. It is unlikely, after all, that a primary student will sit down one day and say to herself, "Well, this is the day I put some real voice into my writing." Young writers usually do not know, unless we tell them, what qualities are exhibited in their work. Further, they trust us to see what is there and to tell the truth about it.

Look again at Jodie's original writing. What comments is she likely to receive from a teacher? How about this one:

Jodie, this is good. Now we need to work on your spelling and punctuation.

This is a well-intentioned comment, but there are some problems. First, the teacher is missing what is *right*, what is *strong*, in Jodie's work. Because Jodie cannot see these things for herself, she goes on to the next piece no wiser about what she has to build on. Wait, you may be saying, the teacher specifically said, "This is good." True. *Good* is a broad, general term, though. This kind of language works between adults because we accept at face value the fact that much of what we say has no real content, explicit or implicit. Consider how we typically greet each other:

"How are you doing?"

"Great—and you?"

This common exchange really means nothing beyond "Hello." We speak to one another from habit. We must not speak to our young writers this way, however. They need detail. If something is good about their writing, we need to tell them what it is.

Second, the reference to spelling and punctuation is likely to suggest to Jodie that these are the two things she most urgently needs to work on. Were that not the case, why would the teacher focus on it? This kind of comment, repeated often enough, will eventually teach Jodie that conventions are the *most* significant element in any piece of writing. This is not to say that Jodie does not have some work to do on her conventions. Her spelling is in a phonemic stage, prephonetic, and most of the punctuation is missing. She is not, however, ready to make all these corrections—yet. Further, her writing shows thinking, and we do not want to overlook this essential part of writing in our zeal to make things "correct." So what *do* we do? Three things:

1. Let's tell Jodie explicitly what is *strong* in her writing.

   Jodie, you are writing in whole sentences! Good for you. Guess what? I can read this even without your help. Want me to read it to you so you can see?

2. We can suggest *one* kind of addition—a writer's secret, if you will—that Jodie can incorporate into her writing.

   Jodie, now that you are writing whole sentences, I think you are ready to use periods to show where a sentence ends. This little clue helps your reader. Would you like me to show you how it works?

3. We can translate Jodie's work into conventional print so that she will be able to read it down the road. This step is optional, but I like it because it preserves text that will soon be "lost" to Jodie as her own reading/writing skills advance and the kind of writing she is doing right now becomes difficult for her to decode.

   Jodie, I'm thinking that we could save your writing about the move and your dog Ben, and I could also give you a "book" version so that you'd be able to read this for as long as you want. Would you like to see what your writing—your ideas—look like in book language?

What have we done here? We have taught Jodie to look at her writing in a different way—to see first what is strong, what is working. We have begun to add one new skill to her writing, the use of periods. She may get the hang of this on the first try; many young writers do. Or she may sprinkle her text liberally with random periods for some time to come; many young writers do this, too. Either way, it is a step forward. Third, we have honored Jodie in step 3 by suggesting that her text is worth preserving and by showing her a way of doing it that links reading and writing.

A LITTLE WARM-UP

For the sake of teaching ourselves how the six traits of writing look "in action," let's leave the primary world for a moment or two (a world in which the traits are sometimes a little trickier to recognize) and see how they play out in some examples from an older writer. You will look at two examples, A and B, and simply ask yourself the old critic's question: What's the difference? As you do so, here's a reminder list of what the six traits are all about that may help trigger some responses.

Ideas
Clarity, focus, and detail all working together to make the writer's message clear.

Organization
The overall design or structure of a piece of writing, including the lead, the flow of ideas, use of transitional words or phrases, and the conclusion.

Voice
The writer's *way* of expressing ideas—the general sound and tone of the piece, the link between writer and reader, the fingerprints of the writer on paper.

Word Choice
The words and phrases the writer selects to get the message across.

Sentence Fluency

The flow and rhythm of language, variety in sentences, natural sound, and degree to which text can be read with expression and interpretation.

Conventions

A combination of spelling, punctuation, capitalization, paragraphing, grammar, and usage (and sometimes layout or presentation) working together to make text easy for the reader to process.

Using this list of reminders, see what differences you spot between sample A and sample B.

Sample A

John felt hungry. He felt he needed something to eat soon. He was ready to eat just about anything. He was that hungry.

Sample B

John stumbled along a dusty North Dakota road headed for a town that in his mind had no name. He had not eaten in over four days, and though he had a little water left, it wasn't enough to fool his empty stomach for long. Biting his lower lip, he leaned against a fence post, turning his back to the hot wind. If he did not eat soon, he did not think he could keep walking. While he had heard of people eating grass, he was not sure whether it was really edible, or whether it could make a person sick. He thought he might have to find out for himself if something resembling lunch did not come along soon. That's when he saw the family, stopped by the road. Were they eating, or was he imagining it?

Note: Before you read the following list, write down (on a piece of scratch paper) what you notice as you compare sample A to sample B.

OK—now read the following list. Perhaps you noted several (or more) of these differences:

- ✔ Sample A relies on generalities, whereas sample B is highly detailed. (*Ideas*)
- ✔ Sample A has short, choppy sentences, whereas the sentences in sample B are graceful and varied. (*Fluency*)
- ✔ Sample B has more voice than sample A. (*Voice*)
- ✔ Sample B seems to be leading somewhere—it has a sense of growing tension and anticipation—whereas sample A seems more a collection of random thoughts. Sample B also has a stronger lead. (*Organization*)
- ✔ The words in sample B are more interesting and specific than those in sample A. (*Word Choice*)

Did you also notice some differences we missed?

THE PRIMARY CONNECTION

Now that you have had a chance to "look within" the text of an older writer, let's take it to another level—spotting signs of the traits in the writing of younger students, where those traits are not always so obvious. Keep in mind that at primary level, writing can take many forms: scribbling, playing with letter shapes, creating letter or word strings, drawing, combining text and art, labeling, listing, and writing sentences or paragraphs. We must learn to look for signs of the traits in all these various forms. A picture, for instance, may contain much detail or voice even from a young writer who is not yet producing text. Gradually, as he or she relies more on text and less on pictures to express meaning, the voice and detail shift into the text also. So an important question to ask, always, is this: "How is this child expressing himself?"

If the answer is "In pictures," look there first. If the answer is "Orally," listen. Remember, too, that students *hear* traits before they express them. In other words, a student recognizes fluency in a poem or song before she writes with fluency—even before she has a name for what she hears. Molly, a kindergartner, loves music and poetry because "That's when we get to clap our hands and move around!" This is Molly's way of responding to fluency—she feels the rhythm, she hears the beat.

TRACKING DOWN IDEAS

Writers who include detail in their work are those who have learned to be good observers—to take a close look at the world. This is what author/teacher Barry Lane calls "fine tuning the binoculars" (2001, p. 17). As we bring the world into focus, the degree of detail sharpens, like this:

Level 1 (beginning—out of focus and fuzzy)

Look! A green thing!

Level 3 (middle—coming into focus)

Hey! It's a ponderosa pine tree.

Level 5 (strong—totally focused, picking up detail)

Wow. There's a 100-foot ponderosa with a red-tailed hawk perched at the top, searching the forest floor for a mouse.

What to do with this old pair of shoes? Gadge says, "I would deliver them to the P.E. teacher and on her days off she could walk in them."

Young writers can learn to spot details and make a mental note of them long before they are ready to incorporate *all* those details into their writing. However, details often do find their way into children's drawings and into what they share orally. We must teach ourselves to look for the little details—and to listen for them—so that we can tell our young writers, "Hey! You were really paying attention. You noticed how the fins look on a goldfish (or the petals on a flower or the eyes on the face of a surprised person)."

What to Look for in Pictures

✔ *Interesting details*—facial expressions, fingers and toes, leaves on the trees, eyes that show emotion
✔ *Unusual details*—a different hair-do, things in the windows of a house, people or animals in motion, smoke rising from the chimney, waves on the water
✔ *Labels*—use of words to expand the meaning of a picture

What to Look for in Text

✔ A message that makes sense
✔ More than one statement on the same topic; for example, "I hate flies. They bite."
✔ Details; for example, "I love my dog because *she is brave* and *she can swim.* She is pretty. She has *two white paws.*"
✔ New information; for example, "Some kinds of dogs do not bark at all."
✔ A strong main idea; for example, "I love picnics" OR "I can cook."

What to Say in Your Comments

✔ I understood your message perfectly.
✔ You wrote more than one sentence on the same topic. That's what I call focused.
✔ I can picture your dog perfectly. You painted a picture for me with your details.
✔ Are there really dogs that do not bark? I did not know that! I learned something from your paper.
✔ I love this topic. Where did you get your idea?

Note: While real-life writing sometimes does call for us to write on other people's topics (an assigned letter, report, evaluation, etc.), writers also need the skill of finding and defining their own topics. If you provide the topic routinely, you will encourage students to depend on you for this. Writers do not always get assignments, topics, or story starters. They have to think. And they have to learn to spot the moments or ideas within their experience that are worthy of writing time. Yes, it takes practice. Yes, sometimes it is hard—and frustrating. The best writing, however, comes from original thinking, not from 30 clone papers on "my best gift ever." As Marcia Freeman reminds us, "We must show young writers that we believe they have something to say. We must help them tap into their personal experiences, expertise, and interests. If we select topics for them and provide many story starters, we send young writers a message: You are not able to pick meaningful topics" (1998, p. 25).

FIGURE 2.1

"Peter Pan flies to Never-land. I know he laughs and he does everything."
Thomas (K)

Some Examples

Look carefully at the samples of student writing included here, noticing any details or other signs of ideas that strike you. Do not be too influenced by my comments because what leaps out at you may not be the same at all as what strikes me. Just remember, the student writer/artist does not know what's there—yet. You can unlock the door with your comments.

In Figure 2.1, Thomas creates a brief summary of *Peter Pan*. It's a bit tricky to read because, like many primary students, he is innovative about placing text, finishing the first line in the middle and then going to line two and popping back up to line one for the ending of the sentence. You have to be patient! Notice how many letter-sound connections he makes. He is also including spaces between words. His ideas are clear and complete, and much of the content is carried by the art. Notice his use of labels. Michael seems to bear a striking resemblance to Captain Hook.

FIGURE 2.2

List of "Things I Love." Liam (K)

Lists are a wonderful way for young children to share ideas without the need for a lot of text. In Figure 2.2, Liam shares all the things he loves: snow, sun, pizza, sand, and ice cream. You can probably think of numerous innovative ways to use lists with your students: things done, remembered, wished for, hoped for. Lists at this early age *are* the writing; later, they may become a basis for writing.

FIGURE 2.3

"Dad Recycling." Meg (K)

APR 1 5 2002

MY DAD IS piting the NOSPAPR
iN the RESOCL BIN.

It is a breakthrough moment when young writers create text that we can read independently—without their help or interpretation, that is. Notice that this also increases the likelihood that the writer will recall what the text says, too! In Figure 2.3, Meg makes a simple but clear statement supported by her picture: "My dad is putting the newspaper in the recycle bin." Apparently dad enjoys recycling since he looks quite jolly about it.

When we think of detail, we long for extended explanations, imagery, sensory details, examples, and anecdotes. For beginning writers, though, we must be realistic. Any complexity of thought is welcome, especially when the writer's message clearly outstrips his spelling skills. In Figure 2.4, Ryan tells us that "Vipers are venomous and they are very fast." A deadly combination.

FIGURE 2.4

"Vipers Are Venomous."
Ryan (K)

Vipers are very vinimes. and tha are vary fass!

FIGURE 2.5   *"Moving Day."* Andrew (1)

FIGURE 2.6   *"My Room."*

The gum hangs from my ceiling. My room looks like a Pigsty. There is a cupcake on my desk that is full of fuzz. It was hard to clean up!

By Zachary, Grade 1

By grade 1, we usually see increased detail emerging both in pictures and in text. For example, in Figure 2.5, Andrew shows a very cheery and detailed picture of moving day. Start looking for the "little things" in this picture, and you will be amazed at this student's observational skills: bricks on the chimney, billows of smoke, bars on the windows, fruit on the tree and a nice hollow for nesting, a smiling sun with avant garde glasses, and of course, the use of text in the picture: "Move."

First grader Zachary has a flair for imagery. In Figure 2.6, Zachary creates a picture of his room that is vivid and anything but enticing. Want to bring out even more detail? Ask some questions: How far down did the gum hang? Was it slick or hard? Fuzzy cupcakes? How fuzzy? What color was the fuzz?

In Figure 2.7, Devon goes for originality—a trait that never receives enough audience appreciation. How nice is her dad? Why, "as nice as some pudding." There's a simile you don't hear every day. Moreover, Devon expands her writing, giving reasons for her affection: Dad takes his children out for ice cream, takes them hunting, and has (apparently) bought them a bear and video camera, the perfect gifts!

Writing is strongest when it's real. In Figure 2.8, Kurt recounts the story of being injured by a boat propeller. He has no difficulty staying focused. Notice the expanded details. Kurt manages to tell a lot without telling too much.

Prompts have their limitations, and for the most part, children do their best writing on their own topics. However, a wide-open prompt such as "The best gift I ever got" sometimes elicits remarkably personal, voice-filled writing because the writer can take it in any direction. Witness Sarah's response in Figure 2.9. Many children, of course, write about the "specialness" of a family, but Sarah gives very explicit reasons: Mom helps her find things, her brother never tattles on her, and it is easy to make Anna smile. This part of her writing is original and rings true. Dad has taken care to bury the dog (Worthless? What a great name.) in a spot where Sarah can visit him every day. That's love.

FIGURE 2.7   *"Nice Dad."* Devon (1)

ThQ Nice DaD.

You ate as NICR as some
        PUDDiNgo
Yo u TaKe us out For icecream,
and you takeme with Grampa
        to go HuNting For Birds!
a ND I like the bear

        aND viDeo camEra.

You ate the Nice DaD.

☆☺☆ Love DeVon
      ILove you DaD

FIGURE 2.8   *"The Time I Got Hurt."*
                  Kurt (2)

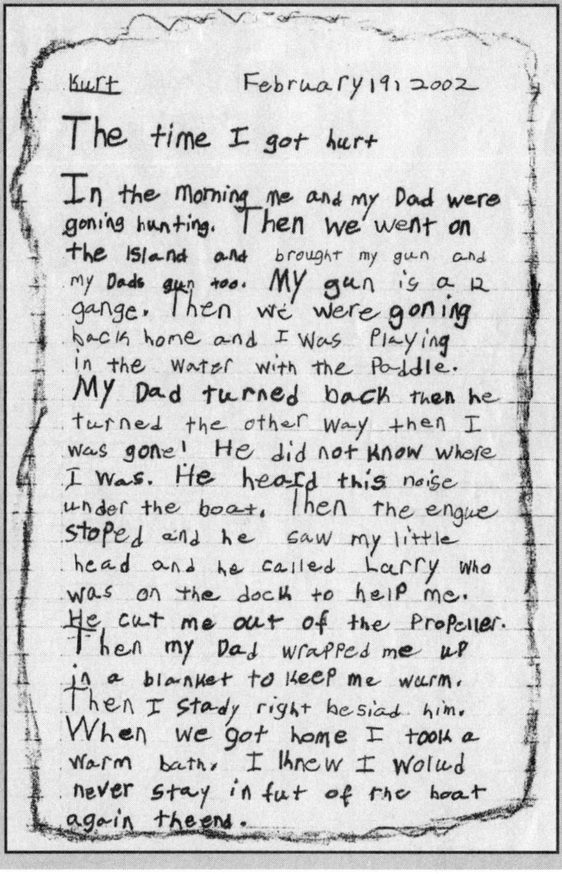

Kurt   February 19, 2002
The time I got hurt

In the morning me and my Dad were
goning hunting. Then we went on
the Island and brought my gun and
my Dads gun too. My gun is a 12
gange. Then we were goning
back home and I Was Playing
in the water with the Poddle.
My Dad turned back then he
turned the other way then I
was gone! He did not know whore
I was. He heard this noise
under the boat. Then the engue
stoped and he saw my little
head and he called Larry who
was on the dock to help me.
He cut me out of the Propciler.
Then my Dad wrapped me up
in a blanket to keep me warm.
Then I stady right besiad him.
When we got home I took a
warm bath. I knew I wolud
never stay in fut of the boat
again theend.

FIGURE 2.9   *"Special Family."*

The best gift thet I ever got was love. Because my
family is so speshel to me. My mom and dad help
me find som thing when I lost it. My brother lets
me play with him som times. He rilly never tattles
on me. I all ways make Anna smile. She is my little
sister. Molleghy all ways makes me lagh she is
verey nice to me. She is just a toddler. I had a
dog, but he dieyd I can visit him every day. My
dad baryd him in the woods. he was verey verey
old. He was back and white. My brother Sam nows
wait he look like. He has a pickcher of him. But I
keep it in my mined. Molleghy was verry little thin
when Werthles was a round. Anna did not get to
see Werthles. But we got lots of pickchers of him.

By Sarah, Grade 2

FIGURE 2.10 *Kristen's idea chart.*

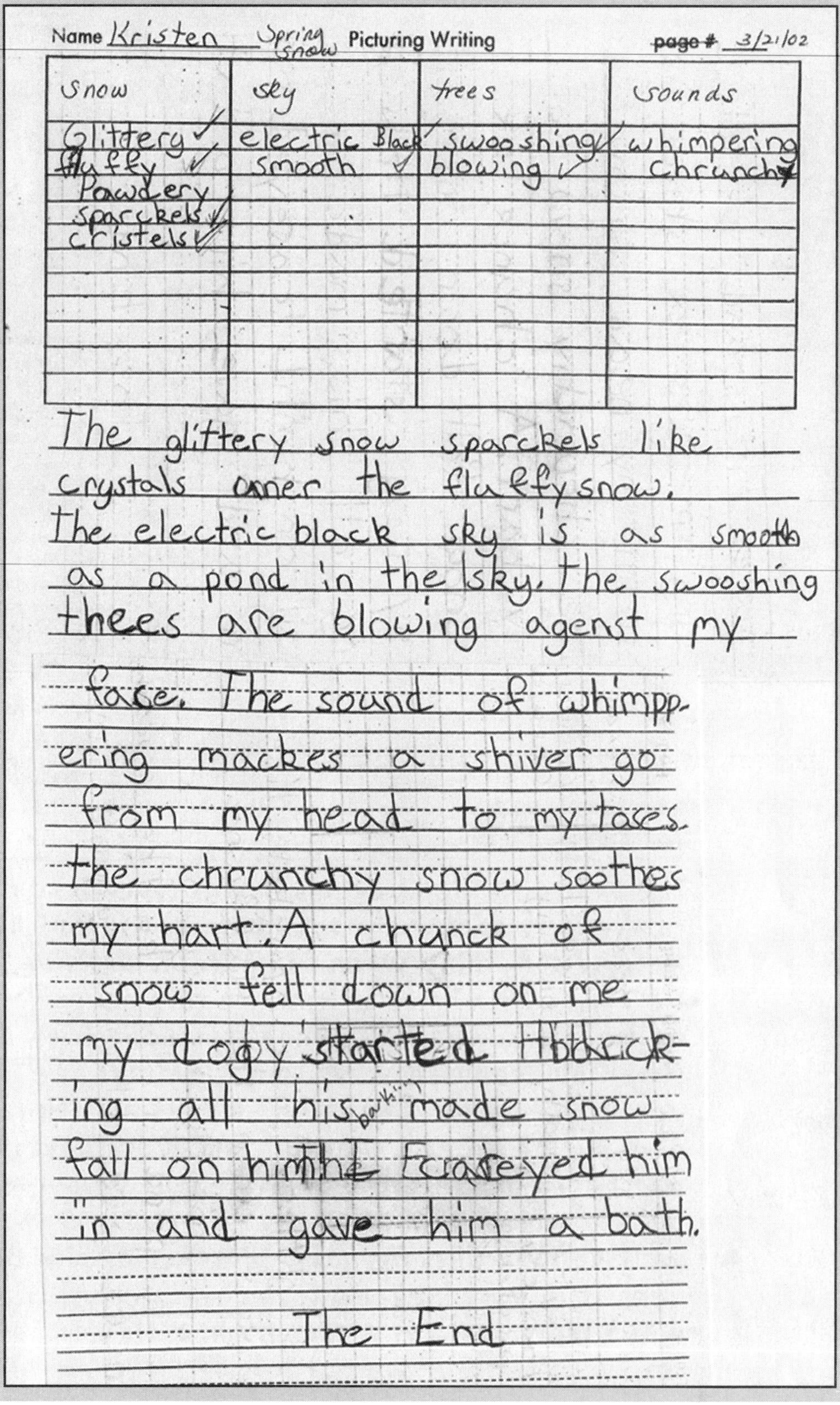

Name Kristen   Spring snow   Picturing Writing   page # 3/21/02

snow	sky	trees	sounds
Glittery ✓	electric Black ✓	swooshing ✓	whimpering
fluffy ✓	smooth ✓	blowing ✓	chrunchy ✓
Powdery			
sparckels ✓			
cristels ✓			

The glittery snow sparckels like
crystals omer the fluffy snow.
the electric black sky is as smooth
as a pond in the lsky. the swooshing
thees are blowing agenst my
face. The sound of whimpp-
ering mackes a shiver go
from my head to my toes.
the chrunchy snow soothes
my hart. A chunck of
snow fell down on me
my dog started bbbck-
ing all his made snow
fall on himthe Fcareyed him
in and gave him a bath.

The End

The question of when and how to introduce the idea of true revision troubles every primary teacher (see Chapter 5 for more ideas on this). Writing/art teacher Penny Clare uses a multistep approach that encourages students not so much to change their writing as to help it grow. In Figure 2.10 you can see Kristen's idea chart, in which she simply jotted some first thoughts. Based on this, she created a picture (Figure 2.11). This led to a rough draft, followed by the final that accompanies her picture. Art is based on detail—looking *at* and *inside* the world around us. Drawing and painting help us focus

FIGURE 2.11   *Kristen's picture.*

The glittery fluffy snow sparkles like crystals. The electric black sky is as smooth as a pond. The swishing trees and the cold wind blow against my face. The sound of my dog whimpering makes a shiver that goes from my head to my toes. The crunching snow soothes my heart. A chunk of snow fell down on me. Plop! My dog started barking. All his barking makes snow fall on him! Plop! Plop! I carried him inside my warm house and gave him a bath. Ahhh!

FIGURE 2.12   *"My Faithful Brain."* Justin (2)

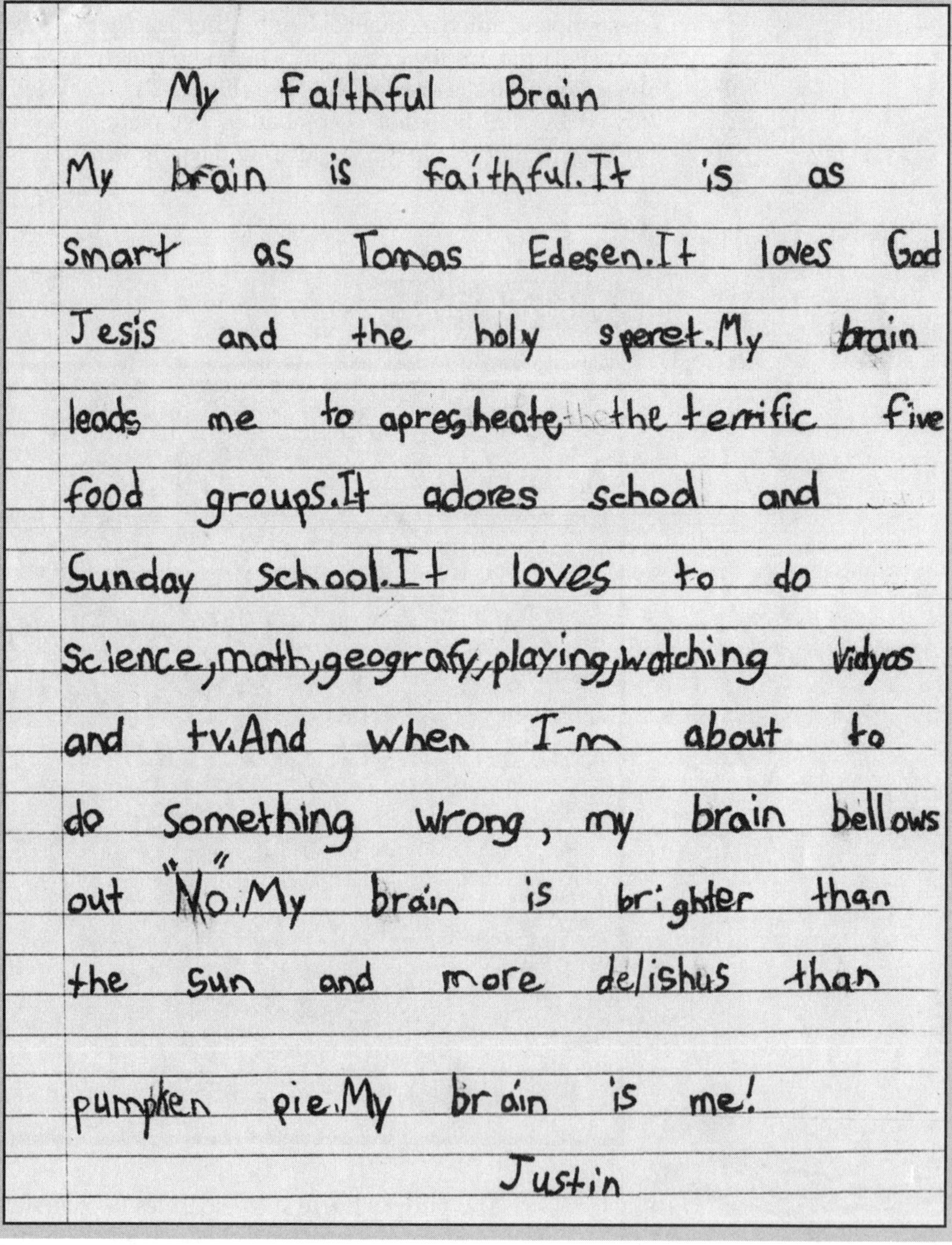

> My Faithful Brain
>
> My brain is faithful. It is as
> smart as Tomas Edesen. It loves God
> Jesis and the holy speret. My brain
> leads me to apresheate the terrific five
> food groups. It adores school and
> Sunday school. It loves to do
> science, math, geografy, playing, watching vidyos
> and tv. And when I'm about to
> do something wrong, my brain bellows
> out "No. My brain is brighter than
> the sun and more delishus than
> pumpken pie. My brain is me!
>
>   Justin

and shape our ideas. We often think of art as the frosting on the cake, but in terms of its role in guiding thinking, art is sometimes the recipe.

Justin's piece (Figure 2.12) is based on a wholly original idea, and has a kind of energy we often see when children write on personal topics. Notice how the range and clarity of details make the voice sparkle in this piece, particularly in the reference to the "terrific five food groups" and Justin's delightful description of his brain "bellowing" a warning when he's about to go off-track.

By grade 3, the ability of students to create striking imagery and sustained stories/essays is growing by leaps and bounds. Notice how Michael thoughtfully groups together images and impressions, creating a collage for us in "What I See Through My Eyes" (Figure 2.13). In an expository piece on alligators (Figure 2.14), Annie is playing with the concept of metaphor after listening to Janell Cannon's enchanting book *Verdi*. In the first paragraph, Annie feels compelled to use as many metaphors as possible, practicing this new skill. By paragraph 2, however, she has fallen into a wonderfully relaxed rhythm, using metaphor to expand meaning and to help the reader picture the cunning and skill an alligator uses in hunting.

FIGURE 2.13

What I see through my eyes

The sun
glistening on a group of trees
A storm has just passed by
Millions of pinecones
laying on the ground
silent as can be.
Snow capped mountains
in the distance
Mount Rainier sitting alone
glittering in the sun
Birds chirping
As they look for their lunch.

By Michael, Grade 3

FIGURE 2.14

"Alligators." Annie (3)

Alligators

Alligators look cool. Their color is almost as green as grass. Their tummy is like the tan desert floor. Teeth are very sharp like needles. The tail is long like the Mississippi River. Its skin is like mountains in a row. The jaws snap closed like a steel trap. Alligators are cool.

Alligators need good skills to survive. They need sharp eye sight. They have to be as still as a log when they are hunting. They are strong enough to drag their victim into the water and hold it there. Alligators have to be sly like a fox in order to know when to attack. They have to have a good sense of smelling like a dog because they rely on their smelling in the dark. Alligators are good hunters.

FIGURE 2.15 *"Black Widows."* Frances (3)

Black Widows

Black Widows are only a little poisonous. Actually only the female is poisonous. They live in warm climates such as North America, Mexico, Australia. In other parts of the world, they are called redbacks or katipos. Unlike most spiders Black Widows have no hair. The female lives up to 18 months and can have from 250 to 750 eggs. On the other hand males can only live for 25 to 40 days. There are 4 species of Black Widows. When they are ready they shed their skins. The Black Widow, Theridiidae, are only 1½ inches wide and also they have 8 eyes and legs. I used to think spiders were scary, but now I think they're cool.
by Frances

In her piece entitled "Black Widows" (Figure 2.15), Frances manages to juggle quite an extraordinary amount of factual information, yet she sustains a tone of interest and curiosity throughout. This is an excellent example of information presented clearly, but it also shows the impact of sheer enthusiasm on voice.

In "The Best Winter of All" (Figure 2.16), Naomi creates a highly detailed and complex story about a young orphan girl named Ruth, her golden retriever friend Denali, and Denali's friend Layla. Naomi's story has been reprinted in book form and is the result of a program called "Image Making Within the Writing Process" developed by Beth Olshansky at the University of New Hampshire. Naomi has used collage art both to stimulate her writing and to expand and refine her thinking during the process: "I made all my collage pictures first. Then I did my words. It was easier because when I was doing my pictures, I thought about my whole story. Later, when I looked at each picture, I saw more detail. I wrote more because I saw more things to write about."

FIGURE 2.16   *"The Best Winter of All."*

On snowy morning in the middle of winter, a lonely Eskimo girl named Ruth was walking through the deep snow. While she was walking by a pond, she spotted a lost golden retriever. She named him Denali after the tallest mountain in Alaska.

Ruth became friends with Denali. Ruth tried to teach him to ice skate on the pond. It was fun for her because she was an orphan and had no friends.

The day went by fast. Ruth and Denali were tired. They needed to look for shelter. They looked up at the full moon. Little speckles of snow fluttered down onto their cheeks. The night was cool and calm. Best of all, they could see the northern light's beautiful colors shooting across the sky.

Ruth saw an igloo under the moonlight. No one was in it, so they climbed in and fell fast asleep.

They dreamed about a big hole in the ice with a fish swimming in it. In the early morning they woke up. They were hungry for fish.

Ruth and Denali set out to go fishing. They found a hold in the ice like the one in their dream. Denali stuck his head into the hole and caught a perch.

When they got back, Ruth found two dry sticks and rubbed them together to make a hot fire. The flames were so high that they danced in the sky. Ruth and Denali watched them. Then they roasted the perch and ate it.

After breakfast, it snowed. They made a snowman. Then they jumped and rolled in the snow. They made snow angels.

They went sledding down a steep snowy hill. The snow tickled their faces.

Ruth made lunch while Denali went ice skating. Denali met a girl golden retriever named Layla. The minute they met, they liked each other.

As it turned out, Layla became pregnant.

Just as the snow was melting and the sky was becoming brighter, she and Denali had five puppies. They were born on the first day of spring.

Ruth was happy at last because she finally had a big family.

By Naomi, Grade 3

CHECKLISTS AND RUBRICS

I discovered that not only could first graders select topics, but they could also present coherent and detailed information about those topics on paper.

—Carol Avery
And With a Light Touch (2002, p. 2)

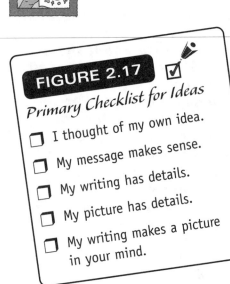

FIGURE 2.17

Primary Checklist for Ideas

☐ I thought of my own idea.

☐ My message makes sense.

☐ My writing has details.

☐ My picture has details.

☐ My writing makes a picture in your mind.

Checklists

Figure 2.17 shows a primary checklist for ideas. You may find the difficulty level of this checklist about right for your students, or you may wish to simplify it—or even add a bit more information. The checklist should grow with you; change or expand it as your student writers gain a stronger sense of what a topic is, what a detail is, and what it means to make a message clear to a reader.

Rubrics

In Chapter 8 you will find primary-level *rubrics* for ideas and the other five traits described here. Those rubrics span five stages of performance from the most rudimentary writers who are just beginning to make marks on paper through a level at which young writers not only create meaning but also expand that meaning with imagery, insight, and detail. Rubrics for older students (or those who are writing at a higher level of skill than grade level might suggest) appear in the Appendix.

SPOTTING ORGANIZATION

Organization for young writers does not usually include a whiz-bang lead, logical sequencing of ideas, and a killer conclusion. It may be as simple as the linking of picture writing with text. Do the two go together? Does each enhance the other? For some young writers/artists, organization begins with the sequencing of pictures, using more than one visual to tell a story or write an all-about paper. Sometimes drawing first helps a student writer organize his or her thoughts. Remember that in its early stages, organization often takes one of three forms:

1. Grouping things that logically go together
2. Telling things in an order that makes sense
3. Coordinating verbal writing (text) with picture writing

The addition of a title and use of the words *The End* are helpful organizational devices for young writers. In grade 8 writing we are dismayed to find students still finishing a piece with *The End*, but at primary level we value the student's recognition that an ending is needed. First things first.

As students grow in their organizational skills, and as they begin to rely on text as much as or more so than on pictures, we find other signs: multiple sentences that stay on one topic, a progression of ideas from general to specific or from the beginning of a story to the end, use of surprise at the close of a story or essay, use of a striking statement or question to kick off the writing, and so on. Even at primary level, some students become quite adept at using transitional words such as *later, then, next, the next day, another reason, first, second,* and so on. These connecting words—or *transitional words*—build bridges between ideas and need to be noticed.

For many students, listing is a comfortable method of organizing information. If you provide opportunities for creating lists—a grocery list, a to-do list, or a recipe, for example—you encourage this simple but effective way to keep track of ideas.

What to Look for in Pictures
✔ Pictures and text that enhance each other
✔ Pictures in sequence that tell a story or develop a concept
✔ Use of a title or label

What to Look for in Text
✔ Use of an introductory device such as a title
✔ Use of words that suggest a beginning: *once, one day, yesterday,* and so on
✔ Use of words that connect ideas: *meanwhile, however, then, next,* and so on
✔ Use of words that show a sense of conclusion: *at last, finally, when it was all over,* and so on
✔ More than one sentence about the same idea (focus)
✔ A progression of ideas or a pattern of some sort: comparison of two things, problem to solution, from first to last, from large idea to small, and so on
✔ A surprise ending
✔ Use of the words *The End*

What to Say in Your Comments
✔ I could follow this from beginning to end. I never felt lost!
✔ You started with one topic—*mosquitoes*—and you stayed with it through the whole paper. That's what I call being focused.
✔ This ending was a real surprise. Surprises make writing interesting.
✔ I noticed you used a word here—*meanwhile*—to connect ideas. Word bridges like this really help me as a reader.
✔ I like the way you started your paper, helping me picture the turtle. That was a good lead.
✔ You began with a problem—the short recess—and then you came up with a solution—having recess instead of lunch. That's a good way to organize information.

Comments, you may have noticed, provide a sneaky but nonetheless effective way of teaching the traits. You can work in the language of the traits (little things like *details, leads, conclusions, linking words, titles, surprise, ideas, focus,* and so on) in a gentle manner. Those words stick with your students, and each one provides one more step up in thinking about writing.

FIGURE 2.18   *"Planting a Rose."* Brock (K)

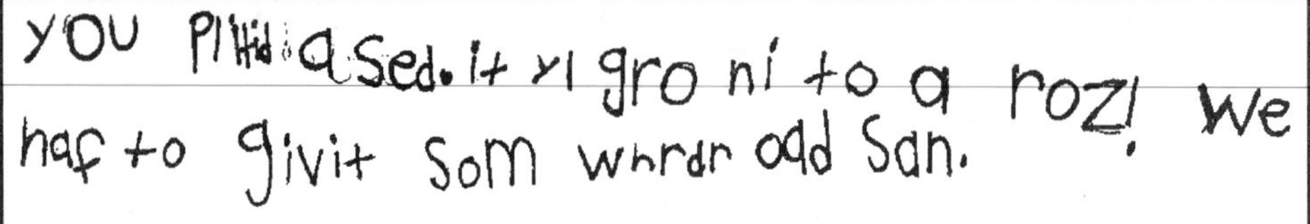

YOU PlHdiased. It rI gro ni to a roz! We
haf to givit som whrdr odd san.

You planted a seed. It will grow into a rose! We have to give
it some water and sun.

Some Examples

Kindergartner Brock (Figure 2.18) displays a wonderful sense of sequencing in a short piece on planting a rose. "Look what you've done!" this piece seems to say. "You planted a rose! Now all you need are water and sun—and soon you'll have flowers!"

In its earliest stages, organization shows itself with such simple features as coordinated placement of text and picture on the page—a spatial organization, if you will. Cognitive organization is evident through the relationship between text and picture. They "go together," we say. If you think this is a small feat to be readily dismissed, I would ask you to consider this: Professional authors (see Chapter 7) are so deft in coordinating illustrations with text that they choreograph the whole relationship like a dance, deliberately determining, page to page, which will carry the force of the message. They guide our eyes from words to pictures and back again in a delicate balance that gives us information while holding our attention. Amanda's piece on playing with her dog and bunnies (Figure 2.19) effectively illustrates picture–text organization.

Text and pictures go together beautifully in Joely's book, "What Animals Don't Do" (Figure 2.20). In her book, Joely also illustrates another highly sophisticated organizational trait—deliberate patterning for effect. Many young writers follow patterns in crafting sentences because it is comfortable to do so; for example, "I love summer. I love the sun. I love frogs." This example is a little different. Joely is using the pattern deliberately to build to her conclusion: "But I do!" The climax page is everything, and it tells us that her use of patterning is purposeful and meant to keep us on the hook.

FIGURE 2.19   *"Dogs and Bunnies."*
Amanda (K)

I AM PLAYING WITH MY DOG AND BUNES.

FIGURE 2.20 *"What Animals Don't Do" (14 pages).* Joely (K)

continued next page

FIGURE 2.20   *Continued*

continued next page

FIGURE 2.20 *Continued*

Tortoises don't go shopping.

Giraffes don't roller skate.

Cats don't do projects.

Fish don't brush their hair.

continued next page

FIGURE 2.20   *Continued*

Gorillas don't write their names.

BUT I DO!

Like many young writers, Joely uses art to stimulate her thoughts. The text is dictated but is totally hers. Sometimes we underestimate the value of dictation to capture longer or more complex messages from young writers.

Sometimes—whether we are noticing organization, word choice, voice, or whatever—moments within a piece stand out. This is the case with Justin's story (Figure 2.21), entitled, "The vakshin [Vacation]." Justin has a growing

FIGURE 2.21   *"The vakshin."*

The vakshin
Have you benn on a vokshin be for. I
went fodast in Florida it is like
California. I went shrthing thair. And I
wipt out. I frict out wine I jumpt of
the shrth bord. I will aowas rentr
wine a fish hit me with he's fin and I
tho th it wse a shark.

By Justin, Grade 1

The Vacation
Have you been on a vacation before? I
went four days in Florida. It is like California. I went surfing there. And I wiped
out. I freaked out when I jumped off
the surfboard. I will always remember
when a fish hit me with his fin and I
thought it was a shark.

sense of what a lead is and introduces his paper with a question. I particularly like the ending: "I will always remember when a fish hit me with his fin and I thought it was a shark." What he is really saying is, "*This* is the moment I remember most." I was delighted that he dared to finish without a cliché wrap-up: "I hope we go back to Florida next year!"

How-to papers are naturals for teaching organization. Although step-by-step structure certainly is not the only organizational pattern writers need, it is a refreshing change from chronological patterning, and it is a fairly simple one for most students to understand because it's easy to tell when steps are left out or are written out of order. Notice the thoroughness of Felicia's instructions in "How to make a snowman" (Figure 2.22).

Andrew's story "Honey Cat" (Figure 2.23), is well-ordered and filled with fresh details. For example, Honey has "wobbly stripes," and "She let me pull a little on her tail. That's not common about cats." I love the conclusion, in which Andrew lets us know that though Honey Cat now belongs to his grandparents, she was his first. Within his first paragraph lies a dynamite lead. Given a bit more experience, Andrew will likely "hear" this himself and will dare to pick right up on those last two sentences; for example, "With more than a foot of snow on the ground, the cat was lucky to find the horse barn." Would I suggest this lead to Andrew right now? No, not exactly. However, because he has so many strengths to comment and build on—fluency, voice, order, detail—it doesn't hurt to toss out one suggestion. I might say this: "The last two sentences in your first paragraph *really* caught my attention—wow. Like the start of a chilling mystery story. I was wondering what would happen if you started with these details—the snow and the cat hunting for the horse barn." Then what happens *happens*. But it will be his, not mine.

FIGURE 2.22   *"How to Make a Snowman."*

First, I would make three snowballs. one small, one medium and one big. second, put the big snowball on the bottum, medium in the middle, and small snowball on the top. next, I would get a carrot for a nose. I would stick it in the middle of the small snowball. Then I would get small rocks for the eyes and mouth. then I will get a hat that doesn't fit me. or you can get any hat. do the same thing with the scarf. Then I would get small rocks again for the buttons. Next, I would get two sticks and stick it in the middle. do it side to side. That's it.

By Felicia, Grade 1

| FIGURE 2.23 | *"Honey Cat."* |

Last Christmas, I was at my grandma and grandpa's house. Every Christmas we go there. They live on a farm. A cat was abandoned by their house. There was more than a foot of snow on the ground. The cat was lucky to find their horse barn.

I was doing chores with my grandparents when I first saw the cat. She had black, white, and brown wobbly stripes. When I saw her the next morning, I thought of a name for her. The name was, "Honey," because she is my little honey. I fed her every day I was there. She let me pull a little on her tail. That's not common about cats. She liked me petting her with strokes from her neck down to her tail. Honey followed me wherever I went but not inside the house.

Honey is now their cat, but at first she wasn't. She's sort of like my cat when I'm there. I kiss her sometimes, because I love her.

By Andrew, Grade 1

Written by Andrew Hicks, May 26, 2001, as a story assigned by Mrs. Giles, his first grade teacher.

In Figure 2.24 we see another of those great "moments." This is only a portion of Kaylee's longer paper about a broken mirror. I was amused by her extraordinary lead; she's exasperated with the old standard "Once upon a time" and charmingly interacts with the audience to let us know that she will find another way to begin.

Why do we not encourage students more often to collaborate as authors and illustrators? We should because when students get together, as Ashley and Shelby did (Figure 2.25), remarkable things happen. They talk, for one thing. And for young writers, talking is among the most effective prewriting (and writing) techniques. They share ideas, feed off each other's imaginations, and share responsibilities for writing and illustrating— just as published writers and illustrators do.

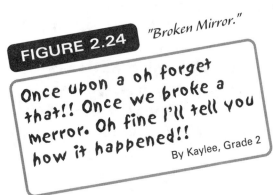

| FIGURE 2.24 | *"Broken Mirror."* |

Once upon a oh forget that!! Once we broke a merror. Oh fine I'll tell you how it happened!!

By Kaylee, Grade 2

FIGURE 2.25 *"We Love Volcanoes."* Ashley and Shelby (K)

Alec cuts right to the heart of the matter with his introduction to the paper "Foxes" (Figure 2.26): "A fox appears in the moon's silvery shadows." This is enticing and masterful.

Pearson takes a bit longer to launch into his story "Fishing in Alaska" (the story really begins with the second paragraph), but once the action begins, it moves at high speed (Figure 2.27). Notice his skillful use of present tense, which gives this story a sense of immediacy. Everything is happening right now! Short sentences (and one fragment) build a kind of tension and energy that give this story wonderful voice.

FIGURE 2.26   *"Foxes."*

A fox appears in the moon's silvery shadows. His orange bushy fur keeps him as steamy as an oven. Hail started to rapidly fall as the fox leaped off through the brisk night. He lunges on a squirrel and dashes to his den. He curls up in a ball as his tail fades away from the dim light and takes a rest from a long day.

By Alec, Grade 3

FIGURE 2.27   *"Fishing in Alaska."*

Hi, my name is Pearson. You are about to hear about the most exciting day of my life.

It's about 8:00 in the morning. I'm going halibut fishing with my dad, my uncle, and my grandpa. We're at the fishing spot. What's this? My dad has one! He's brought it onto the boat. Its tail is slapping frantically. It's a giant sixty-five pounder! It's as big as me!

The waves are crashing over the boat. I'm up. It's raining ice cold rain. I'm freezing. I've got one! It's extremely hard to reel it in. Finally it's over. It's on the boat. Thirty pounds.

My grandpa is seasick so he can't fish. My uncle catches one that weighs thirty pounds, too. My uncle and I catch two more thirty pounders. We go home and have some hot chocolate.

By Pearson, Grade 3

FIGURE 2.28   *"The Day I Got My Dog."*

> The day I got my dog we were really only supposed to be looking. My mom, my dad, and I got into our car and drove down to PetCo (where they sold rescued dogs on Saturdays) and went in to have a look. There were a lot of dogs to choose from.
>
> We were looking around when we saw an adorable puppy in one of the cages. We immediately knew that he wouldn't be there the next Saturday—so we got him.
>
> When we got home, we ended up calling him "Puppy" all day because we couldn't think of a name for him. Then, when I was about to go into my room to go to bed, my mom came down the hall and said that my dad had thought up a name for our dog.
>
> "How about Tucker?" she asked. I agreed and we still have him today.
>
> By Max, Grade 3

Max begins his story "The Day I Got My Dog" (Figure 2.28) so gracefully that it's easy to overlook how effective his lead really is. When he tells us "We were really only supposed to be looking," we know at once what will happen. Notice the conclusion: It doesn't hang around on the back porch—it says a quick goodbye and exits. Max already has a good sense of what to leave out of a story as well as what to put in. Sometimes we do young writers a disservice with the old standard line: "Tell me more." More isn't always the answer, and it usually is not what we really want either. It's the "right" details that count—and this writer not only includes them but puts them in an order that is easy to follow.

See Figure 2.29 for a primary checklist for organization.

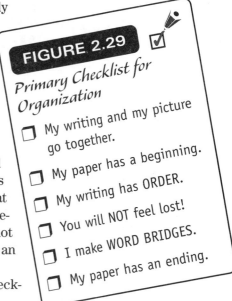

FIGURE 2.29

Primary Checklist for Organization

☐ My writing and my picture go together.

☐ My paper has a beginning.

☐ My writing has ORDER.

☐ You will NOT feel lost!

☐ I make WORD BRIDGES.

☐ My paper has an ending.

ON THE HUNT FOR VOICE

Voice is among the most rewarding traits to teach at primary level because, first of all, it shows up in both picture forms of writing and text writing. Pictures have personality, appeal, individuality—all the attributes of voice. Second though, primary writers tend to be uninhibited in their expression, and lack of inhibition usually promotes voice. In short, this is an area where you can often reward young writers who struggle in other areas—such as organizing writing or using conventions correctly. Remember the wisdom of Donald Murray, who reminds us to build on *strength*:

> *The responsive teacher is an encourager, and there are two important reasons for that. One is that the student doesn't know what is good, what has potential, what is working any more than the inexperienced student [knows] what doesn't work. We learn to write primarily by building on our strengths, and it is important for the teacher to encourage the student to see what has potential, what has strength, and what can be developed [Murray, 1985, p. 157].*

> *Don Murray says the role of the teacher of writing is to laugh and cheer. I try to remember his advice as I listen to writers talk about their writing [Carol Avery, 2002, p. 66].*

Voice is expression personalized. Any time you look at a picture and say to yourself, "Oh, this *has* to be Todd's work," you know it has voice. Of course, sometimes we recognize voice without knowing the artist/writer at all. A picture may make you laugh (or cry). It may be haunting—or may cause you to connect to a memory of your own you thought was buried. You may find yourself mentally characterizing it: It's whimsical, silly, honest, frightening, or stunning. If it creates an emotional response, it has voice. When we say a piece of writing or art has voice, what we really mean is that it speaks to us—somehow, in some way.

In text, voice takes many forms, too. A text may stand out from the others, and that kind of individuality is a form of voice. It is distinctive, unique perhaps. It may also strongly express the writer's feelings: anger, frustration, amazement, worry, whatever. Because voice is personal, it tends to emerge more strongly in certain types of writing (although writers with powerful voice cannot be held down by form). Voice blossoms in personal narrative, persuasive writing, complaint letters (and, really, letters of all kinds), role modeling, journals, and memoirs. A set of directions is less likely to encourage voice, but this is not to say it cannot happen, as in this student's tip: "If the horse you're drawing looks more like a dog, make it a dog" (Lewis, 1994).

Voice also comes from caring about topic, and audience. Bored writers have little or no voice because their hearts just aren't in it. Lucy Calkins says, "When writers learn to listen for the voice of a story, to look for language with a little luck in it, we approach writing with a different sort of expectation. Instead of expecting ourselves to write silly, short texts, we hold our subject in our hands and say, 'This is going to be huge.' We expect to layer our writing with the deepest, richest parts of our lives" (1994, p. 259).

My litmus test for voice is always the same, regardless of the piece or the age of the writer: *Would I share it?* If the answer is "yes," I know that the piece is strong in voice. Think of the writing you love to share aloud with your students, the books that are favorites (for them and for you). Those books are rich with voice. What works for professional writers works for your students as well.

What to Look for in Pictures
✔ A distinctive or unique style or approach
✔ Emotions, as expressed on the faces of characters, for example
✔ Humor
✔ Passion, as expressed through color or style
✔ A piece you would like to share with others

What to Look for in Text
✔ Strong expression of feeling
✔ Text that makes you feel like laughing or crying—or that gives you the chills
✔ Text that makes a connection to a personal memory
✔ Text you remember—and think about
✔ Text you would like to share with others
✔ Text that communicates directly with the audience—for example, a question: Do you like vegetables? Have you ever been to California? Are you afraid of snakes?

What to Say in Your Comments
✔ I loved reading this. I read it twice. *That's* voice.
✔ I could really tell how you felt when your dog ran away.
✔ I had to read this aloud. Then I could *really* hear your voice.
✔ You write like you mean it. I like that.
✔ You write as if you care how the reader feels.
✔ I can tell you care about this topic and you want me to care, too.
✔ This sounded like you and no one else. That's a sign of voice.
✔ This moment right here (point it out) really caught my attention.

Voice is like springtime in March. One moment it's powerful; you feel the sun on your shoulders and smell change in the air. The next—whoosh, the March wind blows, and the moment is gone. That's OK. Moments of voice are indicators of good things to come—and the writer's voice, like the sun, will return. Nurture it. Make sure that you let students know which moments, specifically, have the most power. Writers rarely sustain voice every moment through an entire piece of writing; that takes about as much energy as doing aerobics all day long. It's hard to be on stage 24/7.

Some Examples
In Sarah's paper "Best friend's" (Figure 2.30) we hear strong emotions emerging. Notice the capital letters on "Sad Ending" and "Tears Dripped." Check

FIGURE 2.30 *"Best Friends."*

Once when I lived in Dover I had a best friend named Kristen. She let me go to her Bday partys. We always got surprised. One time a storyteller came and gave us a lot of candy. We had a very good friendship togather until a Sad Ending came. Tear's Dripped from our eyes. I was moving after this day. Every one I new gave me going away presents. Even Mrs. B who was old and lived across the street from me. She really meant alought to me. I will always miss her so. I will always Remember her in my Life. and the day I met her. She was special because She always made my day special.

By Sarah, Grade 2

out A. A. Milne's *Winnie the Pooh* and you'll find capital letters on most significant words. Capitals signify importance. I love the line about Mrs. B: "I will always miss her so." You don't just hear the voice there—you *feel* it.

FIGURE 2.31 *"A Good Friend."*

I really miss my best friend Alyssa she moved to Philadolphea. I think a good friend is someone who can defend you. Alyssa and I meet in kindergarten. We are now pen pals. We had lots of play dates. We would play with my dog. A friend that make's me play with them all the time is a person I don't like. To have a best friend I think you need to know that person for a wyhill. Friends allways cheer me up when I'm in the dump's.

By Kris, Grade 2

Papers about best friends tend to bring out voice with young writers because feelings are strong. It's even better when the writing includes some strikingly original comments, as is the case with Kris's piece (Figure 2.31). She tells us that a good friend "is someone who can defend you." Notice, too, that Kris thinks for herself: "A friend that make's me play with them all the time is a person I don't like." Writers with voice are writers with opinions.

Expressive language often contributes to voice. Wait a minute, though—isn't that word choice? Yes, but because the traits are closely linked, it is hard to change one without affecting the other. Lilly (Figure 2.32) increases the voice in her piece when she calls *Anne of Green Gables* "an old classic" or refers to "fire-burnt red hair" and "wide imaginations" and most especially in her closing line: "Her imagination inspires mine."

Voice is passion, certainly. It's spontaneity, too. Notice how the two combine in Jana Leigh's paper (Figure 2.33). It was the Friday before Mother's

FIGURE 2.32 *Review of Anne of Green Gables*

Dear Mrs. R,

The book I am reading is an old classic and it is called Anne of Green Gables. Anne reminds me of Peppie long Stockings. Anne reminds me of her because they both have fire-burnt red hair and have wide imaginations.

  I liked this book because it has a lot of excitement and Anne is sort of energetic and happy all of the time. Her imagination inspires mine.

Always,
Lilly

By Lilly, Grade 3

FIGURE 2.33 *"No Mom's Allowed."* Jana Leigh (K)

Day, and the kindergarten class was making Mother's Day cards. Jana Leigh was worried because her mother worked as a school secretary. What if she should burst in and see her card ahead of time? Her teacher, Debby, helped her come up with a solution: How do you keep unwanted people out of a room? A sign, of course. Jana Leigh's sign reads "No moms allowed in this class unless you don't have a child in this class. No. Knock." She doesn't add "This means you," but we can read between the lines. Her illustration shows a fist knocking on the door with sound waves emanating.

Alyssha's teacher has just lost her mother and is feeling the pain of that loss. In a heartfelt letter (Figure 2.34), Alyssha assures her that all will be well because her students are so close to her they are like her brothers and sisters. Who could fail to take comfort in such a message?

| FIGURE 2.34 | *"Dear Mrs. Choffnes."* Alyssha (2) |

Date: 4-2-9-02

Cheer up!

Dear Mrs. Choffnes I
know how it feles when
some won dieds. I tos
sad when my gradpa
died he dident ever
see me. We go to his
grave a lot and
bring him a bastest of
flowers. I am sorry
for you. But you have
us as you dont hafe
to cry. We are
your sisters and brothers
so you have lots
of brothers and sisters,
So you have friends and
family. - Alyssha

| FIGURE 2.35 | *"What Hurts my Feelings Most."* |

What hurts my Feelings most is
when people scream at me. I HATE
IT!! It makes me want to punch
them in the face but my dad said
not too. Some times when people
scream at me it makes me cry. My
sister screams at me all the time
but when my sister screams at me
some times I have to punch her. I
do not now why, just because. I
just hope no one screams at me.

By Morgan, Grade 2

Nothing contributes more to voice than flat-out honesty, the kind of frank honesty expressed in Morgan's paper "What Hurts my Feelings Most" (Figure 2.35). You can sense the force of Morgan's feelings from the capital letters, the exclamation points, and the simple but to-the-point disclosure: "It makes me want to punch them in the face. . . ." This is a real-life paper, written from the heart. It is sad and angry at the same time. The voice bites. A paper like this can make a teacher uncomfortable because it is not a fluffy topic (What if you woke up one day and discovered you were the tooth fairy?), nor does it have a happy wrap-up. Yet it is just what Morgan needed to write at this time, and if we honor those feelings and provide an environment in which it is safe to be honest about anger or sadness, we encourage real writing with real voice. And after all, it's better to *write* about

FIGURE 2.36   *"The Bad Day."*

The time when I had a bad day I setet a tantrum. I screming in pels erys. It wusen't a dazzling day for me. Puey I didn't get frens. No TV ether. Its not far that my druther gets good day. I don't like that. Not I sied n-o-t wich prte bo you not understad like that.

By Sujaytha, Grade 1

The time when I had a bad day I started a tantrum. I [was] screaming in people's ears. It wasn't a dazzling day for me. Phooey. I didn't get friends. No TV either. It's not fair that my brother gets [a] good day. I don't like that. *Not, I said n-o-t which part do you not understand* <u>like</u> that.

FIGURE 2.37   *"Only a Dad."* Amity (1)

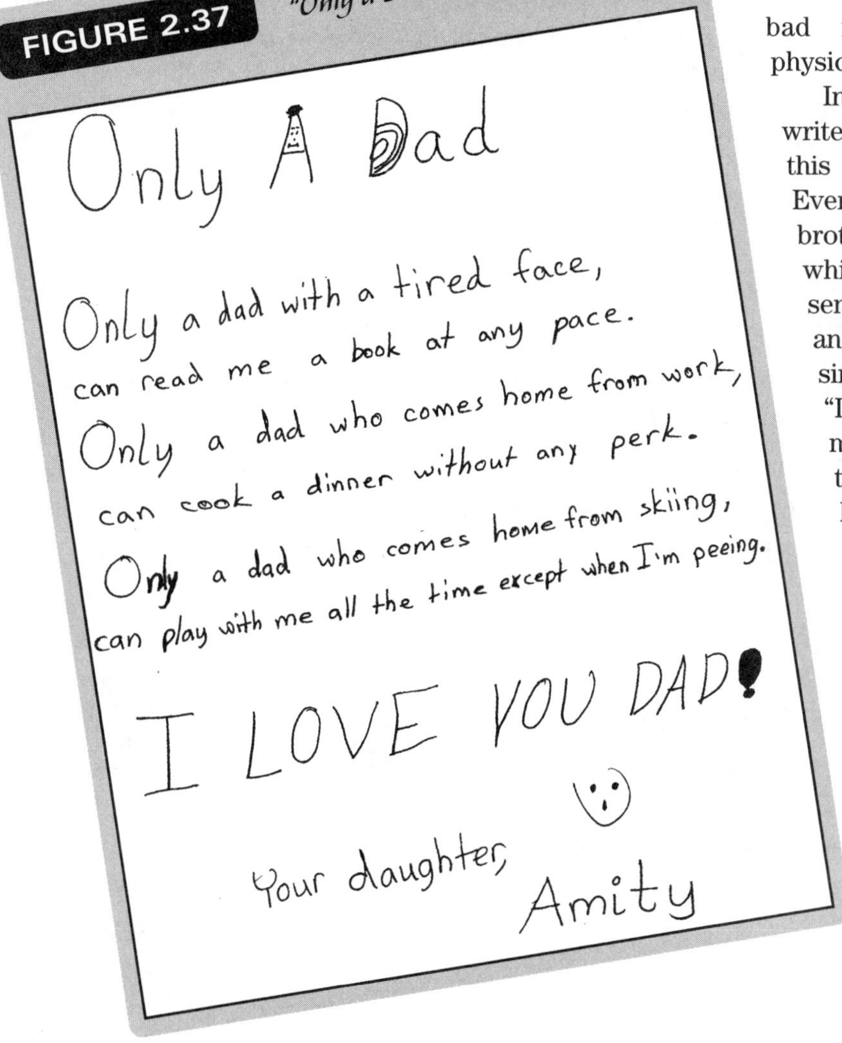

Only A Dad

Only a dad with a tired face,
can read me a book at any pace.
Only a dad who comes home from work,
can cook a dinner without any perk.
Only a dad who comes home from skiing,
can play with me all the time except when I'm peeing.

I LOVE YOU DAD!

Your daughter,
Amity

bad feelings than express them physically.

In "The bad day" (Figure 2.36), writer Sujaytha expresses more anger, this time at the unfairness of life. Everything seems to go fine for the brother (Isn't that always the way?), while Sujaytha struggles with resentment, cut off from friends and TV. We have all experienced similar feelings, and if the line "It wusen't a dazzling day for me" found its way onto one of those filing cabinet magnets, a lot of us would buy it. When we identify and empathize, that's voice.

Amity's poem "Only a Dad" (Figure 2.37) expresses voice in both text and art—neatly combined in her original lettering. The real secret to the voice in this one, though, lies in Amity's clear and deep sympathy for Dad, who is nearly too tired to read but does it anyway and manages to cook dinner— even if it's "without any perk."

Following the reading of Janell Cannon's book *Verdi*, students in Cindy's class were invited to do some imitative writing, and Tommy chose his green math book (Figure 2.38) as his focus. Notice how the voice shifts in this piece, gaining momentum. At first, the book is a "source of learning." Very scholarly, very formal tone here. Later we learn that "the darn thing is thick and heavy!" Just as we suspected. Tommy tells us that "math books are wonderful," but he can't live with this untruth and confesses at the end. My favorite part.

FIGURE 2.38   "Math Book."

My math book is a source of learning. It is verdi. Verdi means green. My math book is made of paper. The paper is glossy. Its cover is dense. It's as hard as wood. The darn thing is thick and heavy! Math books are wonderful. Don't you think so, too? (The 2nd to last sentence isn't true.)

By Tommy, Grade 3

The theme of Amy's paper (Figure 2.39) seems to be "Why does everyone else get the spotlight—especially when I am the interesting one in the family?" This paper is not as angry as Sujaytha's (see Figure 2.36), but it has a definite strong undertone. Amy clearly appreciates the "funny moments" in her parents' videos but also questions why they have overlooked her; it's this attitude that makes her voice strong and individual. Notice also the abundance of details—the frosting-coated finger and dad's big feet. When writers notice small but significant details, we say to ourselves, "Ah, I can really see *and* feel that," and the voice soars. Detail is part of ideas, but serves as a building block for voice as well.

FIGURE 2.39   "Home Videos."

When my sister was born she was funny. I know this because I wacthed Home Videos. These are some things she did: At Christmas she showed my mom her mad face. She grabbed her dress and waiked, for a second. When my mom asked her to show her her happy face she smiled. When my brother was one, when he just turned one that is, he stuck his finger in his cake and did nothing with the frosting on his finger. He also put on my dads shoes wicth were two times bigger than his own feet. Those were some funny moments. My mom and dad tape recorded them. But from what I saw there wqsn't much about me when I was a baby. I didn't see my first birthday tape recorded.

By Amy, Grade 3

FIGURE 2.40 *An Embarrassing Moment.*

It's Halloween! can I have my costume. Im Dorth. Im going. I wint to the frst haes. Im at the the last haes. Tat haes hase a cut scar crol. You have a cut scar crol I saed to the latey. Thacs! Saed the scar crol. That wus the most endarsin momit. I Jupt 3! Fee! are wun was lafen. I awes have inbarsin momits. No wun haes inbarsin momits. Then I fown out its not truw. I dot fill so bad inney more.

By Morgan, Grade 2

It's Halloween! Can I have my costume? I'm Darth. I'm going. I went to the first house. [Now] I'm at the last house. That house has a cute scarecrow. "You have a cute scarecrow," I said to the lady.
"Thanks!" said the scarecrow.
That was the most embarrassing moment. I jumped three feet! Everyone was laughing. I always have embarrassing moments. No one [else] has embarrassing moments. Then I found out it's not true. I don't feel so bad anymore.

Aaron looks back at his story while Hailey listens to see if the story is good.

Photo and caption courtesy of Peter (Grade 4).

Morgan, a second grader, is struggling a bit with conventions (Figure 2.40), and when this happens, there is always a risk that the voice will be buried. With a little decoding, we uncover a well-crafted story about a personally embarrassing moment—commenting on a scarecrow that turns out to be a live person. The story ends with a bit of philosophy, too; the writer thinks no one else has embarrassing moments then learns that this is not so. Here is a paper that needs a fair amount of work on conventions, but we can give this writer some real incentive by taking Donald Murray's advice and showing appreciation for the strengths we see: insight and voice. Have someone read it aloud to you, and you may be startled (like the writer herself) by the detail, organizational flow, *and* voice.

As noted earlier, letters bring out voice. Carly (Figure 2.41) is writing to the school secretary on learning of her (the secretary's) mother's death. Carly puts her whole self into this piece. There is not one shred of artificiality. Not one line is routine or borrowed. She is completely, wholly herself. This is the epitome of voice. Notice the original and strong language, too: "glum for the rest of her sole breaking life."

See Figure 2.42 for a primary checklist on voice.

FIGURE 2.41 *"Dear Mrs. Baker."* Carly (2)

Dear Mrs. Baker,

I know how you feel! Once I was four and I went to visit my unbelievabl great great aunt and she died, two or three months later. When she died I felt like a once contented and proud swan who lost its feathers. Instead of swimming with the other beautiful swans she just stayed in the pussywillos and long green grass, glum for the rest of her sole breaking life. When my teacher Mrs. Burdett broke the news to us about your dear mom, it was heartabe to hear. I know you will never forget your mom, I'm sure she meant the univurse to you!

Love, Carly

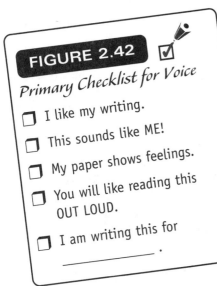

FIGURE 2.42 ☑

Primary Checklist for Voice

- ☐ I like my writing.
- ☐ This sounds like ME!
- ☐ My paper shows feelings.
- ☐ You will like reading this OUT LOUD.
- ☐ I am writing this for
  _____ .

Pieces with this level of voice deserve oral reading and deserve to be read with passion. Read slowly and put your heart and soul into it. That's what the writer did, and her work can only come alive with the best interpretive reading your skill and ear for language will allow. Don't be timid! Give back to Carly in the same generous spirit she has given to us.

IN SEARCH OF WORD CHOICE

When I share books with children, they may describe them as "expressive," "delightful," "outrageous," "fantastic," or my favorite, "rememberable." Unfortunately, these words often do not make their way onto paper. On paper, the same books become "good," "fun," "sad," or "cool." There goes the air out of the balloon.

Very young students often are capable of striking, extraordinary word choice; it may show up primarily in their speech, however not in their *writing*. Don't despair. Encourage what you *hear*, and do some team writing that allows children to express themselves orally and to use the full power of the vocabulary that lives in their minds. Create word walls and personal dictionaries that will put expressive words—the words young writers would prefer to use—right at their fingertips. Be a recorder for your students (so that they can use their oral vocabularies), or let older writers fill this role; they will learn from each other. And don't forget to comment on those early blossoming bits of word choice when you find them.

What to Look for in Pictures
✔ Striking labels or titles
✔ Speech (often enclosed in a bubble)
✔ Language woven into the picture—for example, via signs

What to Look for in Text
✔ Words of *any* kind!
✔ Words you can read and make sense of
✔ Words that replace old, tired standards—for example, something other than *nice, good, fun, cool, neat, really, very*
✔ Strong verbs—the heart of good writing
✔ Words that paint a picture
✔ Sensory words that help you hear, smell, feel, or touch the moment
✔ A stretch to use a new or unusual word
✔ The right word at the right moment—for example, "My socks were *soggy*" (compare *wet*)

What to Say in Your Comments
✔ This is the perfect word—*slimy*. I can feel that myself!
✔ Right here you said, "I raced home." *Raced* is a powerful verb. It has energy.
✔ Your word choice—*creepy, scary*—really gives your paper voice.
✔ I think this word—*delicate*—is a new one for you. I love it when you use a word you haven't used before.
✔ Every word you used made sense to me and helped me understand your message.
✔ You write as if you love words.
✔ I hope you put *zoom* in your personal dictionary. I like it.

FIGURE 2.43 *"My Old Car."*

> This is my story. It's about my old car. It ues to go ccagubop titik crakcrak. Tase because it was vary old. We use to have it. Bet we sal it. Now we have a new one. I ♥ my new car.
>
> By Abby, Grade 1

> My Old Car
> This is my story. It's about my old car. It used to go cagu-bop tick-tick crack-crack. That's because it was very old. We used to have it. But we sold it. Now we have a new one. I ♥ my new car.

Remember that spelling has nothing to do with word choice per se. Many young writers use powerful words they cannot spell yet. It is fine to share correct spelling as you comment on a word as long as you do not make spelling the focus of the comment. One good way to do this is to add the word to a student's personal dictionary. What you want the student to notice is that he or she is using words in a powerful way, words that have meaning, words that get a reader's attention. When students think spelling is the primary goal, they will fall back on words they know, and then everything will become *sad*, *fun*, and *nice* again.

Some Examples

Word choice does not have to be serious all the time. We can enjoy Abby's playfulness in "My old car" (Figure 2.43). "Cagu-bop tick-tick crack-crack." Ever have a car like that? You might sell it, but like Abby, you won't forget it.

The action in sports papers encourages the use of strong verbs. We certainly can see this in Matthew's paper "Basketball" (Figure 2.44). After a fairly routine beginning, Matthew's paper springs to life: "I zoom down the cort. I nailed a three ponter. Swoosh." Go, Matthew!

Jesse was given an idea chart to fill out but wrote nothing. Despite that, she came up with two strong descriptive words—*glittery* and *fluffy*—in her draft (Figure 2.45). Strong words are like hugs. You don't really need 50 to be happy; often one or two will do you. Teach yourself to cheer for each good choice your writers make, and let them know which words get your attention.

"Kangaroo News" (Figure 2.46) has several things going for it—one of them word choice. We learn, for instance, that the "poor kangaroo could not get any relaxation." Andrew hasn't quite got the spelling of this word

FIGURE 2.44 *"Basketball."*

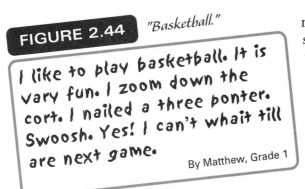

> I like to play basketball. It is vary fun. I zoom down the cort. I nailed a three ponter. Swoosh. Yes! I can't whait till are next game.
>
> By Matthew, Grade 1

down, but what is important is his use of it; it's just right. We wouldn't want him to say, "The poor kangaroo could not rest" just to get the spelling right. We also find out that the other animals would not listen because they were too "rud [rude]." Again, the perfect word. Did you notice the fluency in this piece? True, it is missing periods. Andrew will learn to put those in. For now, notice how smooth the phrasing is and how easily this writer glides from thought to thought [edited version]: "He tried to ask the other animals to be quiet, but they pretended to not hear him. That made the kangaroo very mad, but that didn't stop him. No sir! He kept on trying. He asked and he asked. . . ." This writer already has a good ear for how words should go together. When you get a paper like this, do not mourn the missing periods; read it aloud first so that the writer can hear the flow. *Then* you can say, "I'd like to give you one writer's tip [i.e., periods] to help show where these strong sentences begin and end." Also notice how Andrew's ending builds anticipation for the next installment; this is good organization!

In "Cat's" (Figure 2.47), Yong Jin, a first grader, uses repetitive language, not at all unusual at this age. We value variety but sometimes look for it too soon. Particularly in second-language students or in reluctant writers, certain words—because they are familiar—become "comfort words." It is natural to repeat them, and they can help build confidence, a vital

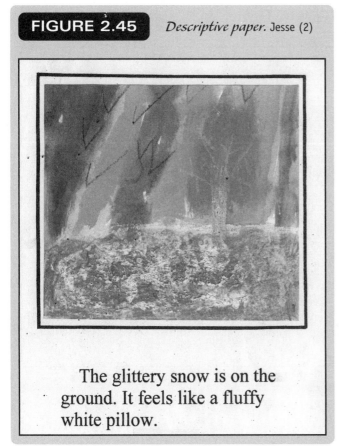

FIGURE 2.45　　*Descriptive paper.* Jesse (2)

The glittery snow is on the ground. It feels like a fluffy white pillow.

FIGURE 2.46　　*"Kangaroo News."*

There was a kangaroo. He lived in australia. And it was very nosiey the poor kangaroo could not get any relacksashon. He tried to ask the other anmals to be quite but the preted to not hear him that made the kanaroo very mad but that didn't stop him no ser he ceped on trying he asked and he asked but the other animmales did not lishen to him they were to rud so see how he stops them in my other kangaroos' news.

By Andrew, Grade 1

FIGURE 2.47   *"Cat's."* Yong Jin (1)

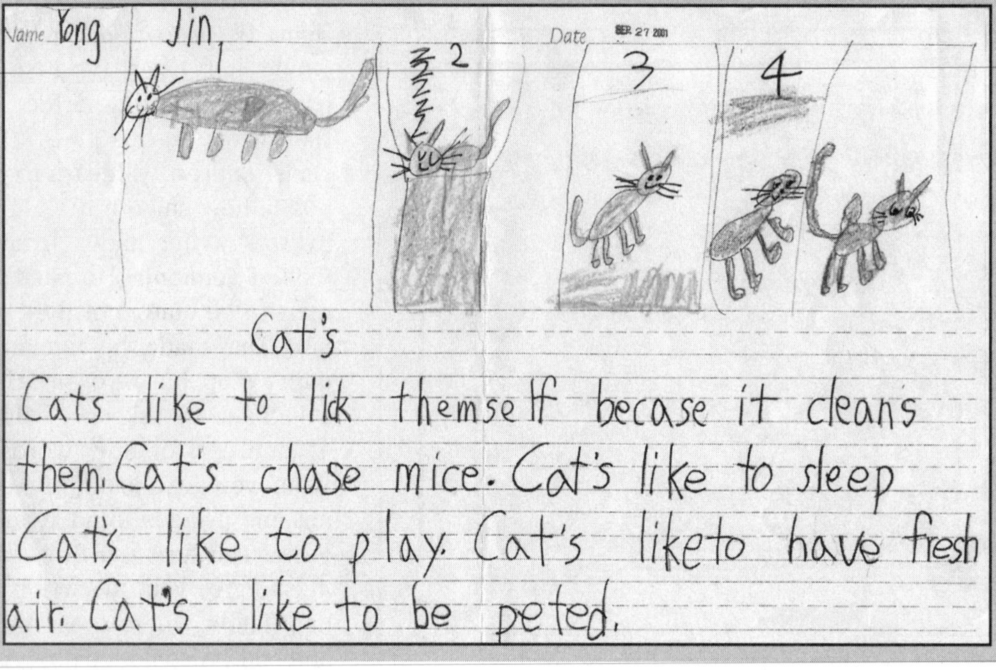

Name Yong Jin   Date SEP 27 2001

Cat's

Cats like to lick themself becase it cleans them. Cat's chase mice. Cat's like to sleep Cat's like to play. Cat's like to have fresh air. Cat's like to be peted.

FIGURE 2.48   *"Red Wolf."* Brandon (2)

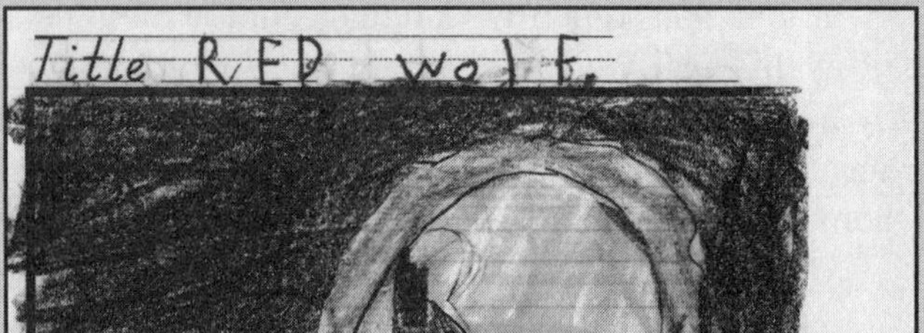

Title RED wolf.

they have black
babeys thet look
like pupes. if
a wolf dosent
respekt the pack...
....he get's ckit
out of the pack.
they live in a
den. they aet rabbits.

stepping stone for any writer. Here is where a personal dictionary can be a huge help. Ask the student what he or she might like to say about cats—or any topic. Make a list of key words in large print. These can go on a large-sized Post-It note right on the corner of the paper. This makes it easier for the writer to incorporate them with ease. Soon new words become comfort words, too. Notice the picture sequencing in this piece. The picture-text coordination is very sophisticated.

As readers, we value words for different reasons. In "Red Wolf" (Figure 2.48), Brandon makes an exceptional word choice—*respect*—to show how each wolf must respond to the pack. It is helpful to say, "I learned something important from this word." It is not just that we *like* the word; it is the *right* word. Precision is an important element of word choice. Notice that Brandon's teacher has written some text on the page—with Brandon's permission. She writes words as he reads his paper to her. These are not corrections. She is interjecting "book text" so that Brandon will be able to read his own writing down the road, and of course, he can use her words for reference, too.

FIGURE 2.49   *Someone Special.*

I Know someone speshul. Only I can see him. He comes out at night. He sems to gloow at me. He wishes throow the trees. He slivers throow the grass. And he maks rippels in the wataer. And he blose with the wind. He's not the swan who swims and drinks from the siver lake. He's not the wind snak who glads with the wind. He's not the grat bear paw that bealogs to the bear of the wild. He's not the butafull flower with one leav and the switist neckter. And He's not the sparkulling purple rock.

By Jamie, Grade 1

I know someone special. Only I can see him. He comes out at night. He seems to glow at me. He swishes through the trees. He slithers through the grass. He makes ripples with the water and he blows in the wind. He's not the swan who swims and drinks from the silver lake. He's not the wind snake who glides with the wind. He's not the great bear paw that belongs to the bear of the wild. He's not the beautiful flower with one leaf and the sweetest of nectar. He's not the sparkling purple rock.

(Revised and edited version shared courtesy of Beth Olshansky, who holds copyright to Jamie's published book, *Someone Special*.)

FIGURE 2.50   *"The Last Snowman."*

Lots of packing.
Three circles tracking.
Two eyes and a carrot nose.
Without any toes.
A scarf, a pipe, and buttons of blue.
Sticks for arms and a black hat too.
Oh no, oh great—
Warm weather here, a snowman's fate!
He's melting, he's dripping,
His body is tipping.
Its hat falls down.
Propping on the snowy wet ground.
He melted. He's gone.
A big puddle in our lawn.

By Conor, Grade 3

Figure 2.49 shows the rough draft (and polished final) from the first two pages of Jamie's book *Someone Special*. This extraordinary example shows us so well why we must read beyond spelling to appreciate the nuances of word choice. In this case, words create energy but also vivid images: "seems to glow," "swishes through the trees," "slithers through the grass," "not the wind snake," "not the great bear paw," and so on. Precise meaning is one reason to appreciate word choice; the beauty of the words themselves is another.

It is not often that a very young student can go for the rhyme and still come up with particularly strong word choice. Conor is the exception: "Lots of packing. Three circles tracking" (Figure 2.50). What an image this is. Then later: "Oh no, oh great—Warm weather here, a snowman's fate!" and just after that: "He's melting, he's dripping, His body is tipping." The rhymes

FIGURE 2.51   *"Sister."* Miles (3)

Sister   Miles

Anonying sister,
bragging   sister,
mad   sister,
mean   sister,
kicking   sister,
poking   sister,
weaird sister,
spying sister,
yelling sister,
But I still love her anyway.

FIGURE 2.52   *Book review.*

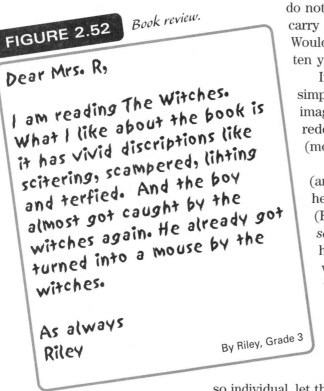

Dear Mrs. R,

I am reading The Witches.
What I like about the book is
it has vivid discriptions like
scitering, scampered, lihting
and terfied. And the boy
almost got caught by the
witches again. He already got
turned into a mouse by the
witches.

As always
Riley

By Riley, Grade 3

do not seem forced because the words are just right to carry the meaning. They're playful, too, and add voice. Wouldn't you love to see a poem by this writer in about ten years?

In Figure 2.51, Miles, a third grader, illustrates a simple way to use a word collage to create a multi-image poem. His sister does not seem to have many redeeming qualities, but of course, he's joking (mostly), as we discover in the last line.

Students learn many new words from reading (and being read to), so it is not surprising that we hear some of them in a book review like Riley's (Figure 2.52). Riley is captivated by *skittering*, *scampered*, *lightning*, and *terrified*—and now that he has used them in his book review, perhaps they will show up in other writings. Asking students to tell you specifically which words they like is one way to encourage exploration.

Some striking phrases appear in "The Blizzard" (Figure 2.53): "family huddled together," "their voices melt in the weather." "Trees have hard times." When you come on a phrase like this, so individual, let the student know: "I have never heard this idea ex-

FIGURE 2.53 *"The Blizzard."*

The blizzard, happening
That was enormous as my
Family huddled together
In the living room.
Few people were outside,
Even if they shout as loud
As they can, their voices
Melt in the weather.
Ponds are frozen,
Trees have hard times
Babies cry in houses
Horses whinny in barns,
Dogs whine and howl.
Their owners they to settle
Them down. I huddle close
To my parents, they calm
Me down. I wish for a
Magic pebble. Nothing
Happens. So, we drank
Soup and went to bed and
Wished good luck for
Tomorrow.

By Celia, Grade 3

FIGURE 2.54 *"Champions."*

Tension mounted as the kick-off drew
near all was scilent exept for
murmers from the crowd
    Jacob (middle forward) passed to
Trent (left fororward) who took it
up-field, but a Cosmos player booted
it down to our end, and I passed to
Jacob who bolted to their goal, shot,
and SCORED!
    They penetrated our defences only
once. How they got in the
championship is beyond me.
    We scored twice more then the ref
blew his whistle in a shrill, sharp
blast. The lightning croud went wild.
WE HAD WON!

By Max, Grade 3

pressed quite this way." Celia's way of sharing her thoughts is unique, and telling her this could give her the courage to be even more adventurous.

Max clearly loves strong words: "murmers from the crowd," "booted it down to our end," "bolted to their goal," and "penetrated our defences." He holds our attention from first to last. I particularly like "How they got in the championship is beyond me" because it rings with voice. This expression reminds us that everyday words can be used with style. Notice how much strong word choice adds to the lead: "Tension mounted as the kick-off drew near...." What a contrast to the more common "Last Saturday we had a game." I was a little confused about whether the team was playing football or basketball, but I loved the action either way.

See Figure 2.55 for a primary checklist on word choice.

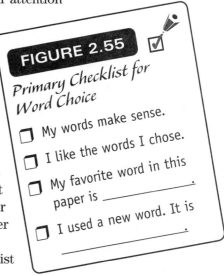

FIGURE 2.55

Primary Checklist for Word Choice

☐ My words make sense.

☐ I like the words I chose.

☐ My favorite word in this paper is _____.

☐ I used a new word. It is _____.

STALKING SENTENCE FLUENCY

At the primary level, one of the first things to look for is use of sentences. Period. That's it! Students speak and think in sentences long before they write them, so getting a sentence—even *one*—on paper is a victorious moment and should be recognized. As students gain skill and confidence, they develop a kind of generative fluency. They just write a *lot*. This too is a victory. You may not feel celebrational when you are reading three pages of text that you do not find particularly interesting. Perhaps you should, though. Look at it this way. We want students to feel a certain comfort level with writing, as if writing were a natural part of everyday life, which it should be. This comfort comes, in part, from writing often and writing a lot. Never mind that not every phrase or sentence is profound. The writer is gaining a sense of balance, much the way a beginning biker does.

Early on, expect to see patterned writing from young students: "I like my dog. I like school. I like my house. I like math." Short, choppy, repetitive sentences would seem to be just the opposite of what we are looking for in fluent writing. This is so, but it is only a first step—like making your way across a river rock to rock. Remember: Look for the positive. The student is writing in multiple sentences and quite possibly imitating a pattern she has heard in oral reading. The student's repertoire of patterns will expand as her ear improves and as she is exposed to more sophisticated text. No wonder what we choose to share aloud with students matters so very much.

As students gain more skill, they usually break free of this repetition, saving it for emphasis and effect. Then the writing looks more like this: "Of all the things in my life, I love my dog the most. I also like school, especially math." This is breakthrough writing—combined ideas and varied rhythm. Some of this can be taught directly; some must rely on example.

Powerful writers and powerful speakers have two wells they can draw on for that power: one is the well of rhythm; the other is the well of vocabulary. But vocabulary and a sense of rhythm are almost impossible to "teach" in the narrow sense of the word. So how are children expected to develop a sense of rhythm or a wide vocabulary? By being read to, alive, a lot! [Fox, 1993, p. 68].

What to Look for in Text*

✔ Appearance of sentences (whether written in conventional text or as letter or word strings)
✔ Use of multiple sentences, whether patterned or not
✔ Use of varied sentence beginnings
✔ A mix of statements and questions
✔ A mix of long and short sentences
✔ A complex or compound sentence mixed in with simple sentences
✔ Use of connecting words—*however, then*—that link sentences together (Yes, this is also part of organization.)
✔ Experimentation with poetry

---

*Fluency is less likely than other traits to reveal itself in picure form (use of dialogue is an exception) because it is by definition an integral part of *text* structure.

✔ Experimentation with dialogue

✔ Dialogue that echoes the way people really speak

What to Say in Your Comments

✔ You are using sentences in your writing. This is exciting!

✔ I notice that you are writing several sentences and not just one—terrific!

✔ Did you notice that you began this sentence in a different way? I love variety.

✔ I noticed you have some long sentences and some short sentences. This gives rhythm to your writing.

✔ I love the sound of this when I read it aloud. Did you read it aloud?

✔ You used some dialogue here. It's fun to hear your characters speak.

✔ This dialogue sounds so real. It helped me get inside the characters' heads.

Fluent writers are experimenters. They try their hands as poets. They make characters speak. They dare to begin sentences in different ways and to try varied patterns, including fragments. They also break the rules sometimes and use repetition for effect. To test the fluency of any piece of writing, read it aloud and listen. *Really* listen. Read it more than once if you need to. Have someone read it to you so that you can focus on how it sounds, not how it looks on the page. If the fluency is there, you will hear it. Set the bar high, but do not expect it to happen all at once. Sentence fluency really must be acknowledged at different levels: level 1: appearance of sentences (or a first sentence); level 2: use of multiple sentences; and level 3: use of varied patterns, structures, and lengths to create a smooth rhythm and flow. Some primary students will achieve level 3 with ease; for others, more time may be needed.

Some Examples

Zhiquae, a kindergarten writer, is just beginning to get the idea of sentences on paper. "Flowers grow. Smell good," she writes (Figure 2.56). Not *quite* whole sentences, but very close—more than single words. We could say to her, "Tell me about the flowers." Zhiquae might answer, "*They* smell good." Then we can say, "You added an important word to this sentence—*They*. We

FIGURE 2.56

"Flowers." Zhiquae (K)

FIGURE 2.57

Single-sentence piece. Khalik (K)

Khalik 2.28.2002

I love JuPITER nD PluTo!

could put that in your writing, if you like." I would write it for her and let her add it with a caret.

Khalik, also a kindergartner, is writing just a single sentence—but it is a complete sentence (Figure 2.57). It is even punctuated with an exclamation point, so we have two achievements to celebrate.

In his paper on fishing (Figure 2.58), kindergartner Alex has moved on to a whole new level: multiple sentences on the same topic. The sentences even begin in different ways. They end with periods, too. If we let Alex know how

FIGURE 2.58

Multiple-sentence writing. Alex (K)

I lic to fish.
Wen I cech som
I pwot tem bac In the
watr. fish.

many things he is doing well, we are likely to launch him into a fluent tear that will have him writing half pages, full pages, and then whole books.

First grader Emily is not only writing multiple sentences on the same topic but is also beginning sentences in a variety of ways: "A long time ago . . . ," "These people . . . ," "They were . . . ," and "When it was late fall . . ." (Figure 2.59). This amount of variety is quite sophisticated for so young a writer. Read this piece aloud to appreciate how smoothly it flows. Also notice the detail in both text and picture. That's a rather authoritarian king addressing the group of disgruntled pilgrims.

With just a bit of decoding, we discover that Olivia is using sentence structure to create tension and mystery—a highly advanced skill (Figure 2.60). Notice that her piece opens with a tranquil ocean scene, the crab scurrying about in search of a home. Enter the school of fish, then the menacing shark. Read

FIGURE 2.59   *"The Pilgrims."* Emily (1)

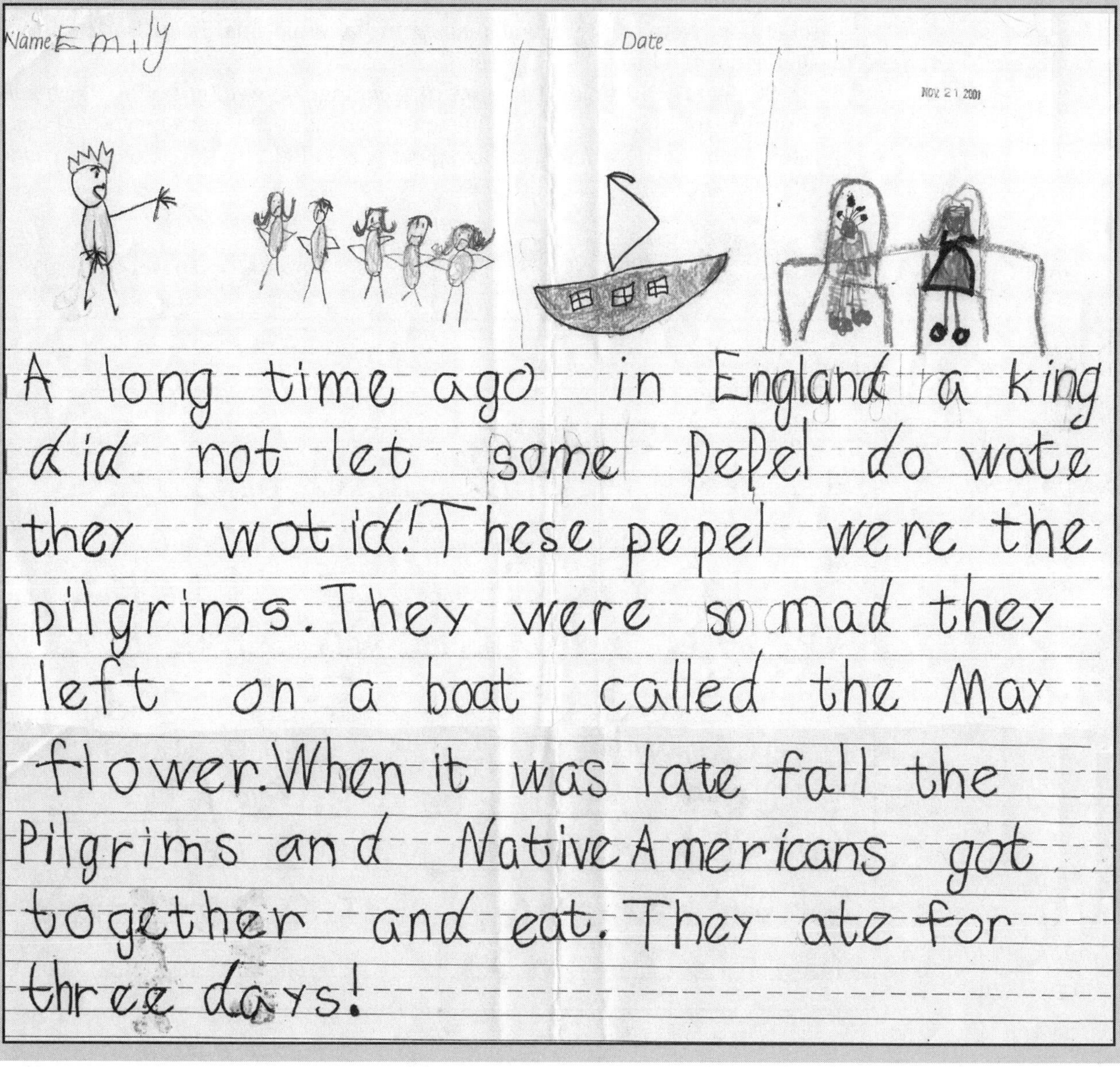

Name Emily   Date

NOV 21 2001

A long time ago in England a king did not let some pepel do wate they wot ld! These pepel were the pilgrims. They were so mad they left on a boat called the May flower. When it was late fall the Pilgrims and Native Americans got together and eat. They ate for three days!

FIGURE 2.60   *"Life of a Crab."*

Looking at the ocean rising idive the sand bneth the wotr, a Crab screy irond tring to find a Home. A sckhoul of fish Swam By. They wrey looking for foed to eat. Of cose they fowd baby plants to eat. But a shark fond something—a lot of somthing—a hole Sckhool of something! But thes how sharks hafe to leve.

By Olivia, Grade 2

Looking at the ocean rising above the sand, beneath the water, a crab scurried around trying to find a home. A school of fish swam by. They were looking for food to eat. Of course, they found baby plants to eat. But a shark found something—a lot of something—a whole school of something! But that's how sharks have to live.

that second-to-last sentence aloud. Olivia has an ear for drama and effective repetition. Note the reluctant realism in her stoic final line: "But that's how sharks have to live."

Students who enjoy listening to, reciting, or writing poetry have ideal strategies for building skills in fluency. Calvin quite impulsively wrote "Lucky's Life" (Figure 2.61) when his beloved cat was killed by a dog. This paper is not

FIGURE 2.61   *"Lucky's Life."* Calvin (2)

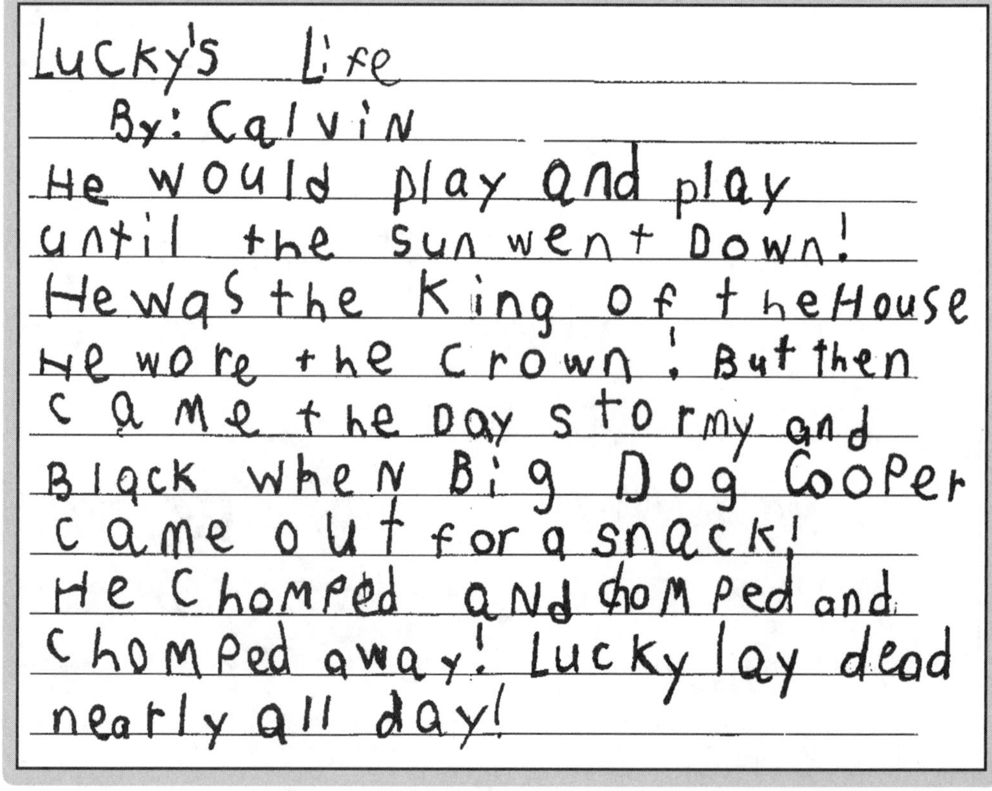

Lucky's Life
By: Calvin
He would play and play
until the sun went Down!
He was the King of the House
He wore the crown! But then
came the Day stormy and
Black when Big Dog Cooper
came out for a snack!
He Chomped and chomped and
chomped away! Lucky lay dead
nearly all day!

—

FIGURE 2.62 *Extended text.*

My first best friend was Alyssa now my best friend is Colleen now I will tell you what a friend is . . . to me. I think it is somebody who cares like if anything happned He/She would be there to help you out because if you fell or you were felling blue. They don't tell secrets about you like if they were with somebody that's a different friend and they wisper to that person and looked at you that it woulded [wouldn't] be a good way to show a friend you liked her. Have you ever hread someone say "look at that new girl she is so uncool well if I hread that I would go talk to the new girl and let her play with me cause I know how it feels to be new. So now you know what I think it is to be a friend.

By Rebecca, Grade 2

in traditional poetry format, but make no mistake, this *is* a poem. It has rhythm and power. Perhaps in poetry more than in any other form we see how much fluency contributes to voice.

Young writers often go through a phase in which written text mimics conversation and, in doing so, omits neat starts and stops. Consider Rebecca's paper, for instance (Figure 2.62). She is a fluent writer in the sense of generating a great deal of text and keeping the flow of ideas going. Now, if we can "disconnect" some of the individual thoughts by eliminating some *because* or *like* links, we can give this text a whole new sound. This is a case where modeling can be extremely helpful. Create a "superlinked" paragraph. Then read your own text aloud before and after eliminating connectives such as *so, because, and, like*. Do not expect students to grasp this rather difficult concept with one demonstration—or two. Keep doing it. Meanwhile, you can feel happy that students like Rebecca are (with ease!) generating extended text.

From Brian, a second grader, comes further proof that poetry builds fluency (Figure 2.63). Notice the different beginnings in this creative piece. Wonderful word choice as well.

Sydney, also a second grader, creates a word poem (Figure 2.64) based on "CAMELS." This kind of activity is greatly enriched with a class brainstorming session to kick it off: What animals live in the desert? What sights would you expect to see? How would it feel to be crossing the desert right now? What might you hear? Word banks enhance word choice but also make fluency easier to achieve. Limited vocabulary inhibits extended sentences.

FIGURE 2.63   *Poem.* Brian (2)

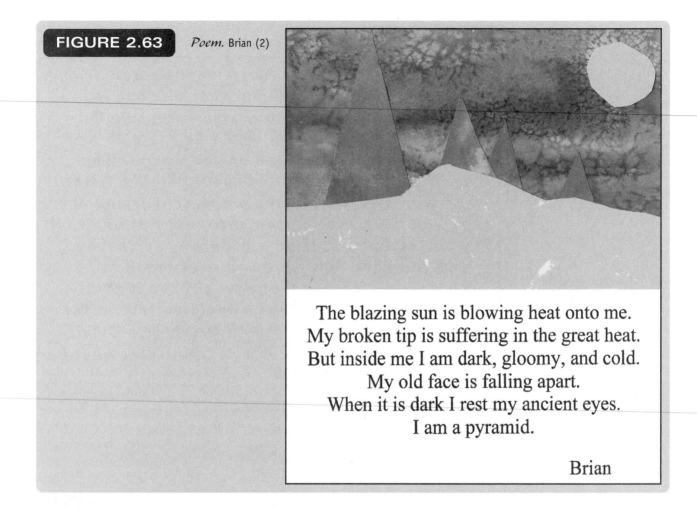

The blazing sun is blowing heat onto me.
My broken tip is suffering in the great heat.
But inside me I am dark, gloomy, and cold.
My old face is falling apart.
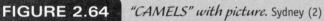
When it is dark I rest my ancient eyes.
I am a pyramid.

Brian

FIGURE 2.64   *"CAMELS" with picture.* Sydney (2)

Color changing all the time
Arid deserts so hot
Mice are sneaky as a snake
Eagles soaring through the air
Light is so bright from the desert sun
Scorpions scuttling through the desert

Sydney

A quick glance at Raechel's piece "Spring" (Figure 2.65) might create the impression that several sentences begin with the pronoun "I." True. However, variety abounds in this piece. Notice the different sentence lengths, as well as the interesting way Raechel puts her thoughts together: "Its colors are like a rainbow, so misty." It does not hurt to say, "That is a beautiful sentence. I love the way it sounds." Raechel also mixes short with long and has some interesting beginnings ("As I dig . . ." and "In the sandy beach . . .").

The whimsical, onomatopoetic poems of Douglas Florian (*Mammabilia*, *Insectlopedia*) are the inspiration for Abby's "Tiger Cub" (Figure 2.66). This is a good example of playful word choice, too, of course, but I chose it for fluency because I loved the rhythm and the way Abby puts the word of emphasis at the end of each line. Some writers do this instinctively; perhaps she is one. It's still true, though, that when it comes to attention, last place in line wins first prize.

Although the fluency in Pearson's "My favorite game" (Figure 2.67) is somewhat inconsistent, this paper has some particularly strong moments. It starts out strong, with notable variety

FIGURE 2.65 *"Spring."*

I can't wait for spring to come for in the spring I hunt for seaglass. In the sandy beach I dig for the smooth colorful seaglass. Its colors are like a rainbow, so misty. As I dig I see tiny pieces hidden beneath the sand. I love to dig for seaglass. I feel so free.

By Raechel, Grade 3

FIGURE 2.66 *"Tiger Cub."*

We are cats hear us purrrr
We have stripes upon our furrrr
We run through the forest like a blurrrr
We are a baby tigerrrr

By Abby, Grade 3

FIGURE 2.67 *"My Favorite Game."*

On a Saturday, I had a baseball game. For the first few games, I only hit singles. But last year, I always hit triples and doubles. So we've been having me take hitting lessons. It was Saturday and time for the game. Little did I know, the next 4 games, (skipping the 3rd,) would be big hitting streaks. I would be part of it. I play center field so I don't get the ball very much. Unless when I back up right or left fielder and they miss. Then we were up to bat. I was 6th. When I was up, the first pitch sailed in. It was low and in the middle. I swung. Contact! It flew past shortstop and landed. I rounded first and stopped at 2nd. The next kid hit a single but I went home. The next inning I hit a single and a double. We won the game. I got player of the game. The game Lucas hit a triple but the next game we lost. Then Conner my feand hit a grand slam 4 run homer. I love baseball.

By Pearson, Grade 3

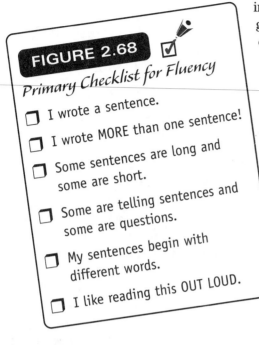

FIGURE 2.68

Primary Checklist for Fluency

☐ I wrote a sentence.

☐ I wrote MORE than one sentence!

☐ Some sentences are long and some are short.

☐ Some are telling sentences and some are questions.

☐ My sentences begin with different words.

☐ I like reading this OUT LOUD.

in sentence beginnings and lengths. There is also nice use of a single fragment: "Contact!" This provides a good opportunity to point out to Pearson (because he is clearly ready) what a fragment is and how it can work—sometimes. If Pearson had written, "I swung. I made contact," much of the oomph would have been lost. Help a student like Pearson (a strong and fluent writer already) to see where the really effective moments are: "Little did I know, the next four games would be big hitting streaks." Then encourage him to read his writing aloud to sharpen an already good ear for language patterns.

See Figure 2.68 for a primary checklist for fluency.

SPOTTING CONVENTIONS

> *. . . I knew this would be a long night. The patient was riddled with embedded clauses and comma splices. Gerunds clung to his sides and participles dangled from his shoulders as he collapsed on the table.*
>
> **—Barry Lane**
>
> *after THE END* (1993, p. 205)

At primary level, conventions begin simply with such elements as text flowing from left to right on the page or use of spaces between words. Discovery of punctuation marks or capital letters is significant, regardless of whether these things are employed correctly. Correct use comes later. Very young writers who are still experimenting with letters and numbers may have trouble recalling which direction letter F or B is supposed to face. More experienced writers are trying to recall whether commas go inside or outside quotation marks.

The secret in assessing (and teaching) conventions is to notice what the student *does* know and to build on that. Remember that nothing is automatic—even writing from left to right. All must be learned.

Although the term *conventions* encompasses a wide range of concerns from spelling to paragraphing, it is spelling that usually gets the most attention. Maybe this is because it stands out. We notice it. Forget a comma, and only a few people get excited. Misspell *because*, however, and the whole world is in an uproar. In looking at beginners' writing, let me suggest that you base your response to conventions more on readability and adventurous borrowing than on correctness alone. Correct use of conventions is a fine goal, but it is not the only goal. Think about it. Do you want students who only write within the safe parameters of the few conventions they feel sure of? Or do you want them to reach and borrow? If you said "yes" to the latter question, then you must reward reaching and borrowing.

What to Look for in Text (Beginning Level)*

✔ Left-to-right orientation on the page
✔ Correct directionality for letters and punctuation marks
✔ Experimentation with punctuation, whether correct or not
✔ Readable spelling (you can tell what the words are)
✔ Use of capitals, whether placed correctly or not
✔ Application of "classroom" conventions—for example, name on paper, date on paper, use of a title

What to Look for in Text (Advanced Level)

✔ Phonetic spelling on more difficult words
✔ Correct spelling of simple words
✔ Terminal punctuation that is correct—or mostly correct
✔ Capital letters on names
✔ Capital letters to begin sentences
✔ Correct use of periods and question marks
✔ Experimentation with quotation marks
✔ Use of exclamation points
✔ Use of commas in a series
✔ Experimentation with more sophisticated punctuation marks—for example, parentheses, semicolons, colons, dashes, ellipses, and so on
✔ Indentation or double spacing to show a new paragraph

What to Say in Your Comments

✔ I see that you have discovered periods (or whatever). Terrific!
✔ You knew this was a question—and used a question mark.
✔ It is so helpful when you put a title on your paper. Then I have a clue about your topic.
✔ I'm glad you remembered to put your name on your paper.
✔ I see that you used parentheses here. Tell me why.
✔ How did you know to use a comma (or other punctuation) here?
✔ This is so close to the correct spelling. Would you like to see how close you came?
✔ You have spaces between all your words now. That really helps your reader.
✔ You used this word five times and spelled it right every time. Is this in your personal dictionary?
✔ I see that you used an exclamation point to show some strong feelings here.

Young writers are borrowers. Therefore, the development of conventions goes in stages, something like this:

✔ Noticing a convention
✔ Borrowing a convention for use in personal text

---

*Conventions, by definition, apply primarily to text. However, do look for experimentation and new skills as text is incorporated into pictures through dialogue, signs, labels, and so on. Also look for visual conventions, such as use of bullets or numbers, or general layout and presentation in a poster, brochure, or greeting card.

✔   Knowing the name of the convention
✔   Knowing the correct use of the convention
✔   Using the convention correctly
✔   Teaching correct use to others
✔   Noticing misuse of the convention
✔   Correcting misuse of the convention in *someone else's* text
✔   Correcting misuse of the convention in personal text

We do our students a service by celebrating the discovery of conventions—then correct use and eventually correction of faulty text. Experimentation is the order of the day for very young writers, who will soon be avid editors if we don't set them to correcting too much too soon.

Some Examples

Consider as you look at conventions whether you are viewing the work of a beginner or a more advanced primary-level writer. Advanced writers tend to be those who can easily generate several sentences (or more) of text. Beginners may still be working on individual words.

Alyssa, a kindergartner, is exploring the world of writing. Her imitative writing does move from left to right on the page, although as yet we do not have recognizable letters (Figure 2.69). The octopus and lollipop are quite recognizable once we know her message. Alyssa dictates the text to accompany the picture. Fluency and strong word choice are evident in her dictation, although she is not yet ready to show these features in writing.

Brady, also a kindergartner, is creating some quite recognizable letter shapes (Figure 2.70) and may or may not be starting to connect letters with sounds (*B* for brother—could be coincidental). He is showing left-to-right orientation, and his letters not only are identifiable but also show correct directionality.

Brian, another kindergarten writer, creates text that is readable without his help: "Me and my penguins are friends" (Figure 2.71). He spells several sight words correctly and also manages the very difficult *penguins*. He also comes very close on *Frensd*, a word with which many older writers struggle. Brian has discovered periods, and they are prominent in his writing; like many beginning writers, however, he uses more than he needs. Notice his use of capital letters, too. Although they are not placed correctly yet, he is distinguishing between upper and lower case—a first step. He is also placing spaces between words.

FIGURE 2.69   *"Octopus and Lollipop."*
Alyssa (K)

FIGURE 2.70   *Early Conventions.* Brady (K)

FIGURE 2.71   *"Me and My Penguins."* Brian (K)

First grader Andrew has the advantage of creating text on a word processor (Figure 2.72). He is beginning to develop some fluency with multiple sentences. Periods and capitals are placed correctly, and spacing is good. Numerous sight words are spelled correctly, and the entire text is readable (with just a bit of work). Some help with the words *magic pebble* and *arrowhead* has made Andrew's task easier. Notice sentence three; it is the only one that wanders from the assigned topic, and interestingly, it has the most voice: "I wish that Mrs. Keefer would let me go outside whenever I want." This is his real message.

The longer the text, of course, the better our sense of a student's real comfort with conventions.

In "My brth" (Figure 2.73), Rebecca struggles with both spelling and punctuation, yet she manages to create a readable piece with quite a lot of voice. Again, resist the temptation to take on too much at once. Begin with what is done well, focusing on one to three strengths: She spells *brother* correctly in the text (although not in her title), along with *house* and *because*. These words could be added to a master spelling dictionary in her writing folder or notebook. She is using periods, but sometimes they come in the middle of a sentence. The question is, Does she hear the text this way? To find out, you could try reading it aloud to her (with plenty of inflection and long pauses), asking her to indicate where the periods should go (wrapping on the desk, nodding, and so on). You may need to read more than once. You can also do this, pen in hand, if you read text that has no punctuation. Let your voice rise or fall to give the student a hint where each period should go. Then you can insert them together. Teamwork makes for a terrific conference format.

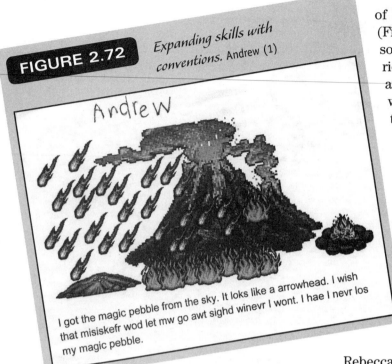

FIGURE 2.72   *Expanding skills with conventions.* Andrew (1)

Andrew

I got the magic pebble from the sky. It loks like a arrowhead. I wish that misiskefr wod let mw go awt sighd winevr I wont. I hae I nevr los my magic pebble.

FIGURE 2.73   *"My brth."*

My brother is a manyack. Because he is wlold. An he bothrs me a lot so wut I do is yel at he so I yel shut the dore an lock it. My brother is rille men so you wid not wot to cum to my house. Be-cause you wid get mad I wish me brother wiol be nis

By Rebecca, Grade 1

My brother is a maniac because he is wild. And he bothers me a lot. So what I do is yell at him, so I yell, shut the door, and lock it. My brother is really mean so you would not want to come to my house because you would get mad. I wish my brother would be nice.

FIGURE 2.74 *"What Taylor Is Like."*

> Taylor is my friend. In my story I would like to tell you all about her because she is one of my bestest friends. She is very nice. She's a very, very, very good friend to have as a best friend. I love her. We read together. Were in the same class. Were in Older phonics and Older Math. We to go cocurr [soccer] together. If we go out to recess we play together. If we stay in we work together. On funtastic Friday if were aloud to we do the same thing together. We always sit by each other at phonics unless some one already is sitting on both sides of either of us. She loves me. (We don't love each other like we love our family.) Were funny. We do jokes. We stick together. We draw together. We do arts and crafts together. We make posters together. We make books together. We try to be on the same tubl [table] for math jornal [journal] so we can do something together. Her clothes are all ways pretty. Her socks are allways pretty. She has brown hair. She has brown eyes. She weares a bow or a braid in her hair when she comes to school.
>
> By Ellie, Grade 1

Ellie's paper "What Taylor Is Like" (Figure 2.74) is a very interesting mix. Although just a first grader, Ellie shows a lot of control over conventions, creating standard sentences with ease and punctuating them correctly. She also uses parentheses correctly—and this needs to be pointed out to her because it's a major step. Her spelling is particularly interesting because she spells some challenging words correctly: *funtastic, Friday, phonics, posters, together, something, school, because, recess, unless, crafts, either,* and so on. On the other hand, the paper has some curious errors: *tubl, jornal,* and *cocurr.* These are relatively simple errors to remedy, though; hand Ellie the words on a Post-It note, and she will (most likely) be off and running. Notice the repetition of some words: *very, love, together, we, she,* and so on. Repetition of familiar words gives beginning writers confidence in their conventions. This is a good thing because it feels good to do things right. At the same time, we always want to encourage a stretch. I would like to list for Ellie those more difficult words—*clothes, phonics, recess, either*—that she has gotten right, along with her use of the parentheses. One key thing to work on?

With a first grader this strong in conventions, I would put the focus elsewhere: How about trying some varied sentence beginnings? Stir a little fluency into this mix, and you will have a powerhouse writer. Her excellent vocabulary is being buried inside patterned sentences.

One of the great things about poetry is that it's loosey-goosey enough to permit freedom with punctuation (and other conventions). Will gets by with virtually no punctuation whatsoever (Figure 2.75). His spelling is excellent (OK, *sneacky*). This writer is ready for something more challenging. Why not focus on end-of-line punctuation for poetry? Ask Will what he hears at the end of each line—a pause (comma), a long pause (dash), a stop (period), a strong stop with emphasis (exclamation point), or a question (question mark). Let him do the punctuating, according to what he hears. Punctuation marks just echo the way we read.

"Little Bull" (Figure 2.76) is a retelling of *Growing Up in Africa's Elephant Kingdom: The Story of Little Bull*, by Ellen Foley. The conventions are Jessica's own, and they are impressive. This level of control represents a sufficiently high expectation for primary level, in my view, even though it is not flawless. Flawless is always a dangerous goal, of course, even for adults. It's too rare. This is controlled, readable, and indicative of a wide range of conventional skills; we should not ask for more.

See Figure 2.77 for a primary conventions checklist.

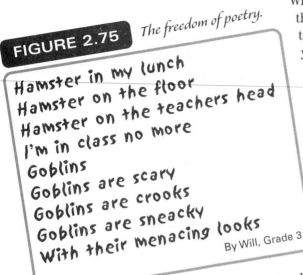

FIGURE 2.75   *The freedom of poetry.*

Hamster in my lunch
Hamster on the floor
Hamster on the teachers head
I'm in class no more
Goblins
Goblins are scary
Goblins are crooks
Goblins are sneacky
With their menacing looks
By Will, Grade 3

Exploring the world for ideas. "If I had teacups like this one," says Kayla, "my Grandpa and Papa would come for tea and cookies. I would wear a pretty pink dress."

FIGURE 2.76 *"Little Bull."*

In a faraway land, shaped just like an elephant's ear, a baby elephant was born. His name was Little Bull. Wraped like a cabbage in his big elephant ears, Little Bull lay very still. Little Bull lifted one ear and heard a chater of birds. Little Bull's playground was the grassy plains. And in a distance, rising up like an elephant's back, was the Great White Mountain. Sometimes, Little Bull tried to get his mother's attention by standing on his head. His humpty dumpty body toppled over every time. That evening Little Bull saw a huge dark mountain move across the sky. That night, Little Bull saw a bowl of stars overhead. The dry season went on and on and on. One day, the rain boweld over the ground. That day, little Bull played with Keekay.

By Jessica, Grade ???

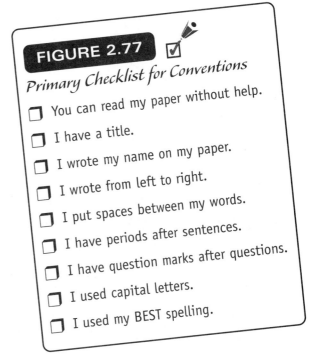

FIGURE 2.77

Primary Checklist for Conventions

☐ You can read my paper without help.

☐ I have a title.

☐ I wrote my name on my paper.

☐ I wrote from left to right.

☐ I put spaces between my words.

☐ I have periods after sentences.

☐ I have question marks after questions.

☐ I used capital letters.

☐ I used my BEST spelling.

LAST THOUGHTS

One of the rewarding things about writing assessment is that through their voices, the writers are always present, always before us. As we learn to look within their writing, they become our teachers, lighting the way for us. As Carol Avery says, "When I focused on children rather than practices, teaching became not only more challenging but also more rewarding and, more important, more effective for the children. I was able to let the children shine through" (2002, p. 6).

CHAPTER 2 IN A NUTSHELL

- Look first for the positive—for what is *there*—not what is missing. Help young writers to grow by building on their strengths.
- Remember to look carefully at both text and picture forms of writing to capture every nuance of meaning and voice.
- Offer suggestions that are specific and manageable—for example, "Quotation marks are like shoes or gloves. They come in pairs and work together, like this. . . ."
- Create and use checklists that "speak" to children. They should address the concerns young writers have and incorporate language young writers can understand.
- Responding to children's writing (or to any writing) is an art. Teach yourself to see what is within the writing so that your students can know the beauty and force of what they create. You are a guide and must point out what will otherwise go unnoticed on the journey. Remember the words of Kathleen and James Strickland: "Assessment gets to the heart of teaching and lets us decide how and when to offer support to writers. Learning to assess students' writing can actually help us to become better teachers of writing" (2000, p. 66).

EXTENSIONS

1. Now that you have had a look inside the writing of numerous students, check out some of the writing your own students are doing. Look for the moments of detail, voice, word choice, or fluency. Look at the beginnings, endings, or *word bridges*—connecting words that link ideas. Look for the numerous conventions your young writers are exploring or incorporating into their own writing and those they have mastered and made their own. Ask yourself, "What comments can I make to encourage them on this journey?"

2. In the chapter "Draw Me a Word—Write Me a Picture" (from *More Than Stories: The Range of Children's Writing*), Thomas Newkirk suggests that several forces combine around the end of first grade (or the beginning of second grade) to move children away from picture writing and toward a more text-focused approach. Among these are the child's own increased fluency, the increased ease of letter formation, the child's increasingly critical view of his or her own artwork, use of lined paper, and a perception (perhaps fostered by our society) that text is more "adult" than picture writing. What do you feel are the advantages or disadvantages of this shift? Based on the samples in this chapter and your experience with your own students' writing, do you see pictures as a legitimate form of written expression? Why or why not? Discuss this with a group.

3. Choose one or more samples from this chapter and review them using the primary-level rubrics in Chapter 8. Check all the strengths you see. If possible, compare your responses with those of a partner or group. Did any of you see or hear things in the writing that others missed? Now try the same exercise with one or more samples of your own students' work. Again, how close were your responses?

4. Based on your assessment of students' work in Extension 3, do you find any descriptors that should be added to the rubrics? Add those to create your own personalized rubrics.

5. Review (and if necessary revise) one or more of the "primary checklists" in this chapter based on your own teaching experience. Be sure that you use actual student samples as a guide in making any revisions. Work with a partner if possible.

6. Work with a partner to adapt one or more of the "primary checklists" for even younger readers/writers. What methods did you use to simplify them even more?

7. Kathleen and James Strickland suggest that assessment helps us become better teachers because it takes us inside students' thinking, enabling us to know them better so that they actually become our teachers. Reflect on this and write your personal response to this idea based on your own teaching experience.

SOURCES CITED

Avery, Carol. 2002. *And With a Light Touch*, 2d ed. Portsmouth, NH: Heinemann.

Calkins, Lucy McCormick. 1994. *The Art of Teaching Writing*, rev. ed. Portsmouth, NH: Heinemann.

Cannon, Jannell. 1997. *Verdi*. New York: Harcourt Brace & Company.

Florian, Douglas. 1998. *Insectlopedia*. New York: Harcourt Brace & Company.

Florian, Douglas. 2000. *Mammalabilia*. New York: Harcourt Brace & Company.

Fox, Mem. 1993. *Radical Reflections: Passionate Opinions on Teaching, Learning, and Living*. New York: Harcourt Brace & Company.

Johnson, Bea. 1999. *Never Too Early to Write*. Gainesville, FL: Maupin House.

Lane, Barry. 1993. *after THE END*. Portsmouth, NH: Heinemann.

Lane, Barry. 2001. *Reviser's Toolbox*. Shoreham, VT: Discover Writing Press.

Lewis, Cynthia Copeland. 1994. *Really Important Stuff My Kids Have Taught Me*. New York: Workman Publishing.

Murray, Donald M. 1985. *A Writer Teaches Writing*, 2d ed. Boston: Houghton Mifflin.

Newkirk, Thomas. 1989. *More Than Stories: The Range of Children's Writing*. Portsmouth, NH: Heinemann.

Strickland, Kathleen, and James Strickland. 2000. *Making Assessment Elementary*. Portsmouth, NH: Heinemann.

3 Teaching Traits Conceptually: Introductory Lessons

Simone (Gr 2) is revising. She's looking for organization and sentence fluency.

Photo and caption courtesy of Michael (Grade 4).

Teaching masters like Janet Emig, Donald Graves and Jerome Bruner tell us students learn best when they mine their spontaneous knowledge for skills they already use. Simply put, we learn by doing; then we go on to do more through learning.

—Barry Lane and
Gretchen Bernabei
Why We Must Run with Scissors
(2001, p. 1)

Writing allows us to hold our life in our hands and make something of it.

—Lucy McCormick Calkins
The Art of Teaching Writing (1994, p. 4)

Poor horsemanship consists in suggesting that man and horse are separate. A horseman afoot is a wingless, broken thing, tyrannized by gravity. . . . for that burst of poetry, horse and rider have one another to thank.

—Thomas McGuane
Some Horses (2000, pp. 18–19)

"NOTHING TO DO WITH MY CURRICULUM"

A primary teacher intrigued me one day when she said, "I can't work with these traits—they have nothing to do with my curriculum." When I asked her to describe her curriculum, she said, "Well, we talk about fun things we could write about. We make lists. Then we have time for writing, and sometimes I help my kids get started. Later, we share what we have written. Sometimes, we make displays." Fun things to write about? Those are ideas. Making lists? A way of capturing ideas on paper. Getting started? Organization. Sharing? Voice—and words, too, of course. Displays? Often, some attention to detail there that might connect to revising ideas or thinking about conventions. In other words, the six traits were embedded in everything this teacher was doing. She was seeing the traits as something separate, a new layer of instruction, an extra "workbook."

It is not like that at all. I think what the traits do, really, is get us organized. My mentor teacher, Ronda, turned the light on for me when I saw her sprawled in the middle of her classroom one August afternoon, her files in apparent disarray around her. When I asked what she was doing, she replied, "It's simple. I already teach all this stuff [the traits]. I'm just reorganizing my lessons so that when I want something on organization or voice or fluency, I can find it. See?" I did see. Ronda also inspired me to color code my files: red for ideas, green for organization, and so on. This is such a simple idea, but it is so helpful. Not new so much, you see, as *restructured*. So many of the best books on writing give us a thousand good ideas but never answer the one question we're burning to know: How do I get started? The traits make it simple. Start with ideas—a message, a topic, something you love to write about. Model it, read books that show how skillful authors express main ideas and details, and then add another trait (*writing*, of course, all the while).

Emphasize what students need. As Ronda told me, "Every class is different. Some are strong in conventions—some have wonderful voice or details. It's when I look at their writing that I know where to spend my teaching time." You'll know, too.

Two things are critical at primary level:

1. Writing, reading, and just plain loving it.
2. Using writers' vocabulary so that such terms as *voice* or *fluency* are at least familiar—even if they are not integral parts of a child's own writing.

You can teach the first by being an enthusiastic writer/reader yourself, by providing time and a classroom environment in which students are immersed in wonderful literature and feel comfortable as writers. Teach writers' vocabulary by using the language yourself at every opportunity. And remember, if it is difficult for some students to grasp the notion of, say, fluency in the context of writing, you could start with the larger notion of fluency. What is it, really? This chapter is meant to give you an inside look at the *concept underlying each trait* as a way of making definitions clearer to young minds (and perhaps within your own thinking as well). Keep in mind that the six traits are not a curriculum, not a program. They are a *way of thinking about writing* that leads to understanding.

TEACHING THE CONCEPT OF IDEAS

Ideas can be taught conceptually in many ways, for they are many things. They are everything we think or imagine or picture in our heads. Ideas can begin with something huge: *Things that grow*. Then, by fine-tuning our mental binoculars, we focus in on our idea and bring it down to manageable proportions: *Plants . . . houseplants . . . my philodendron . . . the philodendron that is overtaking my file cabinet, keeping me out with its leafy arms*.

Let me suggest three key approaches, each of which can be taught separately—even to students who are not yet creating much (if any) text. They are

✔ Ideas as *imagination* and *observation*
✔ Ideas as *pictures in the mind*
✔ Ideas as *messages*

Ideas as Imagination and Observation

Give students something interesting to observe—a rock, say, or a seashell or an orange peel. Ask them to look, sniff, touch, tap, and turn it around to see it from different sides. As they do so, they should ask themselves the questions "What do I notice?" and "What does it remind me of?" A simple object such as a rock may suggest to the imagination a mountain looming in the distance or the shape of an animal. It may take the observer, in his or her imagination, to a wooded glen or the flatlands of a desert. It may remind one writer of her aquarium and another of his grandmother's rock garden. The smell of an orange may take a writer to a kitchen, a picnic, or a grove in Florida.

Observations and associations, especially when recorded, teach children to be keen observers of the world—and mental recorders as well. A writer can have no greater gift. As writer James Dickey (in Calkins, 1994, p. 3) has observed, "A writer is someone who is enormously taken by things anyone else would walk by."

You can enhance this experience by recording your students' observations and rewarding them by appreciating the small details they notice—especially if you did not notice them yourself. Have you ever looked, *really* looked, at people's hands, for example? The shape, the look of the nails, and the lines and creases all tell us who the person is, even if we have no other details on which to rely. Author Rick Bragg wrote of his grandfather's hands, "They hung at the ends of his skinny arms like baseball mitts, so big that a normal man's hand disappeared in them. The calluses made an unbroken ridge across his palm, and they were rough, rough all over as shark's skin. The grease and dirt, permanent as tattoos, inked his skin, and the tar and dirt colored the quick under his fingernails, then and forever. He could have burned his overalls, changed his name and bought himself a suit and tie, but those hands would have told on him" (2001, p. 52). This is observational genius—coupled with supreme inferential skill. And it starts right in your classroom, looking at a simple object as you jot down what your children see and celebrating their skill in seeing.

Ideas as Pictures in the Mind

We see with our eyes, but we see within our minds as well. Ideas grow out of what students hear and what they visualize from what they hear. In *Twilight Comes Twice*, Ralph Fletcher (1997) creates image upon image, a mental collage that defines dawn and dusk in myriad ways. In what remains my favorite passage from the book, Fletcher tells us, "Slowly dusk pours the syrup of darkness into the forest. Crows gather in the trees for last-minute gossip before nightfall." Close your eyes and you can see the syrupy darkness falling slow and thick across the trees, covering them and blurring the shapes. You can see and hear the crows gathered on the branches, chatting with each other.

Now imagine your students creating pictures from what they see and feel and hear as you share a story, a poem, or a moment of your own experience. Students, who draw freely—without fear of "getting it wrong"—create as much meaning with pictures as with text. They incorporate details, and they let us know what meaning a passage has had for them. They may expand meaning, too. Part of Fletcher's art is that he never tells too much. So often our teacher comments include the suggestion, "Tell me more." What we really mean sometimes is, "Tell me the *right* thing—the *just right* thing." Encourage your students to speak through art. Sketching and painting are ways of discovering what that "just right" detail might be.

It is easy to sketch what Ralph Fletcher describes. His images seem to float right off the page and into our hearts and minds as if he were touching a spot within our brains that could take us to a time and place where we had once been ourselves. If, however, a writer is bored or labors with every word, the mental pictures come less easily. Suppose that Ralph had written, "Everything got darker. Then some birds came." This would be tougher to sketch, don't you think? Just as writers can tell too much, they can also tell too little. Therefore, ask your students as they draw what they picture, "What do you see? Is it easy to draw? Do you see enough? You *do?* The little parts of what you see are detail." They hear, they see in their minds, they draw—and often, they expand. Expect their pictures to encompass more than Fletcher—or any author—provides a blueprint for. Their mental pictures will stretch and grow—as long as you let them form on their own and do not too quickly share the pictures from the books (however wonderful!). Oh, it's tempting. After all, we buy picture books partly (sometimes *mostly*) for the pictures. Now and then, however, it is refreshing for the mind to make its own movies.

Ideas as Messages

In the introduction to his wonderful book, *More Than Stories*, teacher and author Thomas Newkirk (1989, p. 1) tells the delightful tale of his five-year-old daughter reading the long list of rules posted at the city's swimming pool. Why, Newkirk wondered, would this young child take such a long time in the cold winter air to study rules that she could only begin to read? The answer was that she wanted to go into the sauna—and could not. It was this print, these rules, that kept her out: "Here we were, about fifty swimmers in all, seemingly controlled by the words written on this poster, words that would, among other things, keep her out of the sauna bath until near the twenty-first century" (1989, p. 1).

The rules carried a message, and that message was, in essence, "You cannot do what you want because you're too young." Often, this is precisely what we mean by ideas—a message. Sometimes the message is clear and concise, sometimes not. One of my e-mails earlier today contained this message: "Sentences go forward and turn into ideas which become the paragraphs that we preserve." It sounds good, doesn't it? But what on earth does it mean?

See how many ways your students can think of that we give messages to each other in our society. Here are a few (they will think of more):

✔ Conversation   ✔ Advertisements
✔ Television   ✔ Newspapers
✔ Radio   ✔ Greeting cards
✔ E-mail   ✔ Bumper stickers
✔ Post-It notes   ✔ Labels
✔ Signs   ✔ Directions
✔ Letters   ✔ Product packaging
✔ Other mail

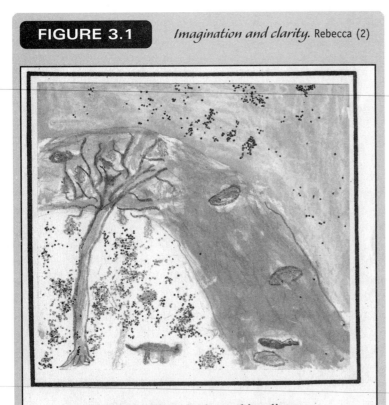

FIGURE 3.1 *Imagination and clarity.* Rebecca (2)

It's spring. There is clean white glittery snow on the ground. It floats like a cloud. The blue electric sky is flashy. The trees are blowing swiftly among the wind. The stream's water waves everywhere as it flows down into a pond. I would like to go outside for the whole day. I think it's a great day. I hope tomorrow is like today.

Rebecca

What separates a good message from a poor one? Simple. You can understand it. It makes sense. This is just a simple way of saying that it has *clarity*. When you ask your students to line up, take out paper, give you their attention, prepare to go home for the day, remember something to bring for tomorrow, or take a notice to parents, you are giving a message. And when you ask, "Does everyone understand? Do you have questions?" you are checking for clarity.

Messages can be very simple, like "Stop!" Or they can be as complex as the Internal Revenue Service tax code. The greater the complexity, of course, the harder it is to maintain clarity; that's the test of a good informational writer, really. A truly gifted informational writer can make tax codes as understandable as traffic signs.

You might teach this message concept by having students write notes home—through pictures or print—about *one* significant thing that happened during the day. Ask them to write Post-It note reminders to each other—again using pictures, print, or a combination. Ask students to create posters for classroom rules, such as behaving courteously. Again, pictures or print—it does not matter. What matters is that the message goes from writer to reader in any way that makes sense. Clarity is the name of the game.

Ideas as "Something to Write About"

When students hear the word *ideas,* they often think of the age-old question, "What shall I write about?" Write what you know, we tell them. Or write what interests you. What *is* that anyway? We ask these questions of our students, but the truth is, often we cannot answer them ourselves. Ever notice how a million things interest you until someone sticks an eight and a half by eleven inch sheet of paper in front of you? Then, amazingly, you cannot think of one interesting thing. So what do you do? As Anne Lamott tells us, there is no "magic formula my father passed on to me in a whisper just before he died." You just sit down and do it. "You begin to string words together like beads to tell a story" (1994, p. 7).

USING LISTS

Of course, we all have stories in our lives, things we notice, things that interest us—and opinions. It is going to be 103 degrees today, and I have no idea how to keep cool (unless I stay at work overnight); my son has a driver's test in two days, and my daughter is being married in three (and again I am wondering why everything happens at *once*); some idiot cut down five old-growth trees next to my office to put in a parking lot that no one needs; and one of the construction workers in our area has decided, quite arbitrarily it seems to me, to drive on the left side of the road at unsafe speeds. Such everyday events and random thoughts are the basis for narrative, descriptive, expository, and persuasive writing—for notes and letters, how-to pieces, essays, and stories. Unfortunately, we do not always write down our observations or story ideas or opinions. We should, though. Otherwise, we may forget. Lists are enormously helpful when it comes to writing. Your students may not know where to begin in putting together a writer's list, however. You need to model this. What are three things you are thinking of writing about *right now?* Write them down. This is the beginning of a list you can share with your students. You can't share it just once, of course. You need to share your list frequently because it will change all the time. Here is my current list of things to write about (I am not going to write about all of these, you understand—or maybe any of them—it's just an idea list):

✔ How to stay comfortable when your ears are popping on an airplane
✔ How do deal with maniac drivers
✔ What to do when a truly angry dog comes after you—and you are alone
✔ How to get up when you are cross-country skiing and fall into a deep snow bank
✔ The story of Pearl (our neighbor's poodle, whom I do not like much) and a prowling coyote
✔ The sheer joy of watching sea turtles at play

This list will look very different by the time this book actually goes to press. It will look different next week. Writing lists change as experience changes—and that's good.

BORROWING

Another good place to go for writing ideas is a writing group—or just a friend who writes. Just as the fish are always better on the other side of the lake, so the other writer is always coming up with a better idea. Barry Lane (2002) is writing a series of stories based on fables, his first being *The Tortoise and the Hare Continued.* . . . I like this idea very much—the notion that stories aren't really over when they're over—there is always another episode. This is a good one to borrow. Author Anne Lamott advises her students, "Write down all the stuff you swore you'd never tell another soul. What can you recall about your birthday parties—the disasters, the days of grace, your relatives' faces lit up by birthday candles? Scratch around for details: what people ate, listened to,

Katie (me!) and Lilly (my first grade reading buddy) look over her book for any missing details.

wore—those terrible petaled swim caps, the men's awful trunks, the cocktail dress your voluptuous aunt wore that was so slinky she practically needed the Jaws of Life to get out of it" (1994, p. 5). I love this advice because basically she is telling us, each of us, "Your life is fascinating, and since only *you* have lived it, only *you* know what to write."

Our students need to talk to one another *before* they write—and to suggest ideas for writing. In *Writing: Teachers and Children at Work*, Donald Graves suggests that we should know our students and their interests in order to help them find topics. Rather than assigning topics, he says, know the child well enough to suggest interests. He even suggests making a chart (and if you have never tried this, it may surprise you to discover how hard it is) listing each student's name and his or her special interests (1983, pp. 22–28). That way, the first conference can focus on topics—not topics we assign but questions that lead children to topics of their own: What is the most interesting thing that ever happened to you? What is your first really vivid memory? Do you have any pets? Do you have hobbies? What do you find fascinating? Annoying? As Graves tells us, "Writers who learn to choose topics well make the most significant growth in both information and skills. . . . with [the] best topic the child exercises strongest control, establishes ownership, and with ownership, pride in the piece" (1983, p. 21). Ownership and pride—that's a recipe for voice. Voice begins with having something to say. "Writers who do not learn to choose topics wisely lose out on the strong link between voice and subject" (Graves, 1983, p. 21).

TEACHING ORGANIZATION CONCEPTUALLY

When we connect organization to writing, we think immediately of leads, transitions, conclusions, orderly paragraphing, patterning, and so on. However, the concept of organization is much larger than writing. It can be taught in several ways.

✔ Organization as *patterning*
✔ Organization as *grouping*
✔ Organization as *making a plan*

Organization as Patterning

Lots of things in life are organized—and you might brainstorm a list with your students. Following is a list of things students have mentioned at various times—and no doubt your students will think of more:

✔ Grocery stores (and other stores, of course)
✔ Closets (not mine, but some)
✔ An ant colony
✔ Traffic
✔ City streets
✔ A buffet in a restaurant
✔ A hotel
✔ A sports team
✔ Colors in a crayon box
✔ Living room furniture
✔ Newspapers
✔ Telephone books
✔ Rows of crops
✔ The alphabet
✔ Dishes in a cupboard
✔ A calendar
✔ A blueprint for a house
✔ An eight-course dinner

Good. Think about how each thing is organized—what sort of pattern does it follow? Alphabetical? Geographic (like a map)? Little to big? Salad to dessert? And so on. Now, what about the things in the world that are disorganized (or random)? Here are some things students have mentioned:

✔ *Some* closets
✔ *Some* desks
✔ Clouds in the sky
✔ Weeds
✔ People running from a fire or accident
✔ A fight
✔ My hair in the morning
✔ Wrinkly clothes packed in a hurry
✔ My notebook!
✔ The laundry when it first comes out of the dryer
✔ My dad's calendar
✔ Our kitchen
✔ Our car

In one group, we see patterns; in the other, not. This is one underlying concept of organization: things in patterns. You can reinforce this basic idea throughout the day or the week by asking students to identify moments or events where things or people fall into patterns—or not: People line up for the bus (that's organized); leaves blow off the tree in the wind (that's not). Soon your students will be seeing organizational patterns everywhere—and you can reinforce this with art. Ask them to draw a picture of something organized and a picture of something random. This reinforces their thinking about the basic notion of organization. Now it is time to extend it, if you wish.

Sometimes patterning is vital; at other times it really does not matter. For example, no one cares whether leaves fall from a tree in a precise pattern. We rather like the randomness. However, take one of the student examples—the grocery store. There, order matters a lot. Why, though? Ask your students this: What if you went to the grocery store and things were totally jumbled: paper towels mixed with oranges, soup mixed with toothbrushes. Would that work? Why? Suppose that you opened your calendar and the dates were out of order. Would a calendar like that be usable? How come? The question here is, How does organization make life easier? Your students will have creative answers, and their answers will provide the foundation for what you want to teach later—that organization in writing makes some writing easier to interpret and to follow. (A poem may be more random than, say, a how-to chapter on fixing your lawnmower.)

■ Don't Forget Puzzles

Jigsaw puzzles make patterns—patterns that are not always immediately obvious. In many ways, assembling a puzzle is a way of solving an organizational challenge: What is the picture or pattern I am supposed to be seeing? Many people (young and older) solve puzzles by beginning with the outside framework. This is rather like coming up with a main idea that frames what follows. Puzzle pieces are linked together with colors or shapes; these are like the links between ideas.

■ Pictures in a Series

Give your students three pictures, related or not, and ask them to put the pictures in order and tell a story based on the arrangement (There does not need to be any right answer to this—it's an exercise in imagination). The pattern they choose determines the story. When they have finished, see if they can shift the order to come up with a different story.

Organization as Grouping

Grouping is easy to teach. It is simply putting things together that go together. You can teach grouping with items of similar size, color, shape, texture, or any other common trait. This practice provides a foundation for creating paragraphs or chapters—for "chunking" information. You can do an interesting grouping activity with something like rocks or coins, where there are numerous possibilities for grouping. Coins, for example, can be grouped by color, size, value, or date—or in a number of other ways your students will surprise you by thinking of. The same is true for rocks and numerous other objects. Grouping can be done in teams, and when you are finished, ask students to share the various methods of grouping their teams have thought of.

Organization as Making a Plan

When you have an event coming up—a conference night, a school gathering, a field trip, or whatever—make a "plan" with students. You may decide to prepare invitations or posters, to celebrate, to write about the event, to take a class picture, or any number of things. Planning is an important component of organizing because it requires anticipation and prediction. When you plan as a group, you ask students to envision what will happen in the future.

This is the idea, really, behind prewriting: making a plan for writing (so what you are teaching is a precursor to the prewriting phase of writing process). Of course, in our lives, when the wedding plans do not work out, we amend them—or abandon them. Somehow, we forgot to give ourselves such freedom with writing, in which outlines can become tyrannical. Where we often go awry with prewriting is in forcing student writers to stick relentlessly to whatever plan they come up with (never mind if it's working!). This defeats the whole point. The planning sets thinking in motion; drafting continues the development of that thinking. An idea evolves throughout the prewriting, drafting, and revising stages—and must be given freedom to do so. Force students to adhere to a prewriting plan (whether a list, a web, or whatever), and you shut down their thinking. Lucy Calkins says, "I've come to think that it's very important that writing is not only a process of recording, it's also a process of developing a story or idea" (1994, p. 8).

TEACHING VOICE CONCEPTUALLY

Of all the traits, I love voice the most because voice is the person speaking to us from the page. Voice is the essence of the writing, the reason for the writing, and the reason for reading. Voice is the place where many students, regardless of technical skill in other areas of writing, are likely to shine. Donald Graves (1983, p. 227) puts it this way:

> *Voice is the imprint of ourselves on our writing. It is that part of the self that pushes the writing ahead, the dynamo in the process. Take the voice away and the writing collapses of its own weight. There is no writing, just words following words. Voiceless writing is addressed "to whom it may concern."*

Let me suggest several different ways of teaching this elusive but vital concept:

✔ Voice as a *metaphor*
✔ Voice as *individuality*
✔ Voice as *mood*

Voice as Metaphor

This first way to teaching voice is the simplest—and it is a good place to begin. One day, when I visited my friend Arlene Moore's K-1 classroom, she said, quite out of the blue, "Jennifer, that dress has so much voice!" Indeed it did. It was a bright rosy pink with yellow loose-petal flowers hand-stitched onto the front.

"I love bright colors," Arlene went on. "It makes me feel good just looking at them." She went on to ask her students what colors they felt had the most voice—and not surprisingly, the striking colors of purple, orange, yellow, and red were popular responses. We then talked about colors without voice—but this time, there was not so much agreement. Some children saw tan as voice-free, but one young writer said that tan was the color of beach sand, which he loved—so for him, tan did have voice. Many students felt that gray lacked voice, until one writer ran to the window and pointed out the number of different grays in the sky; a storm was brewing. "Gray can be a storm color, and storms have voice," he reminded us. Voice is personal.

Arlene likes to connect voice to favorite and least favorite foods, too—"strong voice" foods include the perennial favorite, pizza, as well as ice cream, chocolate, hamburgers, fruit, cotton candy, and so on. "Low voice" foods include tapioca pudding, leftovers of all kinds, liver, undercooked eggs, watery oatmeal, and "anything my sister makes in the blender."

Use your imagination in making metaphoric connections. Anything that taps into the senses will work, including music, art, dance, films, TV shows—even animals. "Zebras and chimpanzees have a lot of voice, and slugs don't," one first grader told me. (Or perhaps "slug" voice is less appealing to us.)

Voice as Individuality

Here's a question I like to ask students: "When you talk to a friend on the phone, how long does it take you to recognize that person?" Not long. Why? Because every voice is different. Try this. Have your students close their eyes, tap one student on the shoulder, and ask him or her to make a simple statement: "Guess who I am." Everyone will guess correctly. That's how individual voices are. You may also wish to play some voices on tape: "Does Mem Fox sound the way you thought she would? What sort of voice does she bring to her own work?"

Voice shows itself in other forms, too, such as art. Show your students works by a few well-known artists, for example, Picasso, Charles Schultz, Bev Doolittle, William Steig, Jules Feiffer, and folk artist Charles Wysocki. What are the differences? What kinds of "voices" are these artists showing in their paintings? Don't worry about whether your students recognize the artists. That really makes no difference at all. You are just looking for their responses to the voice within the art. Who *is* this person? You can also use art from the vibrant world of picture books, of course. Some *particularly* striking examples include

✔ William Noonan [in Carolyn Lesser's *Great Crystal Bear* (1996)]
✔ David Diaz [in Eve Bunting's *Smoky Night* (1994)]
✔ Jean-Michel Basquiat [in Maya Angelou's *Life Doesn't Frighten Me* (1993)]
✔ Kate Kiesler [in Ralph Fletcher's *Twilight Comes Twice* (1997)]
✔ Tom Lichtenheld [in his book *Everything I Know About Pirates* (2000)]
✔ Giselle Potter [in Toni Morrison's *The Big Box* (1999)]
✔ Fred Marcellino [in his book *I Crocodile* (1999)]
✔ Greg Couch [in Lynn Plourde's *Wild Child* (1999)]
✔ Lane Smith [in Jon Scieszka's *Math Curse* (1995)]
✔ Stephen Gammell [in Jim Aylesworth's *Old Black Fly* (1992)]
✔ Ruth Wright Paulsen [in Gary Paulsen's *Dogteam* (1993)]
✔ Steve Jenkins [in Sneed Collard's *Animal Dads* (1997)]
✔ Jannell Cannon [in her book *Verdi* (1997)]
✔ William Steig (in *any* of his books, including but not limited to *Amos and Boris, The Toy Brother, Dr. DeSoto, Solomon the Rusty Nail, The Amazing Bone, Shrek,* and *Grown-Ups Get to Do All the Driving*)
✔ Faith Ringgold [in her book *Tar Beach* (1991)]
✔ David Shannon [in his book *No, David!* (1998)]

Pictures, like text, have mood and tone. Talk about this with your students. Ruth Wright Paulsen, for example, creates a hauntingly beautiful snowscape for *Dogteam* that fits the adventurous, mysterious mood of the book perfectly.

A simple rose is very close to Edgar's heart: "I would give this red beautiful rose that smells good to my little sister that died because my mom always brings her flowers every day."

In all his books, William Steig is humorous and unpredictable. David Shannon's illustrations are silly and sometimes outrageous. Giselle Potter creates amazing details with eyes and mouths and hair; she can sketch a character to make you laugh out loud or break your heart. Stephen Gammell has a wild, wacky, slapdash approach that gives his pictures a spontaneous, explosive, energetic look. Jannell Cannon is stylish but leans toward a mix of reality and fantasy that is more dramatic than cartoonish. Cannon relies heavily on texture and color to create the "voice" imprint of her work; Steig relies more on facial expression and interaction between characters. Their motives and intentions are quite readable on their faces. Tom Lichtenheld's characters are jaunty and defiant as pirates should be, whereas Greg Couch's beautiful creations are dreamy, floating, and fantastic. These words are *mine*, though; let your students find their own. The point here is only that voice can be as strong in art as in text and that no two artistic voices are alike. Once students begin to see the voice in the artwork around them, they also become more conscious of the voice within their own art, the individuality and style that marks each of them. But you must say it—you must emphasize individuality, or your students may not automatically value it. Help them to seek and love the differences among artists so that they will love the differences among themselves.

Voice as Mood

Music offers an even more immediate way of helping students tune into mood. Think of a film you have seen recently—or at any time. How often did the music let you know what was about to happen? You know when the hero is in trouble, don't you? Or when something sad—such as the old, faithful dog dying—is about to happen? Think of the music *you* play when you are in a celebrational mood, at a party or wedding, versus what you might play as background music when you are reading or working. What do you play to cheer yourself up? To mellow out? What pieces of music speak to you?

Right now, while you are thinking of it, jot down three favorite pieces of music. (They do not have to be your three all-time favorites—just three that pop into your head.) Are they instrumental or vocal? Lively? Wistful? How do they make you feel?

With your students, explore the moods of music by playing a variety for them, marches, symphonies, folk music, Celtic music. Compare Willie Nelson to the Beatles; or Rod Stewart; Sinatra; Peter, Paul, and Mary; Beethoven; Mozart; or The Chieftains. Compare Israel Kamakawiwo'ole's light, upbeat version of "Somewhere Over the Rainbow" (*In IZ World*, 1992) to Judy Garland's more heart-wrenching rendition (*Judy at Carnegie Hall*, 1967). Ask students to tell you how each piece of music makes them *feel*. Voice is ultimately about reader response—which begins with listener response. Music is vivid and embracing, but the response your students have to music as it engulfs them teaches them how to respond emotionally to poetry or to prose. That comes in the next chapter.

■ Different Voices, Different Times

You might ask your students this intriguing question: "How many different voices do *you* have?" They may have no idea until they start exploring. Most of us have a wide range of voices: one for pleading with a parent or child to please do whatever, another for cheering on the team on the football field, for conspiring with a close friend, for arguing with a petulant sibling, for greeting a stranger in the office or on the phone, or talking to an infant or a puppy. You may wish to actually have your students try this out. Set up a situation. Let's say that you want the door closed. First, have a student "ask" a parent to do this. Notice the words and the tone of voice. Then ask another student to imagine that his or her very annoying younger brother has left the door open for the "bazillionth" time—what do you say, and how do you say it? Then have a third student teach a toddler how to close the door—what do you say, and how do you say it?

If you tell first graders that mystery stories, business letters, and personal essays all have slightly different voices, you cannot really expect them to understand what you mean—yet. However, when you tell them that we all have many voices within us and that we use different voices at different times, they do understand. You are only planting a seed.

| FIGURE 3.2 | *"Good Memories"* is an expressive piece of personal writing by Skye (2). |

■ Wearing Many Hats

Clothing gives us clues about mood, tone, and purpose. I do not wear my jeans to a wedding or chiffon to the rodeo. If you're a hat collector, you can use a variety of hats to indicate various kinds of voice. A cowboy hat might suggest one thing, a gardener's hat another, and a wide fedora with a peacock feather something else. The message you intend may not be the message your students receive! But you can bet they will recognize colorful versus drab, formal versus informal, playful versus serious. This same visual effect works for word choice, too—and later, for fluency. Sentences, like voices and word patterns, can come to the party dressed to the teeth or in comfy lounging clothes. Play dress-up for voice with your students. Ask each person to come to class with a hat of some kind, and talk about the kind of voice each one suggests.

TEACHING WORD CHOICE CONCEPTUALLY

Choice is the operative word here. You might begin with a set of menus. Ask your students to view them in groups and to make choices based on what they are in the mood for right now. Write some choices down, and explain that writers choose words much the way hungry diners choose foods from a menu or shoppers choose groceries or other things to purchase. We have hundreds of thousands of words in English; yet, for a particular moment, to create a particular picture in the reader's mind or a particular response, only the "just right" word will do—the way sometimes you only want hot fudge or a burger. Writers are picky or, we could say, *discriminating, selective, choosy, fussy, particular, demanding,* or *persnickety.* Some simple ways to teach word choice conceptually include these:

✔ Word choice as *muscle*
✔ Word choice as *the target*

Word Choice as Muscle

Some words have muscle. They can carry a lot of weight. This is another way of saying that they have substance, meaning, impact. Vague words—*nice, big, happy, sad, great, fun*—are pebbles. They do not tip the scale because they do not tell us anything. You can illustrate this with a scale and a collection of rocks and pebbles. As your students encounter a new word, ask them, "Rock or pebble? What do you think?" Glue or tape the rock or pebble to a card with the word printed on it, and place it right on the scale. Be sure, though, to let your students make the choice.

To kick off this game, you need some examples. Start simply, with a word your students use often—such as *big.* We all use it, but it's a "pebble" word, really. It does not say much. What are some weightier alternatives? How about *enormous, vast, bulky, burly, robust,* or *weighty*? Of course, these words are not completely interchangeable. This is the tricky part, isn't it? We can say, "The *vast* landscape stretched before us," but "The *bulky* landscape stretched before us" doesn't work. So, you will need to provide sample sentences for clarification. By the way, lots of letters do not add up to more "weight"—it is more a question of how specific a word is. I am *glad* when a favorite movie is on television; I am *jubilant* when my daughter phones to say that she is coming for the weekend.

One of the best ways to show off heavy language is through literature. In *Verdi* (1997), Jannell Cannon writes about a young python being sent into the jungle to grow up "big and green" as all pythons must. Cannon could have written, "Verdi was a *nice* python. He wasn't *too big.* He was *slow.* He was *happy.* He had *neat* stripes *going down* his back." Instead, she used some heavy language: "Verdi dawdled. He was proudly eyeing his bright yellow skin. He especially liked the bold stripes that zigzagged down his back." We never hear a teacher say, "I'm just so tired of *zigzagged* and *dawdled.* There *must* be another way to say it!" We all like fresh language; we cannot get enough.

Word Choice as The Target

Precision is an important component of word choice. When one of your students uses a particularly precise word, you can paste that word right onto a "Word Choice Target"—right at the bull's-eye. In *Smoky Night* (1994), Eve Bunting describes a street riot. Following the turmoil, a street sign "lies crumpled in the gutter." Not bent. Not broken. *Crumpled.* Does that word hit the bull's-eye? You only have to ask your students, "What do you picture when you hear it? Does *crumpled* tell you more than *bent*?"

In *The Toy Brother* (1996), William Steig tells the tale of Yorick, a mischievous young sprout who hopes to become an alchemist, like his father—and who finds his brother Charles a real "pain in the pants." Charles cannot "fathom" why Yorick doesn't like him more and hopes they will someday become "palsy-walsy." When Yorick accidentally shrinks himself, Charles (who is on a ladybug hunt at the time) finds Yorick "thrashing" through the weeds: "It was indeed Yorick, down to the minuscule wart on his knuckle!" *Pain in the pants*, *fathom*, *palsy-walsy*, *thrashing*, *minuscule*—those are right-on-target words, bull's-eyes. Contrast this version: "Yorick wasn't much *fun*. He wasn't *nice*. Charles did not *get why*." We are on the outer rim of the target here.

What I like about the target is that it helps students to see that you can get the basic meaning across with vague words—like *nice*. Taking extra care to aim for the center, however, is worth it; bull's-eye words wake readers up.

 ## TEACHING FLUENCY CONCEPTUALLY

Fluency is wonderfully rewarding to teach conceptually. It is all about rhythm, grace, and motion. Think for a moment how very many things this applies to in real life—everything from an Olympic ski jumper to your own way of climbing or descending stairs. It could be the ripple of waves or the flitter of a butterfly. Wind in the treetops or a dust devil scooting across the fallow fields of the North Dakota farmlands. To teach this, start with your own graceful movement—again relying on music. This time, though, you are going for movement, not emotional response. Choose something lively, with a strong beat. Ask students to move to the music. They can march, twirl, wave arms, clap hands, snap fingers, stomp feet, sway—whatever has rhythm. You need to move with them. They need to feel the beat. You can teach . . .

✔ Fluency as personal imagery
✔ Fluency as "come alive" poetry you can perform

Fluency as Personal Imagery

Brainstorm. What—in the whole wide world around you—moves with rhythm? They will surprise you with their answers. As they speak, write what they say on an overhead transparency, creating a poem of possibles. Here is one third-grade version:

Fluency Is . . .

✔ Geese in a giant V
✔ Wild horses running
✔ Whales sounding
✔ Bats darting after insects
✔ Water flowing down a mountain
✔ Waves pounding on the shore

- ✓ Clouds shifting, meandering
- ✓ A rodeo clown
- ✓ Dancers in a line
- ✓ A parade
- ✓ Wheat in the fields
- ✓ Grasses bent by the wind
- ✓ Trees swaying in the storm
- ✓ Lighning flashing
- ✓ A chef flipping burgers
- ✓ Gravy dripping over mashed potatoes
- ✓ Skaters gliding
- ✓ Skiers flying
- ✓ People walking down the street
- ✓ A cat stretching
- ✓ A spider spinning its web
- ✓ A spider wrapping up its prey
- ✓ Hair in the wind
- ✓ Shadows flickering
- ✓ Fire
- ✓ Candlelight
- ✓ A bride's dress
- ✓ A pulse
- ✓ A drum beat
- ✓ A conductor's wand
- ✓ A musician's fingers
- ✓ A slowly widening smile
- ✓ My mother's hands

This is fluency!

Your students will think of more possibilities, more images. If it flows, if it moves with rhythm, if it moves with a beat, it's fluent.

Fluency as "Come Alive" Poetry You Can Perform

Want to take it one step further? Introduce some poetry your students can act out. Good possibilities for "come alive" poetry that you dramatize on your feet come from Douglas Florian (*Insectlopedia, Mammalabilia, Beast Feast*) or Shel Silverstein. Read a line and ask students to repeat it, moving, using arms, hands, eyes, and facial expressions to bring the poem to life. One poem I love is Douglas Florian's "Army Ants," from *Insectlopedia* (1998, p. 13). You will get the idea immediately if you stand up, right now, and march—left, right, left right—as you read aloud. This is a marching poem with a strong beat, and students love it. They can perform it in small groups or as a whole class. It is short, so they learn it quickly, but you can say a line first and then have your students repeat (the echo effect only enhances the rhythm):

> Left
> > Right
>
> Left
> > Right
>
> We're army ants.
> We swarm.
> > We fight.
>
> We have no home.
> We roam.
> We race.
> You're lucky if
> We miss your place.

A suggestion: Start the left-right, left-right in a whisper, slowly building to a crescendo. Then fade out again to a whisper at the end. Ask students to actually march around the room as they recite the poem. The marching feels good, and it reinforces the idea of fluency.

TEACHING CONVENTIONS CONCEPTUALLY

What are conventions, really? Rules, many student writers would say. (This is often what we think, too.) Actually, the word *conventions* signifies "traditions, customs, protocol"—the thing to do.

FIGURE 3.3	*Expanding control over conventions.* Jamie (2)

> But I don't want to move, Mom!
>
> Why do we have to move mom. What about Kyle? Kyle's a boy but he's also my friend! My only friend! My brother Ryan makes fun of me because he's a boy. But Mom says just to ignore him when he says that! the next morning, AHHHH, yelled my brother AHHH!!!! W-w what happend I asked. somebody stuck a frog down my pants AHH! Ha Ha I giggled. Grrr I'm gonna get you little pipsqeak!!! AHHH! I cried! AHHH. well this was in the morning wile my mom was still sleeping And both of us got in trouble! Grounded for the day! BORING!!! It turned out that we didn't have to move but my brother's still chasing me for puting that frog in his pants but he needed it so I'm not scared! Not one bit!! AHHH, THE End!

Conventions as Customs

Custom and tradition are woven through almost every part of our life. Ask your students to think about customs or traditions that go with eating a meal, for example. (You may need to coax a bit to get them started.) "These days, we usually eat with silverware, for example, not with our fingers—it was not always so! We eat from plates and bowls. Why? How do you suppose that became a mealtime convention?" Each time your students identify a convention or custom, ask why? "Why did that become the custom?"

Look at other situations, too. Sports, for instance, are riddled with conventions. Conventions are the rules of the game in baseball, basketball, or whatever. But what of other conventions? Such as wearing uniforms, having coaches, limiting the numbers of players who can participate at once (whole towns once played football), limiting the time of the game (once they played until everyone was wounded or exhausted), or having fans sit on the sidelines (years ago, "fans" and players were inseparable).

How about driving? What are the customs or conventions that govern our behavior on the road? What happens if we violate them? How about shopping at the grocery store? Visiting the library? Riding the bus? Walking a dog in the park? Dressing for school? Sitting in class? The possibilities are endless. The point here is to help students see, first, what conventions *are* (customs or approved ways of doing things) and, second, how conventions *came to be* (to make life easier, to make people comfortable, and so on).

If you wish to take it to the next step of looking at conventions in writing, you might begin with some writing that is as convention-free as you can make it. What you are doing is playing with readability. Write letters backward and upside down. Put no spaces between words. Spell words irregularly. Omit words, letters, or punctuation marks. Write from the bottom of the page up or right to left. Then ask your students the key question: "Why? Why wouldn't it work if everyone wrote this way?"

Everything from driving to shopping is easier if you know what is expected. It is the reason there is a certain period of adjustment when you visit a new state, town, school, home, or country. Their customs may be slightly (or greatly) different from what you are used to. Conventions in writing help us sidestep that adjustment period and immediately feel at home in any text, no matter who the author.

A LESSON IN ANATOMY: THE IMPORTANCE OF DOING IT

The lessons in this chapter, of course, are not a substitute for writing. They are only valuable in the context of coaching young writers as they make their own marks on paper. Writers have to write. All the time.

Several years ago I watched a western horsemanship instructor giving a group of seven-year-olds their first lesson. They were excited when she led an ornery old paint horse, Willie, out in front of them, and it was obvious from their expressions that in *their* eyes Willie was not a broken down, sway-backed, best-days-behind-him nag. He was flat-out beautiful. They were virtually quivering with anticipation, wondering who would be the first to take Willie around the arena. They wanted to touch him and make friends, to climb aboard and storm the track and win ribbons—but they had been instructed to "stay on the benches."

Excitement dissolved into tedium as it became increasingly apparent that the teacher's intent—at least for lesson one—was to hold off on any actual riding until everyone had mastered the "anatomy of the horse." Her circle of pupils sat stone-faced and rigid as she pointed to various spots on old Willie's legs, head, shoulders, and back and asked the "riders" in turn to supply the correct terminology. "When do we get to ride?" one of her more intrepid pupils finally asked. The instructor looked vaguely perturbed, remarkably unaware that she had lost the attention and enthusiasm of her class.

Before they left (looking a lot less excited than when they had come in), the instructor handed each student a homework sheet with a sketch of a horse and arrows leading to "parts of the horse" labels many of them could not read. These were to go home to parents for more drill and practice. I was willing to bet the class would be smaller the following week—but then, perhaps that is what she was hoping for. After all, she had eight pupils and only four horses. Teaching is almost always like that.

I was lucky—I didn't have that instructor. Becky, who sat a horse as if she'd been born on one, taught me to ride. For a time, she didn't provide much direct instruction at all. She watched me ride, and she rode with me and asked me to watch her. She and the horse moved as one; I wanted to ride like that—to move like that. I wanted to stop bumping up and down, inelegantly smacking the saddle and feeling my feet fall sloppily out of the stirrups. As I think back now to her instruction, I feel the best word to describe it would be *subtle*. She didn't write evaluations or give me points for heel extension or drill me on terminology. She encouraged me to *ride*—in fact, I was on top of a horse within five minutes of meeting her. "Imagine," she would say, "that your legs are so long they could reach clear around the horse and meet underneath." I literally felt my legs grow. "Imagine," she told me, "that every move you make is felt by the horse and interpreted as a signal of where you want to go." And as soon as she said it, I felt it happening. Over time, she taught me about keeping my hands quiet, reading a horse's ears, thinking "down and back" when loping, keeping a center of balance so that I could ride with my eyes closed, extending my legs so that the weight would go into my heels, and feeling the horse's feet move beneath me. We never did get to the anatomy lesson, but I learned anatomy anyway. I do not remember that part of her instruction at all. What I do remember—what I will *never* forget—is Becky saying, "Trust yourself. Go with the flow." Great teachers encourage and suggest—then they trust.

CHAPTER 3 IN A NUTSHELL

- Trait-based instruction is centered around writers' language. For this reason, it is not a curriculum unto itself, nor a new way of teaching writing. It is a way of *thinking* about writing that supports process-based writing instruction.
- Because traits (characteristics of strong writing) are inherent in every piece of good writing, they are necessarily embedded in writing instruction, even when we do not realize we are teaching them.

- Understanding the core meaning of a trait, what it truly is that we are teaching, enables us to teach each trait conceptually—to teach the fundamental meaning behind the trait.
- Ideas are about imagination, pictures in the mind, clarity of meaning, or a central message.
- Organization is about patterning, grouping, planning—creating a sense of direction.
- Voice is individuality, personality, mood, expression,

and connection to an audience—the right tone of voice for the message and the moment.

- Word choice is about precision, hitting the target, relying on verbs instead of modifiers, and using words that paint pictures in a reader's mind.
- Fluency is rhythm, grace, flow, music to the ears, going for the sound and not just the literal meaning.

- Conventions are traditions, customs, protocol, the sum of what's expected and accepted—whether in writing or in any context.
- Writers learn to write by doing it. The traits, therefore, are not an end in themselves but a means to making writing practice richer and more purposeful.

EXTENSIONS

1. Think of at least one more way—if you can—to present each trait conceptually. To do this, ask yourself, "What is the main thing, the underlying idea, I am trying to teach here?"

2. Think of the instruction you were given in writing. What was that like? Which of the two "riding instructors" did you encounter more often? Or was your experience something different from either?

3. Analyze your own way of teaching. How would you describe it?

4. Do you agree that "just writing" is the single most important thing a writer can do? Explain.

5. What would you say to someone who said, "The six traits have nothing to do with my writing curriculum"? Write a short response based on your own experience and thoughts.

6. What advantages do you see in teaching traits to young writers conceptually? Discuss these with a study group, if possible.

SOURCES CITED

Angelou, Maya. 1993. *Life Doesn't Frighten Me*. New York: Stewart, Tabori and Chang.

Aylesworth, Jim. 1992. *Old Black Fly*. New York: Henry Holt and Company.

Bragg, Rick. 2001. *Ava's Man*. New York: Alfred A. Knopf.

Bunting, Eve. 1995. *Smoky Nights*. San Diego: Harcourt Brace & Company.

Calkins, Lucy McCormick. 1994. *The Art of Teaching Writing*, New Edition. Portsmouth, NH: Heinemann.

Cannon, Janell. 1997. *Verdi*. San Diego: Harcourt Brace & Company.

Collard, Sneed B. III. 1997. *Animal Dads*. Boston: Houghton Mifflin Company.

Fletcher, Ralph. 1997. *Twilight Comes Twice*. Boston: Houghton Mifflin Company.

Florian, Douglas. 1998. *Insectlopedia*. San Diego: Harcourt Brace & Company.

Graves, Donald. 1983. *Writing: Teachers and Children at Work*. Portsmouth, NH: Heinemann.

Henkes, Kevin. 1990. *Julius, The Baby of the World*. New York: Mulberry Books.

Lamott, Anne. 1994. *Bird by Bird*. New York: Doubleday.

Lane, Barry. 1999. *Reviser's Toolbox*. Shoreham, VT: Discover Writing Press.

Lane, Barry. 2002. *The Tortoise and the Hare Continued. . . .* Shoreham, VT: Discover Writing Press.

Lane, Barry, and Gretchen Barnabei. 2001. *Why We Must Run with Scissors: Voice Lessons in Persuasive Writing*. Shoreham, VT: Discover Writing Press.

Lesser, Carolyn. 1996. *Great Crystal Bear*. San Diego: Harcourt Brace & Company.

Lichtenheld, Tom. 2000. *Everything I Know About Pirates*. New York: Simon & Schuster.

McGuane, Thomas. 2000. *Some Horses*. New York: Random House.

Marcellino, Fred. 1999. *I, Crocodile*. New York: HarperCollins.

Morrison, Toni (with Slade Morrison). 1999. *The Big Box*. New York: Hyperion Books for Children.

Newkirk, Thomas. 1989. *More than Stories: The Range of Children's Writing*. Portsmouth, NH: Heinemann.

Paulsen, Gary. 1993. *Dogteam*. New York: Delacorte Press.

Plourde, Lynn. 1999. *Wild Child*. New York: Simon & Schuster.

Ringgold, Faith. 1991. *Tar Beach*. New York: Crown Publishers.

Romano, Tom. 1995. *Writing with Passion: Life Stories, Multiple Genres*. Portsmouth, NH: Boynton/Cook.

Scieszka, Jon. 1995. *Math Curse*. New York: Viking Press.

Seinfeld, Jerry. 1993. *SeinLanguage*. New York: Bantam Books.

Shannon, David. 1998. *No, David!* New York: Scholastic Press.

Steig, William. 1996. *The Toy Brother*. New York: HarperCollins.

4 Trait by Trait—More Ideas for Teaching

Exploring the world for ideas: Ita decides that this pumpkin "needs a haircut!"

Children want to write. They want to write the first day they attend school. This is no accident. Before they went to school they marked up walls, pavements, newspapers with crayons, chalk, pens or pencils . . . anything that makes a mark. The child's marks say, "I am."

—Donald Graves
Writing: Teachers & Children at Work
(1983, p. 1)

Children have language, curiosity, and creative instincts. They have a voice that is often unique. But you have to believe in children's capabilities if you wish to entice the good ideas out of the crevices of their fertile minds.

—Ronald L. Cramer
Creative Power: The Nature and Nurture of Children's Writing (2001, p. 221)

TRAIT BASICS

There is no substitute for writing—for just doing it. So, we begin with an assumption that students, no matter how young, no matter how inexperienced, are writing in your classroom every day about a wide range of things. Having said that, within the context of all this writing, how many ways are there to weave in traits—which is to say, to teach students the *language of writing*?

Over the years, I have had lists of top ten ways to teach traits, seven keys to teaching traits, six strategies—hey, do you see a pattern here? The older I get, the more I appreciate simplicity. I like small books and short lists. And here is something I have learned about teaching: The closer you come to figuring things out, the smaller your lists get. You realize something you did not see at first—how things are connected. So, here it is—the newly revised list of four (only four) ways to teach traits (and woven through each, of course, is the use of trait language, writers' language):

1. Ask your *students* to be assessors (or if this sounds too formal, think of it as asking for their opinions).
2. Use literature to model what you want children to hear and see in good writing (and in weak writing, too). Or—just read aloud.
3. Write as a community of writers. Give students time to write. Believe they *can* write. Be a writer yourself. Model. Show students prewriting, drafting, revision, and editing in action (more on this in Chapter 6).
4. Use targeted lessons that help students strengthen specific skills (such as writing a lead or blending two sentences together).

In Chapter 5 we will look closely at portfolios, publishing, and the revision/editing process as it applies to primary writers. Chapter 6 deals exclusively with modeling—the importance of being a writer with your students. Chapter 7 is devoted to literature connections—books carefully chosen to help you illustrate strong voice, good word choice, and so on. Chapter 7 includes additional lessons, too.

In this chapter we will deal with the fourth method for teaching traits: *using targeted lessons*. As you go through this chapter, keep making the connections in your own mind, too: What am I *already doing* to teach this trait? If you are like most teachers, you will find numerous connections. Think of this chapter as helping you to recognize ways that you are *already* teaching traits.

They Hear It Before They Do It

Here's another thing to keep in mind: For very young writers, traits are first learned aurally. That is to say, they *hear* ideas, voice, or fluency. These elements may or may not show up in their own writing, though, for some time to come. Never mind. "Listen to this lead" *is* a lesson in organization every bit as much as if you were asking your students to write leads themselves. You can learn a lot about writing without a pencil in your hand or a keyboard at your fingertips.

Teaching a Trait Is Not the Same as Assessing It

This is why it makes sense to teach each trait long, *long*, *long* before a student is ready to be assessed on that trait. If we wait for students to craft fifty-sentence essays (so that we can assess them) before teaching fluency, we are waiting too long. If we wait for students to stun us with quotable passages before teaching voice, we are waiting too long. We are gambling that they will "get it" while we wait. Why do that? Instead of hoping that students will stumble fortuitously upon whatever it is we are looking for, let's define what we are looking for and show them how to get there.

TEACHING IDEAS
What You Are Teaching

- ✔ Main idea or message
- ✔ Clarity
- ✔ Detail (and interest)
- ✔ Noticing/observing

How to Get There

■ 1. Go from Big to Small (to "find" your main message)

Keeping It Small. One of the greatest lessons to be learned about writing is keeping it small. This lesson has been taught to me by every truly good writing teacher I have ever encountered (meaning the ones who were writers and readers themselves) and by all my writer friends. Tommy Thomason, head of journalism at Texas Christian University, likes to keep his books for teachers under 100 pages. The hallmark of Tommy's books (other than wisdom and readability): They are all skinny. He always tells me, "If you have more to say, write another book. Teachers are busy people." I believe this. Barry Lane is also an advocate of "small writing"—by which he means focusing in. Barry says, "Don't write about how messy your brother is. Write about how you hate finding hair on the soap in the shower" (1999, pp. 52–54).

In coming up with good topics, you need to think about everyday events, the stuff of real life, what you are seeing and feeling right now—or something you noticed just ten minutes ago. Do not go epic. Do not do "world peace." Let someone else handle the big, brooding moral issues of our time. Cut a one-inch hole in a piece of paper, and peek through. On the other side you will find almost every topic you ever need to write about.

Here are some possible tiny topics (just to give students the idea—these are *not* assignments):

- ✔ Difficulty with a pet
- ✔ A pesky insect
- ✔ Falling down
- ✔ A troublesome brother, sister, or friend
- ✔ A time I wished I had stayed home
- ✔ I thought it was lost for good
- ✔ I thought *I* was lost for good
- ✔ It's so boring, I can't stand it
- ✔ The worst weather ever
- ✔ A TV show not to waste your time on

| FIGURE 4.1 | *Big-to-little chart on "how lions hunt."* |

- ✔ I ruined the toast! (Or whatever)
- ✔ Advice I would like to give a friend (or relative)
- ✔ A habit I wish I could break
- ✔ The advertisement that hooked me
- ✔ The toughest food to give up
- ✔ A chore I could do without

Model It. Many student writers struggle with ideas that are too big to handle well: space, a happy life, school, families. Show them how to take a big idea down to size. You need to model this, and you can model it orally or on an overhead projector. Start with a topic such as *animals*. Create a set of steps like this:

Write your topic on the bottom step: "Animals." Explain that you think this is a very *big* topic and that big topics lead to vague writing. Why? Because there is just too much to say! So whittle it down, making this overwhelming topic smaller and smaller as you go. On step 2, you might write "Wild animals." Better, but still pretty big. On step 3, write "Wild animals of Africa." Better. But still large. On step 4, write "Lions." Now we are getting somewhere. But isn't there something specific about lions you could write about? How about hunting? Good. On step 5, write "How lions hunt." See Figure 4.1 to check out this simple but very useful narrowing process.

■ 2. Hunt for Details

This activity builds on the concept of "ideas as observation" presented in Chapter 3. Begin by bringing in objects for students to examine close up—just as before. This time around, ask students to work in pairs, just talking at first and then recording what they see. They can record with words or pictures—either way, they will need to look closely. Tell them that they are looking for *details*. Good things for examination: driftwood, shells, rocks, pinecones, moss or

FIGURE 4.2a   *Using detail.* Erin (2)

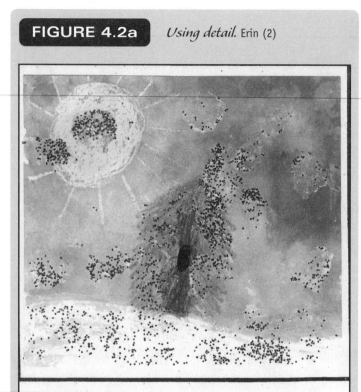

The smooth snow is like a soft feathery pillow.
The chirping birds are singing in the trees. The
bumpy tree trunk is not so soft. The leaves are slowly
swaying against the wind. The ocean colored sky is
filled with shades of light and dark blue. The daisy
yellow sun is shining brightly in the afternoon sky.
The chirping birds are singing loudly. The spring
snow makes me happy.

FIGURE 4.2b   *"What I see through my eyes."*

The sun
glistening on a group of trees
A storm has just passed by
Millions of pinecones
laying on the ground
silent as can be.
Snow capped mountains
in the distance
Mount Rainier sitting alone
glittering in the sun
Birds chirping
As they look for their lunch.

By Michael, Grade 3

other vegetation, flowers, fruit, fabric, their own hands, insects and spiders, fish, or small animals.

If they have practiced observing before, it is time to push a little to make details more explicit. For example, if your students say a rock is "brown," ask what kind of brown—chocolate brown, hen's-egg brown, mud brown, baked-potato brown? Ask them to think in analogies and metaphors: *The cone was as prickly as a porcupine. The corn silk looked like hair. The rock was a small mountain.*

Once their recording is done, invite them to use their observations as the bare bones of a detail poem—each detail becomes a line (see Figure 4.2).

A Variation. Have your students ever looked through a jeweler's loupe? If not, they are in for a treat! You can obtain loupes (and books of ideas, too) from many stores that carry educational or science-study materials. Details loom large through the loupes and invite students to make connections they could never make previously. In a book called *The Private Eye: Looking/Thinking by Analogy*, even very young students make amazing and telling visual discoveries examining their own hands: "craters of a meteor, a garden of cracks, rivers of lightning, elephant skin, threads woven together" (Ruef, 2000, pp. 86–87).

■ *3. Study Pictures*

This lesson is also about details. This time your students look at a picture instead of an object. It could be a photograph, a painting, a picture from a book, a sketch—anything. Greeting cards work particularly well. You can do several things with this. You might start with a list of details—and again turn it into a poem. You can also create a story. What's happening in the picture? Write about it, or put yourself into it—either way. If your students are not fluent writers yet, you can do the writing yourself. Let them supply the ideas. You will need to ask questions: "Who is the person in the picture? What just happened? What is he or she thinking? What's about to happen? Should this be a scary or funny story? How do you know? What else should we tell? Are we telling the reader enough? Too much?"

■ *4. Teach Students the Art of Questioning*

The first time you do this, you will need to supply the main idea and let students ask the questions. You can do this with a story—perhaps based on something that happened to you—or with an essay, description, or how-to piece. I have done this frequently with stories, most recently one based on a nasty little poodle named Pearl and her encounter with a coyote. I begin with a simple statement: "Pearl did not know she was in danger, but the coyote did." Then I invite students to ask me questions: "What do you want to know?" Here are the most frequently asked questions (which I always save):

- ✔ Who is Pearl?
- ✔ Why is she in danger?
- ✔ Does the coyote attack Pearl?
- ✔ Were you in danger too?
- ✔ Did Pearl get hurt?
- ✔ Did she die?

- ✔ What happened to the coyote?
- ✔ Did you rescue Pearl?
- ✔ What was the coyote thinking?
- ✔ What were you thinking?
- ✔ Were you scared?

I do three things next:

1. I keep a list of the questions on an overhead transparency so that I can share them again with students later.

2. I explain to students that it is not my job as a writer to answer *every* question—I will pick the ones I find most interesting.

3. I write a draft based on the questions plus my own memory of the event and share it with students.

Extensions. Ask students (if they are ready) to come up with their own topics. Then, with partners, have them generate questions and use the best questions to help write a draft. You can use questions with literature too, of course. Good authors are forever making striking or startling remarks that prompt questions, as Ellin Keene notes in *Mosaic of Thought* (1997), and she encourages teachers to capitalize on this by inviting students to talk through what they have read and form questions about it:

> *When we sent the children off to share questions with a partner and later to write, ideas flowed. Some began by simply writing the questions. Others were able to take ideas inspired by the questions and write longer pieces. Others drew pictures related to their questions. No one had to be told what to write [1997, p. 105].*

■ *5. Use Oral Skills*

For many writers, talking is an excellent form of prewriting. They need to talk over an idea *before* writing. Like sketching, talking helps writers think through connections, remember details, and put things into place.

Writers with big imaginations but limited keyboarding/pencil-paper experience can occasionally "write" an essay or story on tape. Playing it back helps young thinkers notice the details they have included or omitted, especially if you coach them to listen for this specifically. More advanced writers can write first, then read aloud to record, and play back to see if they have missed anything or have said all they want to say, just the way they want to say it.

Emily (Gr 1) is writing unanswered questions about her partner's writing.
[Photo and caption courtesy of Lilly (Grade 4).]

■ 6. Use Talking to Model Thinking

Talk through a story first, and then write a sketchy version of the same story and read it aloud to your students. Once when I was stranded overnight because of a canceled flight, the airline bused us to a hotel where almost nothing worked. Only one light came on—and it was not in the bathroom. In the morning, tired as I was and trying to get myself together in a dark bathroom, I shampooed my hair with hand lotion, not shampoo (I couldn't read the tiny label in the dark). This treatment gave me a halo of greasy spikes that made me look as if I'd had a bad day on the "Star Trek" set. Students generally love hearing this story, but suppose I wrote it up this way: "One day I had a bad experience! It all started when we missed our flight. We had to stay in a hotel. The hotel we stayed at was not that good. A lot of things didn't work. Thank goodness, we left after only one night."

Notice any details missing? You can bet students will, too. It's the contrast that helps them understand the value of details. Students also enjoy illustrating a story like this for you—as you can see from Figure 4.3.

■ 7. Draw!

Your students can certainly draw on their own, of course, but now and then you can join in the fun, too. Figure 4.4 shows how simple it can be to use a series of geometric shapes to sketch an animal such as a fox. This idea comes from *Draw Write Now*, book seven, by Marie Hablitzel and Kim Stitzer (2000). The idea is to guide students through the sketching process as you discuss the subject of the drawing—in this case, the fox. Students can help you fill in background details by suggesting where foxes live, what they eat, and so on. They can also suggest details—for example, "Add some toenails"—that go beyond this simple geometric sketch. When you complete the sketch (remember, your students are drawing right along with you), you and they can do some research on foxes, making a list of details. Then use what you find to create stories or all-about papers (a simple kind of research paper). From this activity, students learn to use detail in both art and writing, learn to link text to illustrations, and also learn a bit about research.

FIGURE 4.3   *"My Hotel Adventure" as illustrated by Andrew (3).*

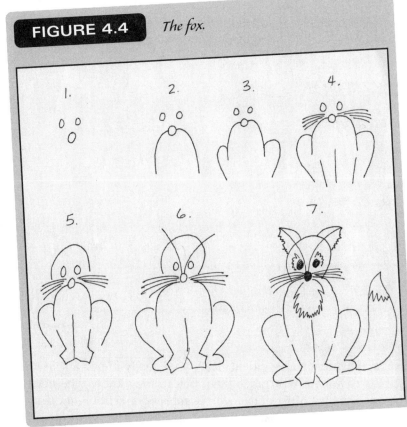

FIGURE 4.4   *The fox.*

■ 8. Use "Snapshots"

This idea comes from author/teacher Barry Lane, who explains it in great detail in his wonderful book *Reviser's Toolbox* (2000, Chap. 3, 74ff). It is a variation on an old theme: *Show, don't tell.* Unfortunately, students do not always understand what we mean by this. As teacher Laura Harper explains (Lane, 2000, p. 217), "I wish I had a nickel for every time I scrawled 'Describe' or 'Explain' or 'Give me more detail' next to an imprecise sentence. . . . Sentences such as 'I walked into my bedroom' actually became worse . . . turning into 'I walked into my big, blue, full, messy bedroom.'"

I like the snapshot idea because students can immediately picture what we mean: *I want to see it, like a photo in an album.* Instead of piling on adjectives, they create pictures. Delia, a second grader, created this snapshot of her family at dinner:

My supper is always the same.

My sister won't eat.

My other sister whines but I just listen to the crickets. [Lane, 2000, p. 75]

This is a simple snapshot, but it is extremely vivid. If this were actually in a photo album, it is the one you would point to and say, "That's so typical! That's *just* how Delia's family looks at dinner!" That's the purpose. Teach this with an example first; then have your students try it.

Vague sentence: "I walked into my room."

Snapshot: "I stomped into my room. I threw myself on the bed and punched my pillow hard. I had to blink my eyes to keep from crying." *(Do you see it?)*

Vague sentence: "It was hot."

Snapshot: "Our shirts stuck to us like plastic wrap. We tried cooling down with ice cream, but it turned to mush before we could get our tongues on it." *(Do you see it?)*

Here are some vague sentences for your students to turn into snapshots:

✔ The dog was mean.
✔ He was tired.
✔ I felt frightened.
✔ She had a nice face.
✔ Grandma was brave.

Tip: Very young writers can do snapshots with pictures, dictation, or a combination of picture and text. It's the concept that counts.

TEACHING ORGANIZATION
What You Are Teaching

✔ How to begin
✔ How to end
✔ Sense of order, patterning, sequencing
✔ How to link ideas together

How to Get There
■ 1. Choose Strong Leads

What is the most boring way you could begin a research report . . . ? We all know. "In this report I will tell you about . . . ."

—Barry Lane
Reviser's Toolbox (2000, p. 30)

In any kind of writing, leads are critical. They are equally important in visual media. Ask students how long it takes them before they know whether they like a TV program or a film. Most of us form an impression within moments, although some of us hang in there longer than others, hoping a dull show will improve. Like filmmakers, good writers know they have to hook readers quickly or lose them. However, young students may not even be aware of the time and effort writers have put into leads; it probably has never occurred to them to think about it. You can heighten their awareness first by comparing and contrasting different possible leads—then by simply asking, "Which one do you like better?" That's it—that *is* the lesson.

Of course, you need contrast to make this lesson work:

Lead 1: "This will be a story about picnics on our apartment roof. Ready? Here goes."

Lead 2: "I will always remember when the stars fell down around me and lifted me above the George Washington Bridge."

Which one do you like better? If you are like most readers, you picked the very magical lead 2, the actual opening to Faith Ringgold's classic *Tar Beach* (1991).
Try another:

Lead 1: "The night Max wore his wolf suit and made mischief of one kind and another, his mother called him "WILD THING!" and Max said "I'LL EAT YOU UP!" so he was sent to bed without eating anything."

Lead 2: "In this story, I will tell you about Max, a boy who acts wild sometimes."

Another easy choice. Lead 1, of course, is from Maurice Sendak's *Where the Wild Things Are* (1963).

As you explore the leads from books you love to read to your students, you will find that most are strong. Here is one of my favorites from Fred Marcellino's *I, Crocodile* (1999): "Ah, what a contended crocodile I used to be. Wallowing around in slimy green water. . . . Snoozing on mudbanks in the hot sun. . . . Scaring the life out of anything that walked by." Imagine the difference if Marcellino had written, "Hi. I'm Fred, and I like crocodiles. Do you? In my book, I'll tell you everything I know about crocodiles. . . ."

■ *2. Use the Visual*

You can use the power of visual media to teach leads (as well as other elements of writing). Play just the first few minutes of any program (TV show or movie) for your students, and ask them to think about what hooks their interest. Perhaps it is a striking image, a bit of dialogue, or something funny—or scary. Some filmmakers plunge right in, whereas others work up to the high points. Either way, as Lucy Dahl recounts in *James and the Giant Peach: The Book and Movie Scrapbook* (1996), "Every movie begins with a script. . . ." Writers guide the way a film begins, how the characters move and when and what they say, how scenes are set up, and so much more. You and your students may enjoy exploring Lucy's tale of how a favorite story became a film. In addition, though, encourage your students to look at visual media through the eyes of a writer and to ask questions such as these: Why does the film begin (or end) this way? If I were the scriptwriter, would I begin (or end) differently?

Alternative. Choose a favorite book, and ask your students to imagine that it is going to be made into a movie. Ask them to work in pairs to come up with an opening scene. How and where should the movie begin? They can sketch the opening scene if they like. They may also wish to come up with some music to set the mood.

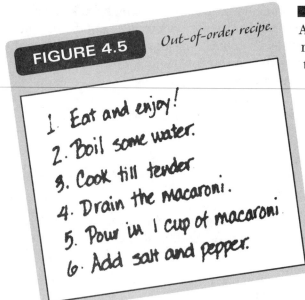

FIGURE 4.5   *Out-of-order recipe.*

1. Eat and enjoy!
2. Boil some water.
3. Cook till tender
4. Drain the macaroni.
5. Pour in 1 cup of macaroni.
6. Add salt and pepper.

■ 3. Make Predictions

A next logical step after listening for strong leads is to make predictions based on what a writer tells you. Try this lead from William Steig's book *Brave Irene* (1986):

> *Mrs. Bobbin, the dressmaker, was tired and had a bad headache, but she still managed to sew the last stitches in the gown she was making.*
>
> *"It's the most beautiful dress in the whole world!" said her daughter, Irene. "The duchess will love it."*
>
> *"It is nice," her mother admitted. "But dumpling, it's for tonight's ball, and I don't have the strength to bring it. I feel sick."*

Make a list of predictions, based on this brief opening. Encourage your students to guess what *might* happen next. It's like going on a journey, imagining what will be around the next bend.

■ 4. Put Things in Order

Take any piece of writing and divide it into five or more short sentences, writing each on a separate strip of paper. Stories work well for this activity, but you can also use directions, recipes (see Figure 4.5), expository writing, advertisements, letters, newspaper articles, or pretty much anything. Try to choose a piece in which sequence makes a difference. For example, order matters greatly in a recipe; it often matters in a poem—but not always.

Give each strip to one student, and give the students time to meet in a group, sort themselves out (so that the sequence makes sense), and prepare to present the writing to the class. As they line up in order, you (or one of the other students) should read the whole piece aloud. When you have finished, ask the rest of the class (those who are not part of the sequence group) to comment on the order. Does it make sense? Is anything out of place?

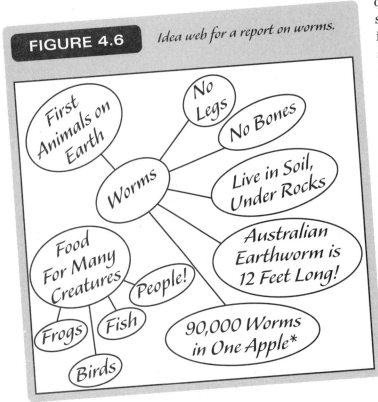

FIGURE 4.6   *Idea web for a report on worms.*

First Animals on Earth

No Legs

No Bones

Worms

Live in Soil, Under Rocks

Australian Earthworm is 12 Feet Long!

Food For Many Creatures

People!

Fish

Frogs

90,000 Worms in One Apple*

Birds

■ 5. Use Idea Webs to Plan

Graphic organizers of all kinds are helpful to older or more experienced students in organizing information. You can model this by choosing any subject about which you have some knowledge and talking through a few elements that you might include in a report. This is the key—*a few*. Do not make the web too complex, or it may look intimidating.

Talk through the web (see Figure 4.6) as you sketch it: "My report will be about worms, so I'll put that right in the middle. Now I'm going to add some details I know about worms. For one thing, they were the first creatures on earth; they have been here for about half a billion years. They have no legs . . . and no bones either. Worms aren't very good fighters, so they need to hide. They live in the soil or under rocks. They hide there because worms are food for many creatures, including frogs, birds, and fish. People can eat some kinds of worms—they're usually not poisonous—but I don't think I'd want to! I also learned that earthworms can be huge! In Australia, they grow up to 12 feet long!" (Information source: *Ranger Rick*, Vol. 34, No. 7 (July 2000), p. 33. Vienna, VA: The National Wildlife Federation.)

Put your web on chart paper, and post it where students can see it easily. Take this lesson to the next step and write a paragraph on worms (or whatever your topic may be) using the parts of your web to organize information. Read the paper aloud as your students study the web.

Note: Author/teacher Marcia Freeman reminds us that many students are not ready for something as advanced as webbing. "Primary writers are not ready for abstract graphic planners such as webs, clustering, mapping, timelines. Teach them to talk, draw, make lists, and make pictures while they gather thoughts before writing" (1998, p. 139). I agree with this core philosophy completely, and if you do find that webbing is beyond your students, by all means forget it. In my experience, though, some students *do* like it—and find it helpful. Perhaps it is just the right combination of picture making and writing for them.

Ellie, a first grader, for example, creates a fairly complex web to organize her thoughts for a paper on things she is thankful for (Figure 4.7a). In Ellie's case, the web becomes just an alternative to talking or listing—but this is not to say that it will work with all children. You must use your judgment. Figure 4.7b shows Ellie's finished paper, which follows the web very closely:

■ 6. Use Lists

Just as webs help to organize information, so do lists, and for many students, lists are simpler. As with webs, the secret is not to make them too big. Here's a list of possible readers' questions based on the same topic: worms.

1. Where do worms live?
2. Are worms ever dangerous?
3. How many kinds of worms are there?
4. Do worms have bones?
5. Can worms see or hear?
6. How long do worms live?

Once I have my list of questions, I can reorder them if I want and put the most interesting question (I think it's "Are worms dangerous?") either first or last. This will give me a punchy lead or conclusion.

■ 7. End It!

Even professional writers struggle with wrapping it all up, so expecting knockout endings from beginning writers is asking a lot. Still, some suggestions may help. Here are a few that are fairly easy for younger writers to understand:

1. *What happened last?* Example: "Finally, we got home safely."

FIGURE 4.7a

"Things I'm Thankful For." Ellie (1)

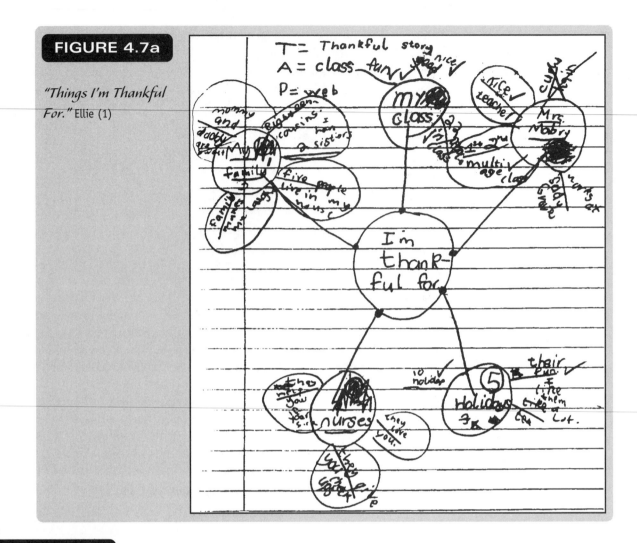

FIGURE 4.7b

I am thankful for my family. My family makes me laugh a lot. Five people live in my house. I have two sisters and 21 cousins. I love my mommy and Daddy.

I am thankful for nurses. They love you. They take care of you. And they give you check ups.

I am thankful for Mrs. M. She is nice. She teaches multi-age 1st and 2nd at Shady Grove.

I am thankful for my class. My class is nice and very fun too. There are older and younger people in my class.

I am thankful.

By Ellie, Grade 1

2. *The most important thing.* Example: "The most important thing when you ride a bike is to be safe."

3. *The thing I remember most.* Example: "The thing I will never forget is how far I could see out the plane window."

4. *Something I learned.* Example: "Fishing is harder and more fun than I thought."

As with leads, share the best examples from the literature you read aloud to your students. I will share some of my favorites in Chapter 7. Listening to what other writers have done is very helpful.

TEACHING VOICE

What You Are Teaching

✔ Putting energy into writing
✔ Recognizing voice
✔ Selecting personally important topics
✔ Connecting to an audience

How to Get There

■ *1. Write Notes and Letters*

Notes and letters work especially well for developing voice because voice is, in part, a writer-to-reader bridge, a way of connecting to an audience. With a letter, the audience is built in. In "How to Write a Letter," Garrison Keillor (1989, pp. 138–139) suggests this frame of mind: ". . . let your friend come to mind until you can almost see her or him in the room with you. Remember the last time you saw each other and how your friend looked and . . . when your friend becomes real to you, start to write." In short, picture your audience. Picture the person's face, the expression as he or she opens the letter. Ask your students to do this.

Students can write to each other, to you, to their parents ("Dear Mom—You are invited to an after-school conference with miss Blair . . ."), to sports figures, celebrities, favorite authors, or people in your community. If they can bring in a photograph to go with the letter (see Figure 4.8), so much the better.

FIGURE 4.8

"Dear Ann, I'd love to go riding with you this weekend. Remember how Smokey bucked you off two weeks ago? Ha, ha. What good times we had! Love, Vicki."

Letters, even when written for a business purpose, are a way of putting ourselves on the page. Donald Murray (1990, p. 34) tells us, "Even in the corporate world, the writer is egocentric, obsessed with self. This is what each writer, no matter the mode or form of writing, has to offer: the individual view and the individual gift." Voice *is* a gift.

Help Students to Discover Personally Important Topics. It is important for students to find topics to write about that they care about deeply, even passionately. If this does not happen, voice tends to remain luke warm. If we want writing that excites us, we need excited writers to produce it. It is hard to come up with a topic that excites someone else; this is why assigning writing is such a thankless task. Restrictive, assigned topics sound something like this: "Think of a birthday gift you really liked. Write a story about receiving that gift. Be sure to tell what happened and how you felt."

There is nowhere to go with a topic like this. It's a form to be filled out. Suggestions, by contrast, often appear as pictures, single words, phrases, incomplete sentences, or quotations—anything that opens mental doors with just a hint or suggestion, but nothing more. Offer your students a "borrowing list" (and post it) *just* for those times when they find themselves staring at a blank sheet of paper and nothing—absolutely *nothing*—comes to mind.

Exploring the world for ideas: Kennedy has found something she is ready to write about: "He has a soft black nose. I would take care of him by giving him lots of leftovers."

✔ The hardest thing
✔ I can't forget it
✔ A good friend
✔ It made me angry
✔ Oops!
✔ I wish I never had to hear it again
✔ It almost worked
✔ I'm happy that . . .
✔ I'm supposed to like it, but I don't
✔ The trouble with _____
✔ Warning: Don't eat _____
✔ My advice
✔ Taking turns
✔ I'd love to do it again
✔ A book you should not miss
✔ Something worth saving
✔ You're old when . . .

Don't abuse your borrowing list—it's a resource for ideas when you're stuck, never a replacement for students' own topics.

> *The first consideration in writing or teaching writing is choice of topic. Real writers choose their own topic; therefore, children should be allowed to do the same. I chose the topic for this chapter. When I suggested it to the editor she didn't say, "No, you can't write about that. Write about this."*
>
> **—Mem Fox**
>
> *Radical Reflections* (1993, p. 36)

The worst paper we see in college writing is the paper in which "nobody's home." We do this to students. We do it to them in school by having them write about things they know nothing about. Worse, we have them write about things they don't care anything about. The writing is for only one person, the teacher. It's written "To Whom It May Concern."

—Donald Graves and Virginia Stuart
Write from the Start: Tapping Your Child's Natural Writing Ability (1985, p. 38)

"I Have a Student Who Only Wants to Write About One Thing!". Keep in mind that some students have a few favorite topics on which they like to write repeatedly. There is nothing wrong with this. Adult writers do the same. Review several books by any favorite author, and you're likely to encounter recurring themes, settings, and even characters. As Regie Routman reminds us, "Students have to care about their writing to write well, and they care about things in which they are interested. One of the mistakes we make is to expect writers to come up with new topics all the time—every day, in some classrooms" (Routman, 2000, p. 213).

2. Show Students How to Put "Personal Self" into Their Writing

When you come up with a topic you would like to write about, one that is personally important to you, model the thinking you use to put yourself, body and soul, into the time and place where you need to be to write. Close your eyes, put yourself just in the moment, take it in, get every sensory detail you can, and talk it through; for example, "I am on a rocky cliff close to the beach. The surf is pounding the rocks so hard we have to scream, but we're laughing, too. I'm walking with my parents, and my mother has the wrong kind of shoes for climbing rocks. Little white sandals with pink roses on the top. Why did she wear those? I think to myself. That was so stupid. Then, she slips, and before any of us can catch her, she has scraped her shin and is bleeding. She's crying, and I try to comfort her, hugging her, but she does not want to be hugged because she is afraid of falling again. All I want to do is put my arms around her, but I'm too short to hold her up. Suddenly, I am furious with the ocean for being so loud. My mother cannot hear my soothing voice. I want to help, but I can't, so I begin to cry. . . ."

In one of the best books ever written on writing, *Writing From the Heart*, Nancy Slonim Aronie talks about making writing our own, sinking into the moment, and knowing the power of our own voices, for each one is unique: "Readers don't need commentary. They don't need detached description. They don't need big words. They don't need imitation Alice Walker. They need you, with *your* language, *your* rhythms, *your* story. They need your heart" (1998, p. 32).

3. Nurture Voice in an Atmosphere of Sharing

Some elements of voice can be taught directly. Some can be *nurtured*. Sometimes teachers say, "If voice is about personality, how can you teach it?" Well, of course, it isn't quite that literal: "Today's lesson, kids—personality. When you finish this lesson, people will seek you out. Now let's begin with that smile. . . ." On the other hand, personality can most certainly be nurtured, rewarded, and fostered. The same is true of voice. You reinforce it by providing an atmosphere in which it feels safe to share and to experiment. You also reinforce voice when you value it and *show* that you value it by reading voice-filled pieces (whether by professionals or by your students) aloud.

Writers also need audience response. We should teach students to respond respectfully to one another, but we have to be careful. Honesty is also important. A kind of forced politeness comes through in comments such as "I really liked your paper" or "That was so good." When students are not sure what to say, here are some *kinds* of comments that can be helpful to a writer:

✔ Name a favorite word or phrase.
✔ Describe something you pictured in your mind as you were listening.
✔ Did the paper remind you of something? What?
✔ Do you still have an interesting question for the writer? What?
✔ Are you curious about what will happen next? Say so.
✔ Did anything surprise you? What?
✔ Did the voice in the paper sound like the writer's speaking voice? If so, let the writer know.

Sharing can be scary for some students (even though it is the high point of the day for others). You can create an atmosphere in which sharing feels safe by, first, sharing your own writing (often) and, second, coaching students on appropriate responses through modeling and examples. Sharing should never feel formulaic, but I think it is helpful to have some ground rules:

✔ Listen with your whole body—eyes, ears, posture.
✔ Think about what the writer is trying to tell you and show you.
✔ Focus on your feelings and thoughts as you listen.
✔ Be honest.
✔ Be kind.

It is helpful if your personal response comes last; it is often the one that will make the greatest impression. Some teachers encourage applause; some dislike it. I think applause is fine as long as it's not a measure of how well students liked the piece of writing—that creates tension and bad feelings. What we should applaud, really, is the writer's courage and willingness to share. This in itself is an achievement—and with this approach, everyone's applause meter is the same.

Students are perfectly capable of writing with voice if we show them how. The same is true for using conversation, meaningful detail, and verbs—even for young writers.

—**Regie Routman**
Conversations (2000, p. 210)

■ 4. Make Room for Alternatives

Same old stories? Same old essays? How about a different form of writing? Instead of a book report, ask students to do a book review, giving the book one to five stars and stating why someone should or should not read it. What if a favorite character from a book escaped? Create a wanted poster. How about an advertisement—say, for chocolate from Willie Wonka's chocolate factory or for the services of Dr. DeSoto, the mouse dentist created by William Steig (1982). Résumés are a good way to get at character and to develop voice as well. Here is a start for a résumé for the witch in "Hansel and Gretel":

Name: Corinne Johnson (nickname: Corie)

Address: The woods

Phone: No phone—people just stop by

Hobbies: Working with children, baking, singing, raising pet scorpions

Experience:

Professional baker: 10 years

Children's camp director: 20 years

Home decorator: 15 years

Professional goal: To star in a movie about my life

Your students also can write poems, songs, journal entries, recipes, weather reports, or news articles:

> Singer and songwriter Jonathan Wolf (who goes by the stage name of Big Bad) was arrested today for assaulting three local business people, owners of The Three Pigs Construction Company. Wolf admitted to being present when two buildings recently completed by Three Pigs Construction suddenly collapsed. However, he denied any responsibility. "I was just happening by," he said. "It was really quite lucky I was not hurt." The pigs, however, tell a different version of the story. "He deliberately flattened the buildings," said Herbert, oldest of the three pig brothers. Wolf admits that his years of singing have given him amazing lungs, but scoffs at the idea he could blow down a house. He called the pigs' charges "ridiculous." A hearing is set for next Tuesday following the grand opening of the Three Pigs Restaurant, which is built entirely of brick.

■ 5. Write in Character

Take idea 4 a step further and ask your students to write in character as someone else. Stepping into the shoes of another person—even for a short while—helps you appreciate that person's perspective, and perspective influences voice tremendously. My friend and colleague Lois Burdett teaches Shakespeare to her second and third graders in Hamlet School in Stratford, outside Ontario, Canada. Her students hear the stories of William Shakespeare and act them out as well. The sight of such young actors in beards, wigs, capes, caps, and boots is stunning and inspiring—but most striking of all is their ability to get inside the hearts and minds of the characters and even Shakespeare himself. "Imagine," Lois tells her students, "that you are on your way to becoming the most famous playwright the world has ever known—and your beloved Globe Theater burns to the ground. How do you feel?" The children are touched by Shakespeare's plight and express their feelings in letters that might have been written by Shakespeare to his wife Anne. In the introduction to one letter (Burdett, 1995, p. 56), seven-year-old Marijke writes, "I hve some dredful noos for you Anne. Our globe Theatre is histery! Gone capush!" Marijke's voice comes through loud and clear in her note. She *is* the playwright who has lost his theater. (For more examples, see Lois Burdett's books, listed under "Sources Cited" at the end of this chapter.)

■ 6. Act It Out

Get students on their feet whenever possible. The combination of speaking (or oral reading) and body language does wonders for developing voice! Choral reading and a readers' theater (in which students read parts aloud from a text) are excellent. The come-alive approach to poetry noted in Chapter 3 also works well. For truly boundless ideas on using drama in the classroom, I recommend Carol Glynn's imaginative book, *Learning on Their Feet* (2001). Carol describes games for dramatizing concepts (such as punctuation, immigration, or the seasons) and for using dialogue or monologue to express ideas of all kinds.

One of my favorites in her bag of many tricks is the use of statues that come to life. Selected students become statues of persons in the neighborhood, for example, a bakery clerk, postal clerk, police officer, teacher, firefighter, person waiting for a bus, person washing windows, person gardening, person walking a dog, and so on (Glynn, 2001, p. 190). Students can work with you in creating a setting; for example, "It was early Monday morning in the town of Summerville. The residents were just coming to life." Students who are not playing parts for this round work with you to create a story of the events of the day; for example, "Mr. Greely was walking his dog Grumbles. Grumbles was pulling hard on the leash, making it difficult for Mr. Greely to stay on the path!" Mr. Greely acts out his part for a short time; then it's on to the next character. Breathing life into the "statues" is an excellent warm-up for breathing life into writing. You will find your students using more verbs in their writing when they have actually acted scenes out.

■ 7. Keep It Snappy

Get a volunteer student to act out the concept/character of "bored" in front of the class. How does "bored" look? Tired eyes, perhaps poor posture (kind of a slump), listless expression, limp arms, and so on. Now ask your students to transform "bored" into "excited"—by telling the actor what to do. (Movement is encouraged!) Then ask them to remember the difference when they write. Which person is likely to compose the piece that will keep you awake—"bored" or "excited"? Tell them, "I want to be able to picture your face and posture—I want to see the face of 'excited' in my mind when I read your writing."

Extend this by showing that even factual writing can be exciting. Here are six facts about sharks, followed by two reports. Which was written by "bored"? Which was written by "excited"? Can your students tell?

Facts

1. Sharks have been on earth for millions of years.
2. Sharks get new teeth throughout their lives—up to 50,000 of them.
3. Some sharks have powerful tails and use them to kill prey.
4. A shark's skin is very rough.
5. Sharks can smell things—such as blood—that are a mile away.
6. Only a few sharks are truly dangerous.

Sample 1 ("Bored" or "Excited"?)

Sharks have been on earth a long time. They are very interesting. If they lose their teeth, they get new ones. Sharks have strong tails. They have a good sense of smell. They have rough skin. Some sharks are dangerous. Some aren't.

Sample 2 ("Bored" or "Excited"?)

Sharks are among the oldest creatures on earth. They were around even before the dinosaurs. Though people are generally afraid of sharks, only a few are dangerous. When sharks do kill a person, it's usually an accident. To a shark, a person swimming sometimes looks like a seal—and that means lunch! Unlike people, sharks get new teeth all through their lives, so if they lose one, it's no big deal. A shark can get up to 50,000 new teeth in its life. A shark's skin is as rough as sandpaper, and if you touch it, it could actually scratch you.

■ *8. Encourage Students to Say What They Mean*

Authentic writing on real topics is, in the end, the best (if not the only) path to voice. A teacher once said to me, "I love the papers about rainbows and blue skies. There is too much violence in the world. We need more students who write about happy things." I disagree. We need more happy students, this is true. But rainbows and blue skies, appealing as they are, are not reality for many students. If we cringe at their reality and force them into some phony fantasy world where all is well, we discourage voice instead of nurturing it. Donald Graves tells us that "People who write with their own voices are people who are not afraid to say what they mean" (Graves and Stuart, 1985, p. 38). While I do not for a second advocate encouraging gratuitous violence in writing (e.g., alien planets warring with one another), it is simply a fact of life that some students feel anger or depression and have a need to write about it. Delving into private lives is stepping over the line certainly, but at the same time, we should be open to honesty and authenticity, even when it does not come packaged in rainbows.

TEACHING WORD CHOICE

Voice is integrally connected to word choice. A strong voice and apt wording keep readers reading for little sparks of surprise and humor.

—Donald Graves and Virginia Stuart

Write from the Start: Tapping Your Child's Natural Writing Ability (1985, p. 38)

What You Are Teaching

✔ Being choosy about words
✔ Identifying favorite words
✔ Using strong verbs
✔ Knowing a verb from a noun—or adjective

How to Get There

■ *1. Act Out Words (Pick One Out of the Basket)*

Everyone is tired of the old vocabulary lists. There must be an easier, more interesting way. Here's one. Choose vocabulary words that your students are likely to really need and use (perhaps some come from books you are currently reading or discussions your class is having). Print each in big letters on a three-by five-inch card, and put the cards into a bag or basket. Pass the bag or basket around, and ask each student to draw one card. The student should come to class the next day ready to act out his or her word. Drama imprints meaning on the mind in a way that memorization alone cannot even touch.

■ *2. Make Posters*

A variation on idea 1 calls for students to make posters. Each poster should include the word itself and a definition. The word could also be used in a sentence. Display posters for a time in your classroom or on hallway walls for everyone to see. Students learn the poster words of others as well as their own.

■ *3. Toss the Ball*

This game can work in numerous ways, depending on the ages of your students and their readiness. The basic game is always the same. Students form a circle and take turns tossing the ball, randomly, to anyone of their choice. One rule: Everyone must get a turn! The person tossing the ball gets to decide what the person receiving must come up with. Possibilities include words beginning with *w* (or any letter), any action word (verbs), any noun (naming word), any describing word (adjective), or the next word in a sentence (the person tossing the ball must say *all* the words so far). The game can be more focused, such as any word that rhymes with *ball*, any word that describes feelings, any word that names an animal, any word you could use instead of *nice*, or any word you are tired of! Use your imagination to vary the game each time you play.

■ 4. Do a Sentence as a Play

While we do not want *parts of speech* to become the whole focus for word choice, it is helpful if students know some basics, such as nouns, verbs, adjectives, and adverbs. If they do not know these basic parts of speech, it will be difficult to share important advice of this sort: "Use specific *nouns*. Use lively *verbs*." Here's a painless way to teach parts of speech—and it's one that students will remember. First, create a short sentence that has at least one noun, verb, adjective, and adverb. It can end with a period or question mark. Write each word or punctuation mark on a separate strip of paper or large card (see Figure 4.9). Be sure the print is big enough for the whole class to read. Here is a sample sentence:

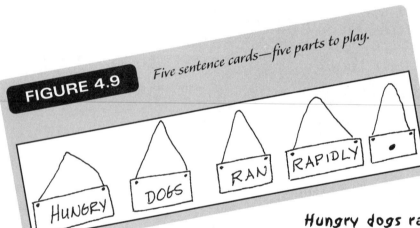

Five sentence cards—five parts to play.

FIGURE 4.9

Hungry dogs ran rapidly.

Students can hold the cards, but this game works better if they can hang them, by string, around their necks so that their hands and arms are free. Invite students to play the various roles—one student per word or punctuation mark. The actor playing *hungry* tells the *dogs* (you can have two students play this part because it's plural) how to look or act. Why? Because adjectives "boss nouns around," if you will. They tell them how to look, sound, smell, and so on. Similarly, *rapidly* bosses *ran* around (because adverbs control verbs). When it's his or her turn, *rapidly* should keep telling *ran* what to do: for example, "Faster—you need to move faster!"

■ 5. Create Advertisements

People who write ads know how important good language can be in persuading us to buy things. Spend some time collecting ads you think are especially enticing—for their word power or visual appeal or both. Talk with your students about particularly persuasive wording. Which products would they buy? Which words "speak" to them? Make a list and keep it in sight so that your students can use words they like. Then create ads of your own. You can use common items your children already have—for example, backpacks, pens, books, or clothing. Or you can branch out, working in some art. Students can find pictures or photographs or create sketches, paintings, or collages to represent virtually anything they may wish to "sell," from pets to vacations.

■ 6. Create Some Small Writing (Greeting Cards, Bumper Stickers, Tee Shirts)

Young students love writing books—of course! Yet some of the strongest writing is little: greeting cards, Post-It notes, bumper stickers, and so on. Why? Because the writer has only a few words with which to get the message across—so not a word can be wasted. As with any writing, it helps to have a sense of purpose, so you might suggest ideas like these:

✔ A poster advertising our school play
✔ Post-It note reminders for people who keep forgetting things!
✔ A greeting card for someone who needs cheering up
✔ A bumper sticker for drivers who tailgate
✔ A bumper sticker for a driver who loves his or her car
✔ A thank-you card for someone who took care of your pet or your plants

■ 7. Revise "Weak Verb" Pieces

This lesson will emphasize the *choice* part of word choice and encourage students to be on the lookout for strong verbs at the same time. Start with a passage from a book you like—one with strong verbs. Here's a short passage from Chris Van Allsburg's *Two Bad Ants* (1988, pp. 4–5):

> The news <u>traveled</u> swiftly through the tunnels of the ant world. A scout had <u>returned</u> with a remarkable discovery—a beautiful sparkling crystal. When the scout <u>presented</u> the crystal to the ant queen she took a small bite, then quickly ate the entire thing. She <u>deemed</u> it the most delicious food she had ever tasted [underlining mine].

Notice the strong verbs in this passage: *traveled, returned, presented, deemed.* You could rewrite this passage for your students (prior to showing them the original), replacing these strong verbs with weaker substitutes, for example, *went* (for *traveled*), *come back* (for *returned*), *gave* (for *presented*), and *called* (for *deemed*). Try reading the passage aloud now with these substitutions. Not nearly as satisfying, is it? Ask students to brainstorm some possible replacements for the weaker verbs you have come up with; for example, "What could we say instead of *went*?" See how many possibilities they come up with; then share Allsburg's original—just for comparison. It is not necessary for them to come up with an exact match. The emphasis here is on the *choice* part of word choice—coming up with as many choices as possible.

■ 8. Keep Personal Dictionaries

As students learn new words, from reading, from conversation, or from direct instruction, encourage them to keep personal dictionaries in their notebooks. These "dictionaries" do not need to be totally alphabetized, but it is helpful to keep all the *b* words together, all the *n* words together, and so on. These dictionaries may be small at first, but they will grow! Encourage students to share words with each other, too, and to borrow. See Figure 4.10 for an example.

■ 9. Collect Favorites

In *Dr. DeSoto*, William Steig (1982) writes of a charming mouse dentist who refuses, at first, to take on a crafty fox as his patient. The fox, in terrible pain, finally persuades the soft-hearted DeSoto to remove his tooth—then stumbles home still under the influence of anesthetic:

> The fox, still woozy, said goodbye and left. On his way home, he wondered if it would be shabby of him to eat the DeSotos when the job was done.

FIGURE 4.10 *Ali's personal dictionary.*

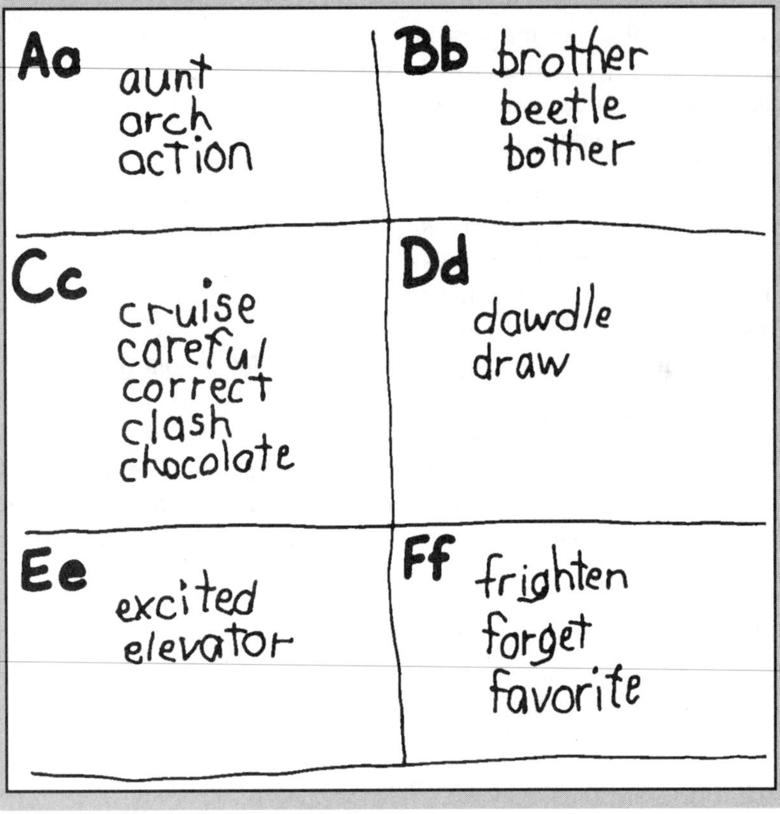

Aa aunt arch action	**Bb** brother beetle bother
Cc cruise coreful correct clash chocolate	**Dd** dawdle draw
Ee excited elevator	**Ff** frighten forget favorite

I love the way an author like Steig with a million-dollar vocabulary chooses homey but underused words like *woozy* and *shabby*. Immediately, I want to add those to my personal list of favorites not because they're new but because I'll forget them if I don't.

■ 10. Create Alphabet Books

This is another thing to do with favorite words—or with words that go with a particular topic: vacations, math, school, siblings, pets, parents, sports, bad days. It is OK to have more than one word per letter! When you are finished, create an "Alphabet of Tired Words": *G* is for *great*, *B* is for *big*, *A* is for *a lot*. You may not have a tired word for every letter—that's fine. Keep the book going, and by the end of the year, you may be surprised at how many of those letters you fill up!

■ 11. Guess What It Means

Words do not always make sense the first time we hear them. However, we learn meanings from the way words are used—from context. Lists are an ineffective way to teach meaning because they rarely include examples of words in action. For in-depth understanding, we need to see and hear words—more than once. Students need encouragement to guess at word meanings, which in turn expands listening skills. Suppose that you gave your students this list of words:

✔ *despised*
✔ *avoided*
✔ *predator*
✔ *ravenous*

Would they know them all? Perhaps not. They might make some very good guesses, though, on hearing this passage from Janell Cannon's *Crickwing*:

> *Crickwing despised his nickname, and he avoided hearing it by staying far away from the other creatures. He would sneak out to find his food when the night was darkest, knowing that the forest was crawling with predators even worse than ravenous toads [2000].*

Notice how Cannon gently hints at word meanings. Notice too how completely unnecessary it is to know *every* word in order to get a strong sense of the text.

TEACHING SENTENCE FLUENCY

What You Are Teaching

✔ Sentence sense—What is a sentence?
✔ An ear for variety
✔ Different sentence patterns

How to Get There

■ 1. Notice Sentences in Students' Writing

Students' early sentences typically do not *look* like sentences at all—until we decode. Bea Johnson offers this advice:

FIGURE 4.11   *Paper on going to the park.* Christopher (K)

Note the sentences children write. They never use the simplistic sentence structure commonly used in the vast amount of the early-basal-reading series. Peruse the children's writings contained in [my] book. You will not find one "See Dick. See Dick run!" type communication. The children consistently use long flowing sentences to communicate their thoughts in a natural way [1999, p. 138].

Figure 4.11 shows a paper by Christopher about visiting the park.

When confronted with a piece of writing like this one, it's tempting to see at once all the things that need attention: Capital and lowercase letters are mixed, spelling could use some work, punctuation is unconventional with periods and commas inserted randomly—and there is no period at the end. Spacing needs work, too. All true. Yet we need to ask ourselves, "What is the most important thing for Christopher to know about his writing right now? The answer is: That he is writing in full sentences. This is the beginning of fluency. If we recognize this, we can say, "Christopher! You're writing whole sentences.

Here you have two ideas combined in one sentence—*Today is cloudy and I like to go to the park*. Terrific."

■ *2. Keep an Open Discussion on "the Sentence" Going*

Around the early part of first grade is a good time to begin asking students the big question, "What is a sentence?" Don't expect them to have the final answer, of course. Just put the question into their minds, and keep raising it. Keep in mind that this is not an easy concept to define, even for adult writers. Of course, we all have definitions swimming in our heads: A sentence is a complete thought. A sentence is a subject and predicate (*That* was a helpful one). The truth is, however, that we gain a sense of what a sentence is simply by listening to people speak—or read aloud. I like Bea Johnson's definition because it's simple and sensible: A sentence is "a group of words that tell about someone or something and what that someone or something is doing" (1999, p. 137).

To expand students' understanding of this or any definition, ask them to explore sentences. You might create a simple piece of writing on the overhead projector and count the sentences. You might say to one of your multisentence writers, "Sarah, let's count the sentences in your piece and see how many you have." You can also write a sentence *slowly* on the overhead projector and ask students to let you know when it becomes a sentence:

The . . . bear . . . found . . . the . . . berries.

■ *3. Show How Punctuation Divides Sentences*

End punctuation is a handy tool. Without it, we would have a tougher time telling where sentences begin and end. You can show this to students with some easy steps. First, write just one sentence on the overhead projector (or chalkboard), and omit the final punctuation:

My dog had puppies

Ask your students if this is a sentence. (Yes.) Now ask if anyone knows what is missing. Someone likely will mention the missing period, but if not, you can answer for them and put one in. Explain how the period shows that the sentence is over. Now try a more extended piece of writing, with capital letters and periods (or question marks) missing:

My dog had puppies she had four puppies in all they were the cutest things I have ever seen in my life

Read this piece aloud with inflection and pauses, showing with your voice where the sentences end—where the punctuation should go. Ask your students to tell you as they read/listen where they hear each sentence end. Then show how capital letters and periods help make these endings clear:

My dog had puppies. She had four puppies in all. They were the cutest things I have ever seen in my life!

■ *4. Read Fluent Passages Aloud*

In Chapter 7 you will find numerous books that are excellent examples of fluency—and no doubt you have many of your own to add to the list. In order to emphasize fluency, you need to read with plenty of expression, and as students become ready, you need to ask them to listen for specific things:

1. Do you like the way this sounds when I read it?
2. How many different ways does this writer think of to begin sentences?

■ 5. Focus on Poetry—and Music

Poetry is *by nature* fluent. So, when you read poems aloud, you *are* teaching fluency. Share poems often. Give your students opportunities to compose poems, too. Rhyming is fun, but poems do not have to rhyme all the time. You can turn prose into poetry just by formatting it differently; for example,

> Rhyming is
> FUN.
> But poems
> do not
> have to rhyme
> *all* the time.

Students also have fun writing songs. They can borrow melodies from well-known pieces and write their own lyrics. It helps to sing one or two to get them warmed up. Then provide a list of well-known songs from which to borrow melodies and rhythms, and watch the lyrics flow. Do this as a group activity (with you as recorder and lead lyricist) if students are not ready to do it on their own. Here are a few melodies that are pretty well known (but your students may have favorites they prefer to use):

✔ "I've Been Workin' on the Railroad"
✔ "Row, Row, Row Your Boat"
✔ "Bingo (Bingo Was His Name-O)"
✔ "Yellow Rose of Texas"
✔ "Three Blind Mice"
✔ "Deep in the Heart of Texas"
✔ "You Are My Sunshine"
✔ "Twinkle, Twinkle, Little Star"
✔ "Down in the Valley"

■ 6. Create Rhyme Mobiles

Many students enjoy creating poems with rhyme, and you can provide a resource by creating collections of rhyming words. Lists work fine for this too, but mobiles are more fun. Use the front and back of one large (eight and a half by eleven inch) sheet for the top of the mobile, one set of rhyming words on the front, and one set on the back. Create crossbars beneath from which to hang two more sets of front-and-back sheets—five sheets in all. Laminate them if possible, and hang the mobile in a writing corner, within reach so that writers can spin it around to check for what they want. Change lists occasionally, asking for students' help to generate new ones. You will have ten sets of rhyming words. Figure 4.12 shows how this might look.

■ 7. Break the Monotony!

Sentence patterning is quite typical with young writers. Yet many manage to break free of this mold (usually at the end of grade one or beginning of grade

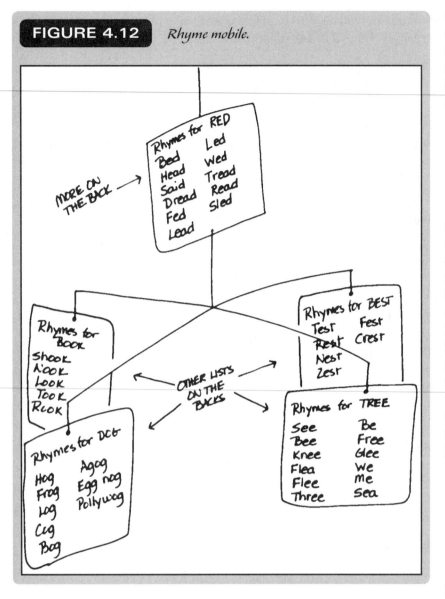

FIGURE 4.12 *Rhyme mobile.*

two) when introduced to the possibility of varying sentence beginnings. A good way to begin is by modeling. Create a piece in which all sentences begin the same way; for example,

> *We had fun over the weekend. We went to the beach. We met some friends who went walking with us. We all had a picnic on the beach.*

The first time through, just read the piece to students and ask them what they notice about your sentences. Some may pick up the repetition right away. If not, read it once more, asking your students to listen to the beginnings. Let them know that you are not happy with every sentence beginning being the same. Invite them to help you to think of different ways to begin each sentence. Let them do as much as you can before jumping in with the solution. Here is one possible result:

> *Last weekend, we had a great time. Saturday morning we left for the beach. Some friends met us there, and we all walked together. Later, we had a picnic right on the sand.*

End by reading the two side by side and asking your students, "Which one sounds better?" By the way, do not expect all students to love the fluent one! Many students love patterns and will choose version 1. Do not be discouraged—it takes awhile to develop an ear for fluency.

■ 8. Play "Create a Sentence," a Sentence Construction Game

This game is played with teams. You need two sets of three- by five-inch cards on which you print words—one word per card. Print the word with a capital letter on one side and without on the other side. In this way, if the word comes at the beginning of a sentence, students can make the right choice. You also need cards with periods, exclamation points, and question marks for the end punctuation. The game works like this: You can have from three to six students on each team. The rest of the students will be the judges. When you give the signal, teams must begin forming a sentence using their cards. Each student takes one card, and the team must form a sentence by standing in line, in order, with the correct punctuation at the end. The first word must have a capital letter at the beginning. You decide what kind of sentence you want. You might say

✔ "Give me a sentence with four words."
✔ "Give me a sentence that begins with *I*."
✔ "Give me a sentence that asks a question."

The team that gets their sentence together most quickly gets one point. Judges must check final sentences to be sure that everything is correct. If students forget a word, put in an extra word, mix up word order, forget a capital letter at the beginning, or leave off the end punctuation—no points! If both teams make mistakes, the team that corrects the errors first wins.

■ 9. Sentence or Fragment?

Students learn to hear the difference between a sentence and a fragment with practice—and many may be good at this right from the start. Make six sentence-fragment pairs by writing them on strips of paper and putting them into a paper bag. Each bag should contain a different set of twelve—six sentences and six fragments. Keep them short and simple. Make the print *big*. Give one bag to each team of three or four students and ask them to sort the fragments from the sentences as quickly as they can. When they finish, ask teams to check one another's work. See if they have any disagreements. If they do, write the questionable "sentence" on the overhead projector, and talk about it with the whole class. Keep asking that question: What is a sentence?

■ 10. Phone Yourself!

Out of three PVC joints from any home building and repair store, you can make a handy plastic "phone" into which students can read and speak—with amazing results! The pipe enhances the voice so that students hear themselves with exceptional clarity. "Phoning yourself" and reading your own writing aloud is a good way to check fluency. It builds voice as well. It is also an aid in conventions because many conventional errors are caught with the ear, not just with the eye. Shy students who do not feel comfortable sharing with a small group or even a single partner take comfort in being a "group of one" for that first reading. Not-so-shy students simply enjoy hearing their own voices. Figure 4.13 is a simple sketch of how the PVC "phone" looks when assembled; other configurations work just as well, so pick any pipe fittings you like.

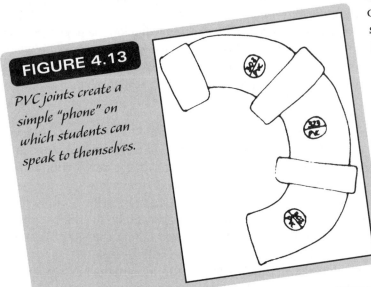

FIGURE 4.13

PVC joints create a simple "phone" on which students can speak to themselves.

■ 11. Use Imagination to Create Puppet Dialogue

Dialogue is a critical part of fluency, but one that is often overlooked. Before students are ready to create dialogue on paper, they can create it orally. Using puppets keeps them focused on "speech," with fewer side comments. You may wish to provide a hypothetical situation with which they can work; for example,

- ✔ Two friends meet who have not seen each other in a long time
- ✔ Two people argue over who should get the first turn down the slide
- ✔ One friend is upset and another is trying to comfort him or her
- ✔ One friend does not like school and another does
- ✔ One friend tries to talk another into sharing his or her lunch

■ 12. Listen to Books on Tape

One of the best ways to teach fluency is to read aloud. It is wonderful, though, for students to hear other voices, too; each reader has his or her own special style. Besides, when you play a book on tape, you get to listen, too. (Don't forget to include music—it's an excellent way to teach fluency.)

TEACHING CONVENTIONS
What You Are Teaching

- ✔ A proofreader's "eye" and "ear"
- ✔ Awareness of conventions
- ✔ Sense of self as editor

How to Get There

■ 1. Let Students Edit Their Own Work—as Much as Possible

Very young students cannot (usually!) insert quotation marks in the right spots, use semicolons with skill, or spell ten-letter words correctly. Fortunately, this is not all there is to editing, though. Begin with what they *can* do, and gradually increase editorial responsibility to match their skills and knowledge. For example, even the youngest students can put their names on their papers. When they check to make sure that they have remembered to do this, this is editing. Later, you can add additional skills: putting a date on the paper, putting a period (or question mark) at the end of a sentence, putting spaces between words, starting a sentence with a capital letter, and so on. Figure 4.14 presents a simple editing checklist that works well with young students.

■ 2. Model Instead of Correcting

We often make the mistake of thinking we are "teaching" conventions when we correct students' work. We are, of course—only we are teaching *ourselves!* Students may interpret substantially corrected pieces as a form of rejection rather than help. This inhibits writing. And writing—a lot—is the only way to get good at it. Consider the wisdom of Bea Johnson: "Celebrate kids' writing, rather than correcting it. . . . Remember, in kindergarten and first grade, the philosophy is to let children write. If you red-mark them, you will inhibit the vital freshness of their writing" (1999, p. 136).

This does not mean that you should not pay attention to the kinds of errors you see. Not at all. You can deal with a few in conferences (see idea 3). Deal with the rest by making yourself a list and then modeling each one for the class. Perhaps many of your students are running words together and putting no

FIGURE 4.14 *Simple editing checklist.*

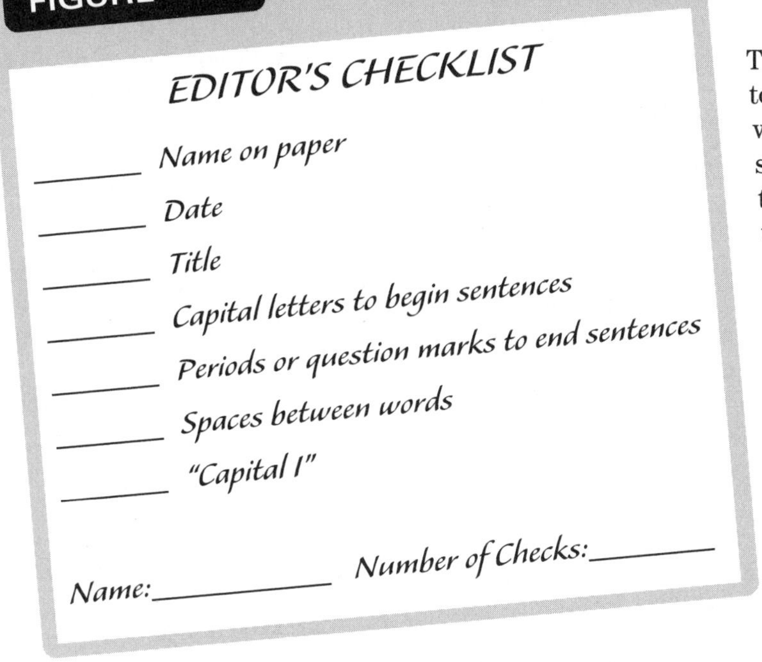

EDITOR'S CHECKLIST

_____ Name on paper

_____ Date

_____ Title

_____ Capital letters to begin sentences

_____ Periods or question marks to end sentences

_____ Spaces between words

_____ "Capital I"

Name:_____   Number of Checks:_____

spaces between them. Model this problem and the way to fix it.

Thefatoldcatcouldnevercatch-thatspeedybird.

Then say to students, "See how hard this is to read? Let me show you what happens when I write the very same sentence with spaces between the words. First, I'm going to mark this sentence with slash marks between the words. Then I'm going to rewrite it so that it is easy to read. Watch and read along with me.

The/fat/old/cat/could/never/catch/ that/speedy/bird.

"Now let's rewrite it and read it aloud again."

The fat old cat could never catch that speedy bird.

Model just *one* problem at a time. I know—you want to fix it all—right now! Be patient. Focus on one thing; then let your students try it. Keep the editing challenge at their level, meaning not what they can understand but what they can *do*. Maybe our sample sentence is too difficult for your young editors to do by themselves. Simplify. Young editors are often stumped because the editing we ask them to do is too hard; this is why they often cannot edit their own work. Their writers' minds race ahead of their editors' skills. Let them work on simple text first—before they take on the complexity of their own work:

Isawabird.

Even young writers, in teams of two, will usually figure this one out. If not, you will be there to help—and they will get it soon enough. Of course, this is only one lesson.

■ 3. Keep Editing Conferences Focused

Start with sincere praise for something the child has done well, including both picture and text, writing a whole sentence, writing more than one sentence, remembering to put his or her name on the paper, and so on. The achievement may be small, but your noticing it will make all the difference. Then you can share one "writer's secret" (a phrase I borrowed from Lois Burdett). This gentle form of making a suggestion says to students, "What I'm about to tell you is special—and will help your writing." A writer's secret can be anything at all—as long as it is focused. Here are a few possibilities, some very tiny and some a bit more significant: "Did you know that if you put a capital letter at the beginning of your sentence, it's easier for the reader to tell where your sentence begins? Could I show you?" *Or,* "If you . . .

✔ Put a period at the end of your sentence . . .
✔ End a question with a question mark . . .
✔ Put a title on your paper . . .
✔ Use a period sometimes instead of the word *and*, making two sentences . . .

✔ Spell the word *write* with a *w*, like this . . .

✔ Use quotation marks to show someone speaking . . .

If you like, you can use a large Post-It note to write a "writer's secret" reminder to the student. At the next conference, check to see what progress has been made. If the student is ready for another step, you're on your way! If not, you can always try it again. Either way, you are keeping editing manageable.

■ 4. Encourage Temporary Spelling

Temporary spelling scares some people who wonder if those early spellings will "stick." They will not. In fact, temporary spelling has some real benefits when explained to students as "using what you *know* and what you *hear* to spell each word as well as you can." First, it encourages students to try more expressive and interesting words by removing the obstacle of "I can't spell that one." And second, because students are continually trying to make letter-sound connections and to "get it right" without a crutch, temporary spelling actually *improves* later conventional spelling.

> *Research says that temporary spelling helps the child learn the sounds more effectively than most phonics instruction, which comes at an inappropriate time. . . . Allowing the child to come up with temporary spelling and to produce written language by himself increases his understanding. Piaget wrote that in order for children to understand something, they must construct it themselves—they must reinvent it* [Johnson, 1999, p. 56].

Bea Johnson notes that educators' and parents' fears that temporary spelling will somehow "take hold" and prevent the development of more conventional spelling skills are unfounded. First, children rarely spell an invented word the same way consistently; they are *constantly* experimenting and teaching themselves *how* to spell, not latching onto erroneous spellings that will haunt their careers as writers. Moreover, our logical understanding of how learning occurs—and *must* occur—tells us that experimentation and mistakes are not only inevitable but also desirable. The child who is willing to stumble and take a few bumps learns to walk faster than the one who sits safely on a pillow perusing *Ten Steps to Correct Walking*.

■ 5. Encourage Word Banks and Personal Dictionaries

Students need easy-to-use, convenient resources from which to draw. Primary students are hungry borrowers. The more you can fill their worlds with print—print used correctly and easy to get at—the more borrowing you will see. An adult dictionary (or even one for older students) is an awkward tool for most primary writers. However, word walls and personal dictionaries are user-friendly and encourage expansion of both vocabulary and spelling skills.

■ 6. Brainstorm Word Possibilities Before Writing

Students usually do not know what they will write before writing. Few of us do. But sometimes, when you have a topic in mind—a trip to Philadelphia, let's say—it is handy to know how to spell *some* of the words you are likely to be using: *Philadelphia, freedom, history, George Washington, bridge, monument, traffic, airplane, exciting, tourist, taxi, hotel, restaurant, shopping,* and so on. These words can be incorporated into personal dictionaries for handy reference later, too. You will not be able to write down every word for every child—there is never time—but you can allow ten minutes for creating a word wall from which everyone can borrow (this works well if students are writing on a common theme—animals, weather, memorable trips). If it works better for you, allow each child up to two or three words.

■ 7. Celebrate the Discovery of Conventions, Even Before They're Correct

Students often "discover" periods, colons, semicolons, ellipses, dashes, and a host of other conventions before they know how to use them correctly. They simply like the look of them and feel that they have meaning. They want their own text to have meaning and significance, too. Text may be peppered with periods, for example, as a precursor to the writer's learning correct placement. This peppering is a *step toward correctness* and should be acknowledged.

■ 8. Teach Editors' Symbols Appropriate for Grade Level

Around the end of kindergarten or the beginning of first grade, you can begin working on some simple editors' symbols that will empower your students to feel like professionals when they edit their own or others' work. They will also open your students' minds to an understanding of what editors do. Editors' symbols are like a kind of shorthand—almost a secret code. If you teach them this way, you make editing fun and playful, not drudgery. And here's the thing: Very young writers do not have to rewrite. When they use editors' symbols, the corrections have been made. Job done. Figure 4.15 provides a simple list of editors' symbols appropriate for young writers. I have listed them in the order in which I would teach them—but you should feel free to change this order to suit your own instruction.

■ 9. Provide Interesting Tools

Editing is much more fun with a favorite pen. Go for wild colors, bold shapes, or big, comfortable pens with an easy grip—even neon. Whatever gets your young editors excited.

■ 10. Play the Treasure Hunt Game

Before students are even ready to work with conventions, they do recognize them. Reinforce what they know, and teach them some new terminology at the same time by playing the treasure hunt game. Spend five or ten minutes simply hunting for a variety of conventions. You can use any text for this, but I like something with big print and a lot of variety. Because her text is generally rich with dialogue, Janell Cannon uses a wide range of conventions, including exclamation points, question marks, ellipses, quotation marks, and italics. Fred Marcellino's work (*I, Crocodile*, 1999) is also

FIGURE 4.15   *Easy symbols for young editors.*

Symbol	It means	Use it like this
∧	Put something in.	likes Paul∧cats.
ℓ	Take this out.	Don is a ~~big~~ huge guy.
∧/#	Put in a space.	Amy loves∧apples.
⊙	Add a period.	The horse saw us ⊙
≡	Make this letter a capital.	We live in oregon.
/	Make this letter Lower case.	Do you eat /Bacon?
_____	Underline this title.	Our teacher read the book Crickwing to our class.

exceptional for illustrating how conventions help make meaning clear and put inflection into speech. Marcellino uses ellipses and dashes with flair. Show students a page of text from one of these authors or any author who uses conventions with skill (and voice—yes, conventions do enhance voice). Simply ask your students at first to find various conventions—and to put their fingers on an example when they find one. For instance, please find

✔ A comma	✔ A capital letter
✔ A period	✔ The word *and*
✔ A question mark	✔ The word *crocodile*
✔ Some ellipses	✔ A word that ends in *e*
✔ An example of italics	✔ Dashes
✔ A name	

After playing the game this way a few times (and getting a little faster each time), ask students to tell you the meaning of the convention; for example, "You found quotation marks. Good! Why did the writer use them here?" Knowing the conventions by name and knowing why each one is used gives students a huge leg up on using them correctly in their own writing.

■ 11. Keep Expectations Realistic

"As a society," Donald Graves (1983) tells us, "we allow children to learn to speak by trial and error. But when it comes to reading and writing, we expect them to be right the first time." Maybe it is because conventional errors are so noticeable. Maybe it is also because we know how to respond to conventions—they are either right or wrong. We are not nearly as sure-footed when it comes to responding to voice or ideas or (toughest of all) organization. When we correct everything on every piece of writing, though, we make our ultimate goal in conventions all too clear: perfect writing *all* the time, every time. How realistic is that? Do you achieve it? Do you know anyone who does? Although Chapter 8 deals with conventional expectations in rubric form, I would like to suggest some grade-level possibilities I think are realistic. They do not reflect perfection but rather focus on something more interesting and achievable—editorial growth (as always, please use your own observations and experience to modify these):

Kindergarten
✔ Playfulness with letters and numbers
✔ Some correct directionality with letters
✔ Ability to distinguish between capital and lowercase letters
✔ Ability to write one's own name
✔ Ability to write a few sight words
✔ Incorporation of some punctuation (periods, exclamation points, commas) into writing, whether placed correctly or not
✔ Conscious attempt to put spaces between some "words"—not always achieved
✔ Ability to write a complete sentence (although it may be in letter-string form)
✔ Ability to use at least one editorial symbol: the caret (∧).

First Grade
✔ Increasing experimentation with letters and numbers
✔ Correct directionality with letters in most cases

✔ Ability to recognize and reproduce a reasonable facsimile of all letters of the alphabet

✔ Full ability to distinguish between capital and lowercase letters—and often to use one or the other appropriately

✔ Ability to write numerous sight words and to make good phonetic guesses at some more difficult words

✔ Readable spelling in most instances (i.e., reader can figure it out without author's aid)

✔ Successful attempts to space properly in most sentences

✔ Ability to write a complete sentence—and often to compose in multiple sentences (usually with punctuation)

✔ Ability to recognize and use several editorial symbols: caret (for insertion), delete symbol, caret with pound sign (for adding space), symbol for inserting period

✔ Ability to write (correctly or in recognizable form) many proper names: own name, names of family members, names of friends, names of pets, name of city and state, name of street, name of school, names of some other states or countries, names of some famous persons

Second Grade

✔ Experimentation with increasingly difficult words

✔ Correct directionality with letters in nearly all cases

✔ Ability to reproduce a readily recognizable facsimile of all letters of the alphabet

✔ Consistent, appropriate use of capital and lowercase letters

✔ Ability to write own name and names of friends, family members, pets, and most other familiar proper names

✔ Ability to write and spell an increasing number of sight words and more difficult words correctly and to make good phonetic guesses at others

✔ Readable spelling on virtually all written work (i.e., reader can figure it out without author's aid)

✔ Consistent, correct spacing on all written work

✔ Ability to write and punctuate multiple sentences with relative ease

✔ Attempted use of paragraphing when needed

✔ Correct use of most terminal punctuation (periods, question marks)

✔ Incorporation of an increasing range of internal punctuation (commas, quotation marks, semicolons), sometimes used correctly, sometimes not

✔ Ability to create bulleted or numbered lists

✔ Ability to recognize and use the editorial symbols in Figure 4.15

Third Grade

✔ Continued experimentation with increasingly difficult words

✔ Consistent, correct directionality with capital and lowercase letters

✔ Ability to reproduce fully readable print and/or cursive writing *or*

✔ Sufficient keyboarding skills to compose multiparagraph pieces

✔ Consistent, appropriate use of capital and lowercase letters

✔ Ever-increasing personal vocabulary of correctly spelled words and use of fully recognizable phonetic spellings on new words

✔ Increasingly consistent distinction between common homophones: *to, two; know, no; their, there*

✔ Readable spelling on virtually all written work (i.e., reader can figure it out without author's aid)
✔ Consistent, correct spacing on all written work
✔ Ability to write and punctuate multiple sentences with relative ease
✔ Ability to organize multisentence writing into paragraphs
✔ Increasingly correct use of terminal punctuation (periods, question marks) on virtually all written work
✔ Correct use of some internal punctuation (may include commas, quotation marks, dashes, semicolons)
✔ Ability to create bulleted or numbered lists
✔ Ability to recognize proper titles and to underline or italicize as needed
✔ Ability to recognize and use the editorial symbols in Figure 4.15 with ease
✔ Ability to write an increasing range of proper names correctly

Children vary tremendously in their skill with conventions and the rate at which they internalize conventions. Some writers are spelling numerous words correctly and using highly sophisticated grammatical constructions in grade one. Others struggle with these same issues all their lives. Therefore, the lists I present here are general guidelines and cannot be more. I encourage you to modify them based on your own teaching experience and consultation with other teachers. What is helpful, I think, is not so much a list that is imposed as "must-achieve goals" but a set of guidelines that help us to watch for, recognize, and celebrate moments of growth in our children's writing.

> *If there is one rule that applies to every child, it is that progress is always uneven. Children never follow any series of stages exactly and sometimes appear to be regressing in one area as they advance in another.*
>
> **—Donald Graves and Virginia Stuart**
> *Write from the Start: Tapping Your Child's Natural Writing Ability* (1985, p. 169)

■ 12. Give Students Editing Practice—Often

Editors learn their craft by editing. Two things are critical: One is to do it often. Editing now and then will not get the job done. When students edit only what they publish, they do not get enough practice to become truly skilled. Second, young editors (all editors, in fact) need to practice on text that is *not their own*. This is so because they have no personal attachment to such text and do not mind making corrections; in addition, errors are much easier to spot in someone else's work. Ever notice a dusty table in someone else's house? So easy to spot, isn't it? Editing is just like that. Three, four, or five times a day, whip out a blank overhead and write about whatever you are currently doing or thinking—make one or two mistakes, and ask your students to find them. For example,

Im enjoying writing today

There are two mistakes here that will take your students anywhere from ten seconds to a full minute to find, depending on ability level. Make the corrections in front of them and go on. Do this often. Give them written text to edit on their own as well. Keep it short. Make it a game.

■ 13. Invite Parents to Sit In on Editing Lessons

Parents worry over conventions endlessly. This happens for multiple reasons. Like it or not, our society does judge people on their conventions. When is the last time you became annoyed (I have friends who actually become enraged)

when you heard a media representative make a grammatical error? Parents also worry because they remember their own writing instruction, and for many, it was a painful process of red ink–covered pages and cryptic, accusatory marginal comments. They lived through it, though, and feel it might be best if their children also traveled the rugged trail to conventional correctness.

Invite parents to sit in and watch as you teach your children to be editors. Watching young editors spotting errors, using editors' symbols, correcting text, and using editorial language gives parents much-needed confidence and a sense of relief that their children are not just being corrected but actually are learning the skills they need to edit on their own.

> *Telling writers they've made a mistake is not teaching. If the child can already do what I've corrected, then correcting is only reminding. And reminding is not teaching. If the child doesn't understand the error, then correcting isn't enough.*
>
> **—Donald Graves and Virginia Stuart**
> *Write from the Start: Tapping Your Child's Natural Writing Ability* (1985, p. 177)

■ *14. Include Samples of Students' Editing in Portfolios*

Students need to recognize their improvement as editors, along with their improvement as writers. Therefore, make sure that portfolios include samples of editing practice—at least five (dated) from various points throughout the year.

■ *15. Ask Students to Double-Space*

This seems like such a simple thing, but we so often forget to ask students to leave room for editing. (It is like leaving room for cream in the coffee.) Text that is double-spaced and has wide margins is much easier to edit than text crammed together on a page. If your students use a word processor, have them double-space anyway and print out a copy for editing once they have made any other changes they wish to make. Most of us catch errors in printed text more readily than on a computer screen.

 # SOME FINAL QUESTIONS

Do I need to teach all six *traits to primary learners?* Yes—I think so. If you do not, you see, it is like presenting writing as a fragmented thing rather than a holistic concept. Writing is not *just* ideas or *just* conventions; it is a compilation of many things—and this is the whole point in working with the traits— to help students see what elements help shape writing and influence reader response. So, yes, teach them all, right from kindergarten. Do not have a *unit of instruction* on each trait, though. Relax! Just *talk about* voice and word choice. Read examples and ask students to listen for fluency or a good lead or detail. Weave the traits naturally, gracefully, into the instruction you are already doing.

Do I need to teach the traits in order, for example, ideas, organization, voice, and so on? Many teachers find this a comfortable approach because, again, it helps you organize how and when you will present various lessons or pieces of literature. Be careful, though. Do not get so locked in that you are afraid to comment on the wonderful voice in a student's piece just because you are working on organization right then. Balance is the key. It is mostly a matter of emphasis. Tell your students that they will be learning "some interesting things about how professional writers work." Perhaps you begin by emphasizing detail. Then leads (one important part of organization). Then personal voice. And so on. Stay flexible, however—flip back and forth as you need to.

What about conventions? Isn't that a special case? Absolutely. Do not wait to touch on conventions until you have *all* other traits in place. You will want to work on conventions *as you are working with other writing traits*, such as ideas or organization. Start simply, asking students to check for their names or names and dates on their papers. Gradually, add more conventions to match their editing skill.

How long should I spend on one trait? For older students, I suggest taking plenty of time—even two to three weeks. For primary students, though, you may quickly lose the larger picture if you try this. Pick a feature or two of each trait to emphasize. With ideas, for example, your "key features" might be a main idea or message and details. For organization, they might be leads and endings. Do not feel that you have to teach every single element of every trait. Remember, your purpose is to lay a foundation of writers, language for students to build on as they grow. You may only need a few days per trait to do this as long as your students have lots of time to write as you discuss the features of writing. Keep in mind that the traits are only a key to unlock the mystery of what makes writing work; *writing itself is the thing*!

What if my students are struggling writers who find some of these activities difficult? How do I simplify writing activities for them? No matter what the level of your students, it is critical to view them as writers and to provide time for writing. This is the *only* way they will gain skill and comfort. In addition, though, use the tools they do have: speaking and listening, for example. As you model, they can respond and offer suggestions. They can talk to each other about their writing, your writing, or books you share. They can listen to literature and listen to you as you share writing samples—and talk about whether they have voice or detail. They can dictate pieces. Or they can talk as you (or someone) makes notes. They can use tape recorders and enhance their text with art. They can memorize poems and act them out or use drama to express feelings or characterizations or to practice dialog. Writing *is* the focal point, to be sure, but it is not the only path to writing instruction.

CHAPTER 4 IN A NUTSHELL

- It is important to teach all traits at all grade levels in order to present writing as a coherent "whole."
- It is not, however, necessary to teach every element of every trait. Keep instruction simple.
- Focus on writing and process. Use trait language to help children "read" their own writing and understand process.
- At primary level, put these goals ahead of others: gaining a writer's vocabulary (to build understanding) and experiencing joy in writing (to build passion).
- As you look at this book—or any book on teaching trait-based writing—you are likely to discover that *you are already teaching traits*, for they are nothing more than the foundation of good writing.

EXTENSIONS

1. Think of your favorite writing activities. Which traits are you teaching? (Do not be surprised if you are often teaching more than one trait.)

2. Which traits strike you as the most fun to teach? Do you have favorites? Look again at the list of activities for that trait. Can you add to it?

3. Is there any trait you have been afraid or unwilling to try? Look again at the list of activities for that trait. Is there one thing you would feel confident to try, just to make a beginning?

4. Think about Donald Murray's philosophy of learning to write by building on our strengths. Are there some traits where you see your students finding more success than in others? Which ones? Why do you think that is? Would it make sense to begin your instruction with those traits?

5. Some schools have tried a trait-a-year approach to teaching six-trait writing (for example, ideas in kindergarten, organization in grade 1). Do you see this as a fragmented approach to instruction? Why? What disadvantages could there be in such an approach? List them here:

6. Is it important to teach the traits in a specific order? Why or why not? Write your thoughts here:

SOURCES CITED

Aronie, Nancy Slonim. 1998. *Writing from the Heart*. New York: Hyperion.

Best, Cari. 2001. *Shrinking Violet*. New York: Farrar, Straus and Giroux.

Burdett, Lois. 1995. *A Child's Portrait of Shakespeare*. Winsor, Ontario, Canada: Black Moss Press (distributed by Firefly Books, New York). Web site: *lburdett@shakespearecanbefun.com*.

Burdett, Lois. 1995. *Shakespeare Can Be Fun Series*. Winsor, Ontario, Canada: Black Moss Press (distributed by Firefly Books, New York). Web site: *lburdett@shakespearecanbefun.com*.

Calkins, Lucy McCormick. 1994. *The Art of Teaching Writing*, Revised Edition. Portsmouth, NH: Heinemann.

Cannon, Janell. 2000. *Crickwing*. San Diego: Harcourt.

Churchman, Deborah. 2000. "All About Worms." In *Ranger Rick*, Vol. 34, No. 7, pp. 32ff. Vienna, VA: The National Wildlife Federation.

Cramer, Ronald L. 2001. *Creative Power: The Nature and Nurture of Children's Writing*. New York: Addison-Wesley Longman.

Dahl, Lucy. 1996. *James and the Giant Peach: The Book and Movie Scrapbook*. New York: Disney Press.

Fox, Mem. 1993. *Radical Reflections*. San Diego: Harcourt, Brace & Company.

Freeman, Marcia S. 1998. *Teaching the Youngest Writers*. Gainesville, FL: Maupin House.

Glynn, Carol. 2001. *Learning on Their Feet: A Sourcebook for Kinesthetic Learning Across the Curriculum K–8*. Shoreham, VT: Discover Writing Press.

Graves, Donald H. 1983. *Writing: Teachers and Children at Work*. Portsmouth, NH: Heinemann.

Graves, Donald, and Virginia Stuart. 1985. *Write from the Start: Tapping Your Child's Natural Writing Ability*. New York: NAL Penguin.

Hablitzel, Marie, and Kim Stitzer. 2000. *Draw Right Now, Book Seven*. New York: Barker Creek Publishing. Web site: *www.dwnow.com*. Portions of this book are reprinted in *r.w.t. the Magazine for Reading. Writing. Thinking*, Vol. 3, No. 4 (March 2002), pp. 20–21.

Johnson, Bea. 1999. *Never Too Early to Write*. Gainesville, FL: Maupin House.

Keillor, Garrison. 1989. "How to Write a Letter." In *We Are Still Married*. New York: Viking.

Keene, Ellin Oliver and Susan Zimmerman. 1997. *Mosaic of Thought*. Portsmouth, NH: Heinemann.

Lane, Barry. 2000. *Reviser's Toolbox*. Shoreham, VT: Discover Writing Press.

Marcellino, Fred. 1999. *I, Crocodile*. New York: HarperCollins.

Murray, Donald M. 1990. *Shoptalk*. Portsmouth, NH: Heinemann.

Ringgold, Faith. 1991. *Tar Beach*. New York: Crown Publishers.

Routman, Regie. 2000. *Conversations*. Portsmouth, NH: Heinemann.

Ruef, Kerry. 2000. *The Private Eye: Looking/Thinking by Analogy*. Seattle, WA: The Private Eye Project. Web site: *www.the-private-eye.com*.

Sendak, Maurice. 1991 (original 1963). *Where the Wild Things Are*. New York: HarperCollins (Harper Trophy Edition).

Steig, William. 1986. *Brave Irene*. New York: Farrar, Straus and Giroux.

Steig, William. 1982. *Dr. DeSoto*. New York: Farrar, Straus and Giroux.

Van Allsburg, Chris. 1988. *Two Bad Ants*. Boston: Houghton Mifflin.

5 Making Changes

- *Keeping Portfolios*
- *Revising*
- *Reflecting*
- *Publishing*

Here is Danielle (Grade 1) looking closely for changes she wants to make in her story. We call this revision.

Photo and caption courtesy of Ariana (Grade 4).

UH-OH—ARE PORTFOLIOS STILL WITH US?

Portfolios became hugely popular for a time in the late 1980s and early 1990s and then (for many) enjoyed a ride into the sunset for which some people, I think, actually stood and cheered. This is a shame—but it is understandable, really, to anyone who has visited many classrooms where portfolios are or once were popular. Despite the valiant efforts of many portfolio champions—including Donald Graves himself—many teachers viewed portfolios as a mission, something quite separate from regular teaching, and they did *all the work*. I understand this. When my son left college last year, I vowed I would not spend five minutes cleaning his apartment for him. But you know? There was that cleaning fee at stake.

As educators, we want our portfolios to look good—impressive. We want students to select their best, most shining moments to include—and how will they know which moments those are if we do not point them out? We also want them to reflect on their growth as writers, but how will they know what to say if we do not tell them? So, we select, we order, we stack and file, we reflect—and then we collapse. Well, who wouldn't? It's stressful to be wise and insightful about the writings of twenty-five or thirty students. Raise your hand if you would like to do this again.

Of course, this do-it-yourself approach misses the whole point. The idea behind portfolios was never to create beautiful packages, although scrap-booking can be rewarding, if you like it. The point was to teach students to look thoughtfully at their own work, to make personal choices about what would be saved and why, and to write their own reflections, even if they were not perfect. As Regie Routman explains, nothing meaningful happens until we demonstrate what it means to look inside your own work and see what's there—or to compare two pieces and see what growth has occurred.

> *There is no guarantee that when we ask kids to evaluate themselves, they will do so in a reflective way or that their learning will improve as a result. . . . Students may look at their work and select pieces to include, but they will not make thoughtful judgments about their work until we demonstrate how to do it and get them to value the process [2000, p. 561].*

If we teach our student writers, including the youngest among them, to recognize detail, good organization, voice, strong word choice, or fluency when they see it, they begin to understand what, specifically, to look for—and out of *the writing they do each day as part of the classroom routine* they can build a portfolio that will knock our socks off. Even more important, however, they will teach themselves (and us and parents) how they are growing as writers. As author/teacher Barry Lane points out from his experience with Vermont's large-scale portfolio-based assessment, "A portfolio is a window into a student's learning and can be as useful to the student as to the teacher" (*After THE END*, 1993, p. 203).

Model It First

Do you keep a portfolio—or a folder—of your own writings? If not, you might think about starting one. In this way, you can show students why you save particular pieces, how you chose them, and what each one tells you about yourself as a writer. Perhaps one shows your voice breaking free or your organizational skills sharpening. Another might show small victories, such as learning whether *bear* or *bears* is the correct plural (either, actually). The pieces I save are not always my very best. I may save them for personal reasons, to preserve a memory, or because they are pieces I wish to work on further. I saved a hastily scrawled description of my grandmother's kitchen that later turned into a short story about her cat Snooky, as well as a poem. When you model your reasons for making your own personal choices (what to save as well as what to leave out), you show your students the basic idea behind the portfolio, and their work becomes a hundred times easier.

Keep It Simple

The portfolio idea lost some of the popular vote, I think, because people saw it as huge. They imagined giant files in which students painstakingly collected and stored everything they wrote. By year's end, some would have had to tote their portfolios around in small wagons. This would be comparable to our saving every note, card, letter, e-mail, memo, grocery list, reminder, report, book review, poem, or story we created. What sane person would do this? If students are *selective* about what they save, a portfolio might be as small as five or six pieces. Then, if a student were to lay those five or six pieces out at the end of the year, he or she likely would see *big* steps in writing skill.

> *In one class that combined first grade and kindergarten, some of the first-graders were convinced on first glance that some of the kindergartners' work must have been put into their writing folders. They themselves could never have produced such a silly-looking jumble of letters [Graves and Stuart, 1985, p. 111].*

To see how powerful this overview can be, look at the following miniportfolios, with just a *few* samples each. I am not suggesting that portfolios need to be *this* small either; I am including these examples to make a point. Although these are not giant collections, look how much they tell us. Add just one or two more items, and you would have a whole writer's biography.

■ Sample 1: Kiya's Journey

Kindergartner Kiya has four entries in her portfolio, running from November to April. In Figure 5.1 she is writing in a letter string and using her picture to carry

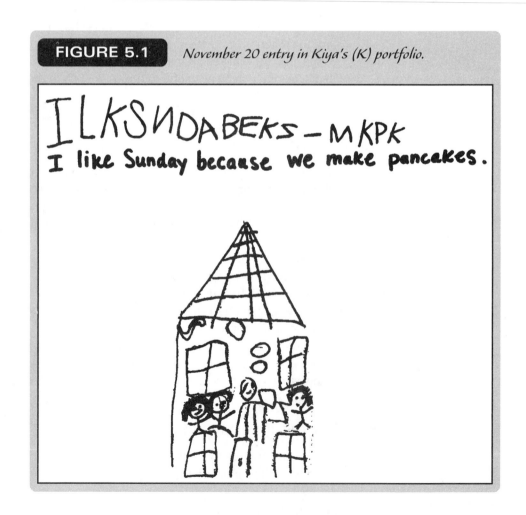

FIGURE 5.1 *November 20 entry in Kiya's (K) portfolio.*

I LKSNDABEKS — MKPK
I like Sunday because we make pancakes.

much of the meaning. She is writing in full sentences and making numerous letter-sound connections. Notice her use of the blank for the word (*we*) she does not know. At this point, her writing includes all capital letters and no punctuation. The picture is full of detail; notice the high-flying pancakes and the happy faces of the pancake eaters.

By January, Kiya is constructing writing that we can decode without any difficulty (Figure 5.2). She is writing much more conventional text, with a mix of lowercase and capital letters and is using apostrophes and periods. She has learned to capitalize the pronoun *I*. Her picture and text are connected—just as they were in her November example. Both show early indications of organization.

In March, Kiya is writing more extended text (Figure 5.3). She continues to use punctuation, although, as this example shows, it is inconsistent. Writing is

FIGURE 5.2 *January 24 entry in Kiya's (K) portfolio.*

FIGURE 5.3 *March 21 entry in Kiya's (K) portfolio.*

FIGURE 5.4   *April 18 entry in Kiya's (K) portfolio.*

I m going to get n_ new S_s! shoes!

APR 18 2002

never a steady climb up the mountain; writers pause occasionally, hit plateaus, or even get sidetracked. Nevertheless, this expanded sentence shows a big leap in fluency and greater comfort with the generation of text. Kiya is also willing to experiment with new, less familiar words, for example, *slbt* (celebrate). She also has noticed that words are sometimes split at the end of a line, and so she is trying this technique out in her own writing, a reminder of what good borrowers young writers can be. Kiya still relies on pictures to carry a portion of her detail; we might infer that quite a large group will gather for Grammy's birthday and that they will be pretty happy about the whole thing.

Kiya's April example (Figure 5.4) takes an interesting turn. Here she puts much of her writing energy into her picture, which is far more detailed and expressive (this is voice) than any preceding. Compare this drawing with the figures in her November picture to appreciate the growth in her observational skills and sense of perspective. Here we even get bows on the shoes. On the other hand, Kiya is a bit less daring with the text, preferring to use blank lines for the sounds that she is unsure of in "new shoes." Never mind. She is very close to coordinating the text with the picture, and within a few weeks, we are likely to see the expanded text of Figure 5.3 combined with the detailed picture of Figure 5.4.

■ *Sample 2: Hannah's Journey*

Hannah's very simple portfolio includes just three pieces of writing. Again, though, we can see signs of real growth and change. In Figure 5.5 Hannah creates a sketch of herself holding a baby. It is "labeled" with imitative writing that reads "My Baby Sister." The picture has detail. Both figures have smiling faces, and Hannah's arms embrace her baby sister. Notice the bed above, with covers turned down. Hannah has not yet begun to experiment with letter shapes.

FIGURE 5.5   *September 3 entry in Hannah's (K) portfolio.*

In Figure 5.6 we see a change from October. Here Hannah is writing with letters and making many letter-sound connections in this complete sentence (a big step forward from the simple label in the preceding sample). Notice that although her text goes mostly left to right, she takes the

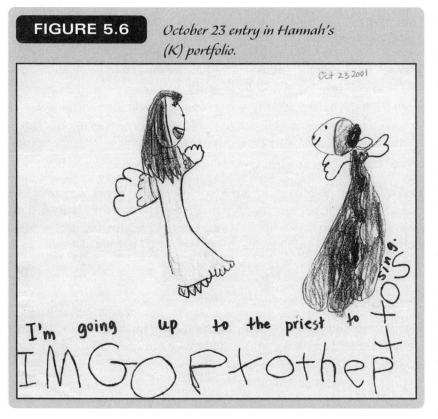

FIGURE 5.6 *October 23 entry in Hannah's (K) portfolio.*

liberty of running up the page when she runs out of room. Her drawings are more detailed than those from her first sample; we see lips, hair ribbons, and frills on the dress she plans to wear for this big event.

Big things have happened in Hannah's writing by April (Figure 5.7). She is writing more than one sentence and including detail—not just a tooth but a "wiggly" tooth. Her text goes left to right on the page, incorporates conventional spacing, displays both capital and lowercase letters, and includes some punctuation. In addition, this text (compare Figure 5.6) includes many sight words plus more difficult words (*tooth*), all spelled correctly. Hannah can now convey her messages to a reader with ease. What a change from late October.

Small as these examples are, I think each clearly shows the value of preserving work samples at various periods in a writer's year and marking those periods with dates. No one example by itself tells us even a fraction of what we

FIGURE 5.7 *April 11 entry in Hannah's (K) portfolio.*

learn by putting those samples together and "reading" the story they tell. So, don't set out to do a "portfolio project" or launch yourself on a "portfolio mission." Instead, do this:

1. Teach yourself the criteria within each of the six traits so that you know what to look for as you review your students' writing.
2. Teach students the traits so that *they* can see changes in their own writing.
3. Encourage your students to save and date a few pieces throughout the year, adding them to their portfolios/folders/writing collections.
4. Encourage students to comment on the changes they see, orally or in writing.

Suggestion: Just for practice, let your students review Kiya's and Hannah's portfolios and comment on the changes *they* see. Don't worry if they don't mention everything noted in this book. What's important is the practice of looking—a good warm-up for noticing changes in their own writing.

READY FOR REFLECTION?

When are students ready to do some serious reflecting on their writing? Sooner than you might think. Even very young students can notice and comment on things like these:

- ✔ I am using periods now.
- ✔ I am writing real words.
- ✔ You can read things I write.
- ✔ I can write a whole sentence.
- ✔ My picture has a face.
- ✔ I have two pictures, and they tell a story.
- ✔ In this paper I remembered to use a title.
- ✔ I have an ending.
- ✔ I describe things.
- ✔ My paper has details.

It is the *noticing* that matters, not the length of the reflection. You are simply teaching your students to compare individual pieces of writing and to comment on the changes they see. The more you talk about the six traits of writing, the easier this will be. It is easier to see or hear voice in your writing when you know the word and know what to listen for. It is easier to spot detail if you know what it looks and sounds like.

Michael, a third grader, likes to write mystery stories. He is in a class that has been working on the traits of ideas, organization, voice, and word choice. See if you can spot elements of each trait in his story "The Closet Monster" (Figure 5.8).

Michael's teacher asks her students to reflect on their writing, and to make this task easier, she provides some leading questions. They can, however, write about anything they notice. In Michael's reflection (Figure 5.9), you will hear some echoes of the traits, indicating his growing understanding of what makes writing—his or anyone's—work.

Notice that in answering the first question, Michael quotes from his paper to support his assertion about good description. This causes him to go back and take another look at his work, a vital step in teaching revision.

FIGURE 5.8   *"The Closet Monster."*

Hi, I'm Michael. I'm looking for what I call the closet monster.

I'm looking for the closet monster because last night around midnight I woke up from a rattling sound coming from my closet. I went over to check out what it was. I opened the closet door and nothing was there. I thought to myself it must of just been the wind. When I went back to get into my bed I saw a gigantic shadow move swiftly across my room. Then I was mabey thinking I had someone or something in my room that wasn't supposed to be here, and I had to get out of my room and quick because it was giving me the creeps. I stayed up looking around for whatever was in my room. Just then there was another rattling sound coming from the closet again. I creeped over to the closet and nothing was there. CRASH! My lamp came down on the other side of the room. Right after the lamp came crashing down I caught a glimpse of something scurry under my bed. My knees were trembling as I slowly crept over and nelt down in front. I pulled up the bed skirt and looked undernieth and there was something furry with big, black, round eyes. I jumped back in shock. My heart beat was going 10 times it's normal rate.

To be continued

What was under Michael's bed? Will Michael ever get it out of his room. Tune in next time for *The Closet Monster.*

By Michael, Grade 3

FIGURE 5.9   *Michael's (3) reflections on his writing.*

Something I did particularly well:

I think in this piece of writing I described things particularly well. Like "A gigantic shadow moved swiftly across the room."

If you were to work on this piece to make it better, what could you do?

I would try to yose different kinds of words to start off each sentence.

What did you learn from this writing that you can use in the future?

I learned if you write more description then more people understand your writing.

Celia (Figure 5.10) shares a brief reflection on "The Blizzard," a poem that appears in Chapter 2 (Figure 2.53) as a sample of strong word choice. Notice how Celia's reflection focuses on her thought process and deliberate consideration of detail.

REVISION: FROM ROUGH TO READY

Students tend to define revision in their minds in one of two ways:

1. Fixing the paper (especially the spelling)
2. Doing it over

Neither is particularly attractive, and how surprising is that? For a beginning writer, completing a piece of writing can feel huge, like completing a pyramid. Who wants to hear, "Would you mind *fixing* that pyramid? It's got a little tilt to the left." From the student writer's perspective, you (mean old reviser of pyramids) have two semireasonable choices:

1. Live with the writing as it is (clearly the more sane choice).
2. I will write something *else* for you since you're so picky.

"If you did not like the pyramid," the writer reasons, "I'll build you a bridge, but no, I am *not* redoing the pyramid. Get a grip."

How do we deal with this? First, it is helpful to show students what revision really is. It is not fixing, correcting, or (necessarily) redoing—especially

---

FIGURE 5.10   *Reflections on "The Blizzard."* Celia (3)

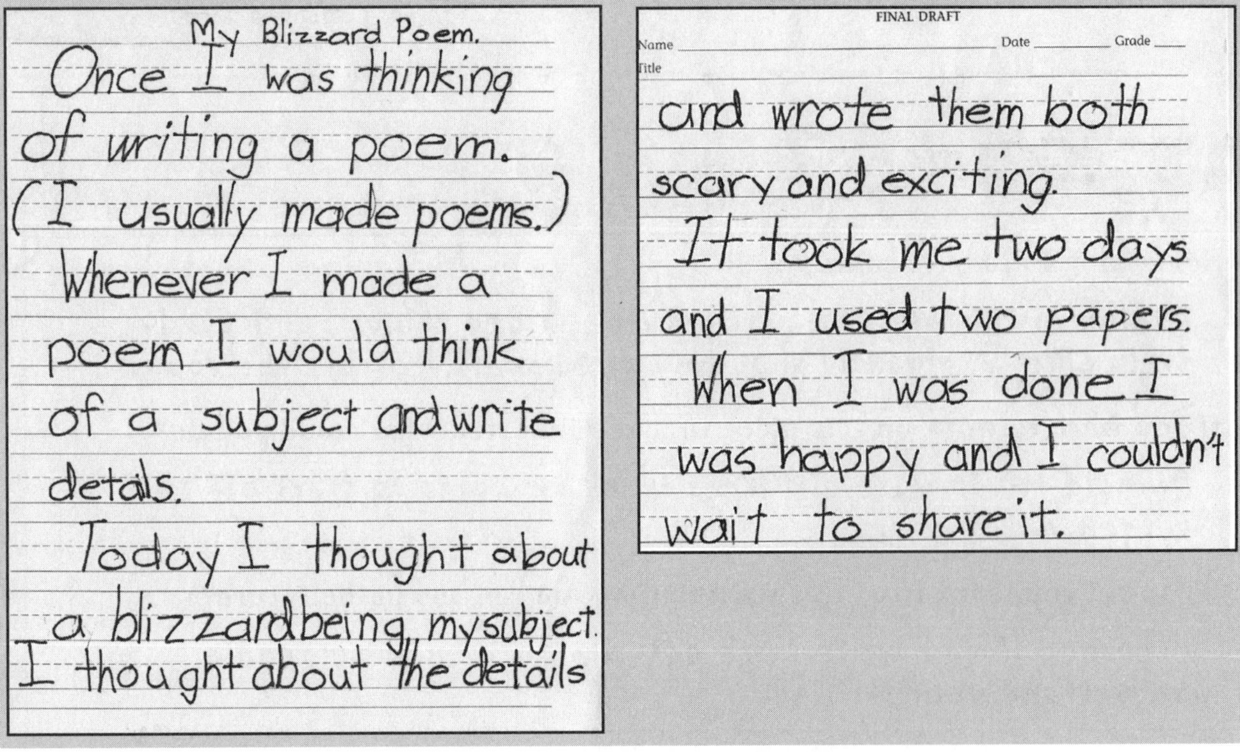

My Blizzard Poem.
Once I was thinking of writing a poem. (I usually made poems.) Whenever I made a poem I would think of a subject and write detals.
Today I thought about a blizzard being my subject. I thought about the details

FINAL DRAFT
Name _____ Date _____ Grade _____
Title

and wrote them both scary and exciting. It took me two days and I used two papers. When I was done I was happy and I couldn't wait to share it.

not at the primary level. Revision becomes more complex as writers get older and grow more skilled, but this is because both their writing and their thinking have grown more complex. Revision *is* thinking—and rethinking or reconsidering, if you will. If you have ever, even once, made a comment and wished you had said something else, put it another way, added a comment, left something unsaid, or used a different tone of voice, you have grasped the basic nature of revision. Unfortunately, once you have said it (if anyone was listening), it is usually too late to do it differently (although many of us try later, in the shower, in the car, or walking down the road). In writing, though, sometimes you get another crack at it before anyone sees or hears it. This is the beauty of revision in the writing world.

To understand how revision works, try this simple exercise. Think of someone (it can be a pet if you like—it does not have to be a person) that you see daily or at least very often. Right now, without thinking too hard about it, draw a one-minute sketch of this person (or pet). Go ahead—put the book down and *do* it. Then come back.

Got your sketch? Now, set your sketch aside for a moment and try to get a picture of the person (or pet) in your mind. Really try to bring his or her face and body into focus. Think of color, size, expression, attitude—little things like hair, hands, feet, way of standing or moving, eyes. Now look at your sketch again. Is there *anything*, any small detail, you missed? Anything you could add that would give more character or life to your sketch? Add it now. Do not take more than another minute.

Guess what. You have just revised your sketch. Revision is sometimes—often—as simple as adding or changing *one small detail*. Adding is an early (and significant) form of revision. Later, students also may choose to move things around. Later still, they may be ready to delete information or unneeded words. This is the most difficult stage of revision, and even adult writers fight it, so we should not be surprised if second graders are not wearing out pencils deleting extra words. Remember, a piece of writing is a hard thing to "build." You do not tear it apart without a lot of thought (and often some pain).

Revision Strategies

■ 1. Make a Decision

Carol Avery teaches us that revision does not begin with marking up a paper; it begins with making choices. "Demonstrate returning to writing by reading what was written earlier, and ask children to reread their pieces from the previous day and decide whether to make changes, continue the piece, or start a new piece" (2002, p. 73). Read this one more time just to get the full impact: Make changes, continue, or start fresh. *This* is where it begins. Putting the writer in control over what will happen with the writing. Not every piece needs to go through the whole writing process. Some can be tossed aside. Some are unfinished, and the writer can pick up where he or she left off. Others call for change. Just knowing these three choices gives writers an enormous head start on revision.

■ 2. Learning Through Modeling

Model the sketching activity you just tried, and ask your students to do it with you. Share your sketches, and talk about the kinds of changes you made, big or small. Refer to your changes as *revision*.

Explain that revision is something you *get* to do as a writer—not something you *have* to do. It is a privilege, a right. Like deciding how you want your own room to look. You have a certain vision of your own space, right? Most of us do not like it when we are told that we have to keep that space a certain way. We need to feel protective of our writing, too. This is not to say that writers should not be open to suggestions; however, there is a vast difference between suggestions and commands.

Ask students to help you with your revision of a simple piece. They can do this by offering suggestions or asking questions. Start with a very simple piece of writing, such as this one:

I was driving home. I saw a deer. It was very pretty.

Ask for questions: "What would you like to know?" Perhaps your students will have questions like these:

✔ Where was the deer?
✔ What was it doing?
✔ What did it look like (besides pretty)?
✔ What were you thinking when you saw it?

If they don't, though, you can encourage them: "Wouldn't you like to know . . . ?" Then, answer the questions by writing a more complete version on the overhead projector, as shown in Figure 5.11.

As you create a revision like this, talk through the changes you are making as you make them; for example, "I think I'll put these first two sentences into one longer sentence. I'm not sure I need to say the deer was pretty because most people know that. When I saw it, it was running along a fence, so I'll put that in. It had two very small fawns and was trying to cross the road with cars coming both ways. The poor deer looked terrified! Lucky for the deer, it was fast. It darted across with both fawns. They were all safe. Do I need to add anything else? [PAUSE] Maybe I should change the title. It was a very close call, so that might make a better title than 'The Deer.' Let's read it once from the beginning so that you can tell me what you think of my revision."

This revision is fairly long. You do not need to make yours this long—or even close. It's up to you. This revision adds a lot of detail. Another might focus on a specific feature, such as sentence beginnings.

When you model revision, several things are key:

1. Use as many suggestions from your students as possible.

2. Add your own ideas to theirs—being quite spontaneous as you do.

3. Do not try to do too much at once.

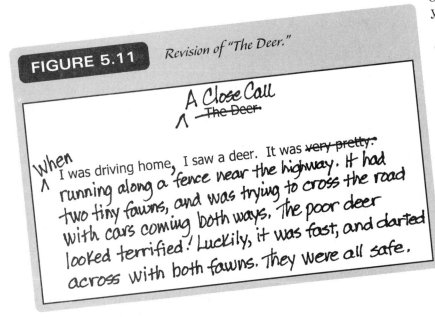

FIGURE 5.11   *Revision of "The Deer."*

A Close Call
~~The Deer.~~

When
I was driving home, I saw a deer. It was ~~very pretty.~~
running along a fence near the highway. It had
two tiny fawns, and was trying to cross the road
with cars coming both ways. The poor deer
looked terrified! Luckily, it was fast, and darted
across with both fawns. They were all safe.

4. Talk as you go.
5. Read your revised paper aloud so that they can hear it as well as see it.
6. Let them know that you like having a *chance* to revise.
7. Do *not* expect their revisions to look like yours.

Most of your students will not be able to revise in just the way you are modeling it. This is less important, however, than their opportunity to see you revise—see you go through the process. They can appreciate what you are doing (even if they cannot do it all yet), and you are planting seeds for actual work they will do later. As Laura Benson eloquently points out, "When children do not make progress as writers, we must look to ourselves. Giving our students layers and layers of modeling along with massive amounts of time to practice their writing are the hallmarks of successful writing programs" (2002, p. 20).

■ *3. Delete and Insert (℈ and ∧)*

To make this strategy work well, you need to make one simple but very *important* suggestion to your young writers: *Double-space all work.* Do this as you model, too. It leaves room for revision. There is nothing like having room. *Big* margins are also a help. Trust me—if your students fill a page with text, side to side, top to bottom, they will not want to make changes and insertions. Would you?

Older writers (about midyear grade 3 and on) can create new drafts when revising. For younger writers, indicating change is often enough, especially if getting text down on paper in the first place is something of a chore. Encourage use of the caret (∧) to show the addition of a word, phrase, or whole sentence. Use the delete mark (℈) to show deletion of the same. Expect to see more insertions than deletions. It is difficult to get rid of language we have put to paper, much like tossing out favorite knickknacks. You encourage this if you model it and invite your students to egg you on a bit. As you begin your revision on the overhead, ask them, "What do you think? Shall I be timid or bold with my revision today?" What do you suppose they will say?

■ *4. The Beauty of the Arrow (→)*

Some revisers are ready to move text around or to make larger insertions. There is nothing like the ever-helpful arrow for making this kind of change. Second grader Nina is quite an advanced reviser, using arrows together with crossouts to show changes in her draft (Figure 5.12). Notice how she replaces her comment about rolling in the leaves with the more relevant statement about feeling happy to get spring clothes. This deserves a response: "Nina, you made a great revision here, sticking with your topic and adding an important detail about your feelings. I like this revision."

■ *5. Good Old Cut-and-Paste*

My friend and colleague Tommy Thomason, author and professor of journalism at Texas Christian University, spends numerous days working with students in his wife Debby's kindergarten classroom. "It keeps me grounded," he likes to say. Like so many of us, Tommy has discovered that the problems writers face remain largely the same, from kindergarten right through college—and beyond.

FIGURE 5.12 *Revision of "Spring."* Nina (2)

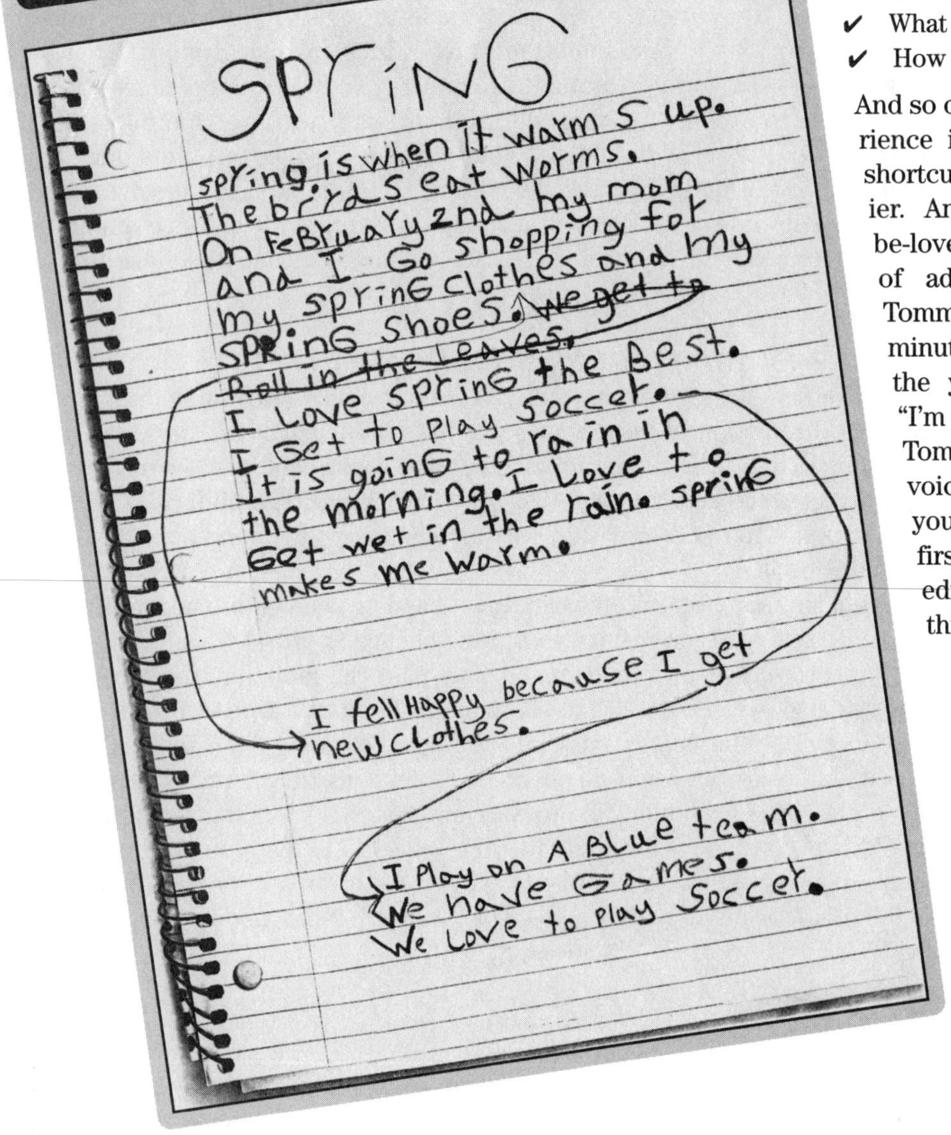

> SPRiNG
>
> Spring is when it warms up.
> The birds eat worms.
> On February 2nd my mom
> and I go shopping for
> my spring clothes and my
> spring shoes. We get to
> roll in the leaves.
> I Love spring the Best.
> I get to play soccer.
> It is going to rain in
> the morning. I Love to
> get wet in the rain. spring
> makes me warm.
>
> I fell Happy because I get
> new clothes.
>
> I Play on A Blue team.
> We have Games.
> We Love to play Soccer.

He is not surprised to see Debby's kindergarten students struggling with the same difficulties that plague professionals:

✔ How do I get started?
✔ What do I say first?
✔ How do I think up a title?

And so on. One advantage of experience is that we all learn little shortcuts that make writing easier. Among them is the much be-loved cut-and-paste method of adding information. When Tommy stopped by for a two-minute conference with Sergio, the young writer announced, "I'm done. Wanna read it?" Tommy said, "I like to hear the voice of the writer—why don't you read it for me?" Sergio's first version (which we have edited) went something like this:

My Trip to the Zoo

Last Saturday I went to the zoo. My aunt took me. We went to McDonald's first. I liked all the animals, especially the tiger. He was cool. I liked all the animals very, very much. I had a lot of fun. Later, we went home and I went to bed.

Tommy asked if the tiger was the white tiger at the zoo, knowing there wasn't one. "Naw," Sergio replied. "It was just a regular tiger." As he went on to describe it, Tommy pulled out his three- by five-inch notepad (the one he always carries with him when working with students) and made some notes. Sergio added four new sentences about the tiger (a lot for a writer so young).

When Tommy read them back to Sergio, he got a clear picture of the tiger in his head. "Know what they call that?" Tommy asked. "It's called good writing. When an author describes something so you can see it in your head, that's detail. Would you like to add these new sentences to your paper?"

Here's where Sergio hesitated.

So Tommy asked, "What if you could put those four sentences in your paper without rewriting? You know, a professional author wouldn't recopy this when you could put it together with a shortcut."

Sergio eagerly agreed. A few snips with the scissors, some tape and staples later, Sergio had a much expanded, highly detailed story to share with his friend Juan, who also loves tigers. He also had a new sense of revision.

■ *6. Save It for Next Time*

One of my all-time favorite suggestions comes from my friend Barry Lane, who says, "Understand that one method of revision is to write a new paper" (1993, p. 212). Sometimes this is the very best approach of all. Students can learn from the writing they are doing, the writing you are modeling, and the literature you share, and next time around, they can take another crack at it. Just the way you do when you say the wrong thing.

When Should Students Begin to Revise?

How old should students be when they begin to revise? This is an excellent question, one to which there is not, I think, any simple answer—but some common sense can guide us. It makes little sense, in my mind, for very young writers (or early beginners of any age) to extensively revise what is strenuously difficult to put on paper in the first place. At this age, revision, in the sense of "lessons learned," as noted in strategy 5 above, can be for next time. *Next time you write*, perhaps you will think to

✔ Add a detail.
✔ Create a picture to go with your paper.
✔ Think of a title.

You can (and should), of course, model revision for students of any age. Just because you model it does not mean you expect them to *do* everything you do. You are simply showing them conceptually what revision is all about. And it is often realistic even for young writers to add one detail or change one word.

Meanwhile, encourage young writers to develop some real fluency—comfort with the idea of writing. This (much more than revision) is the key goal for early beginners. Chances are that you do not remember learning to write. Very likely, however, you recall learning to drive (at least those portions you didn't mentally block out). Remember how important it was just to log miles, to get the feel of the car? If you are like most of us, you certainly did not do everything correctly at first. You forgot to signal a turn, or you signaled a quarter mile in advance. You cornered too sharply or too slowly. Or maybe, like me, you attempted to accelerate during your driving test without first turning on the engine (it is incredible how many points they knock off for that). Then one day it all feels comfortable—not *easy*, necessarily—but natural. Writing needs to feel like this. When a writer stops thinking about how to hold the pencil and begins to think, "What do I really want to say next?" or "Does this make sense?" or "What is my main idea?" then the time has come for revision. How old is the student at this point? Probably mid- to late-third grade—on average. As with anything, however, some students will be ready in grade one and others not until late grade three or even grade four. The following behaviors can be a guide to revision readiness: The writer

✔ Is focusing more on the content of the piece than on the logistics of making letters or words.

FIGURE 5.13 *Word list and rough draft.* Ellie (2)

Name Billey ___ Picturing Writing Gr.2 JAN page # 39			
BKy!	Suny	Problem	Water
aBlue Pink	Orange	Boat Feller	Tin the cbot sead
white	yellow	Swiming	
	it is sparkling with		

"The Turtle is swiming she hers brdim bloom
but she does't no what it is. Then she gets ran
over. Then billey has a cut on hier shell.
but Litfle does't fell it and she swims near
a beach. She is swiming fast

FIGURE 5.14 *Revised final.* Ellie (2)

As the turtle swims she hears a "broom
broom" sound. She doesn't know the sound
was from a boat's motor. Suddenly she
feels something sharp on her back. It was
almost like a big knife digging into her shell.
She began to swim faster.

✔ Has a main idea or message in mind.

✔ Is able to read his or her text aloud and ask, "Does this make sense? Is this what I want to say?"

✔ Has a conceptual understanding of revision as "rethinking," not as "fixing."

✔ Has seen the revision process modeled by the teacher and has in his or her mind some possibilities and strategies for revision.

Some Examples

I chose these examples because I think they show clearly what early revision *can* look like. Although the changes in detail, voice, and fluency are significant, they are small. Beginning writers do not (usually) discard whole pages of text, create new paragraphs, start over totally (reworking the same topic), or set out to do extensive research because the detail is weak. Big changes like these are for later—when extensive practice has made writers not only faster and more fluent but also more confident about playing with their writing. Beginning drivers usually do not go from Maine to California. They go around the block. These beginning revisers are going a *little* farther than just around the block, but they are not at the major overhaul stage yet; in their early revisions we see the promise of deeper thinking and larger changes to come.

Second grader Ellie begins with a brainstormed list of details on *sky, sun, problem,* and *water* (Figure 5.13). Notice that these headings guide Ellie into creating descriptive writing—details—as well as a story (this is the *problem* part). Her draft appears below the chart. Ellie then uses art to expand her thinking and build on her details. In this case, the art serves two purposes. It illustrates her story, and it also stretches her thinking, helping her visualize more than she can see in her mind from the words alone. She also reads what she has written aloud, and this too helps her to think of new ways to say things. With a little editorial help (the wording is her own), Ellie creates the revised version we see in Figure 5.14.

FIGURE 5.15 *Rough draft.* Olivia (2)

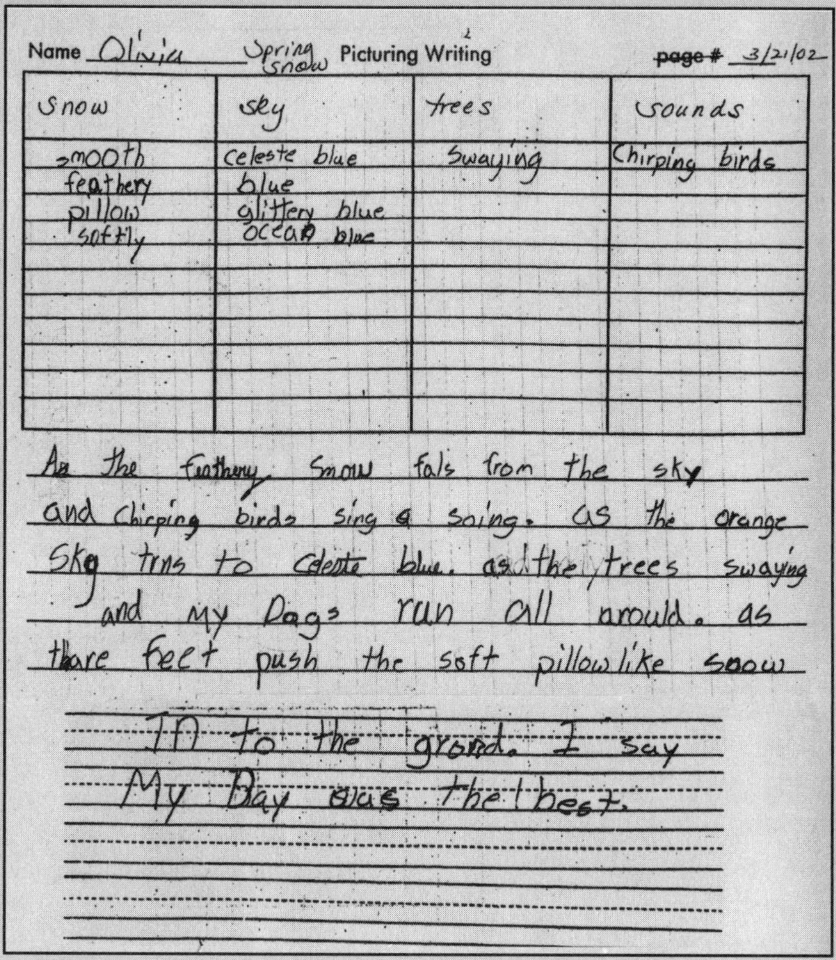

Name Olivia ___ Spring snow Picturing Writing ___ page # 3/21/02

Snow	sky	trees	sounds
smooth	Celeste blue	Swaying	Chirping birds
feathery	blue		
pillow	glittery blue		
softly	ocean blue		

As the feathery Snow fals from the sky and chirping birds sing a soing. As the orange Sky trns to celeste blue. as the trees swaying and my Dogs run all arould. as there feet push the soft pillow like soow in to the grond. I say My Day was the best.

(Read both versions aloud to really appreciate the extent of her changes.)

Olivia, also a second grader, follows basically the same process in creating a descriptive piece about a snowy day. Her rough draft (Figure 5.15) focuses primarily on capturing the details from her brainstorming chart. By the time she creates her revision (Figure 5.16), she has used both her picture and reading aloud to help her rework sentence patterns and to add a wonderful ending. (Again, read both versions aloud to hear the differences.)

■ *Inside Revision*

If we remember what revision really is, it helps us be more patient about seeing it appear in children's writing. If we think of it as correcting or improving, then all our attention goes to the draft, not to the writer. When we remind ourselves that revision is "reseeing," or revisiting in our minds, then our attention goes to the writer's thinking. It is important to teach revision not so much because we want dazzling writing (although this is often the bonus) but because we want young writers who can *think*. Writers who revise learn the invaluable habit of thinking like readers. They learn to ask whether a message is likely to make sense to a reader, whether an image is clear, whether the voice is appealing or appropriate, or whether a phrase is sparkly and fresh or worn from overuse. Even very young writers can get in the habit of taking one more look, reading their writing aloud and "just thinking about it for a minute," even if no actual changes result. This thinking lays a valuable foundation for the time when they are ready to revise.

We in turn can be realistic in our expectations, not expecting true revision from students who are still working to form letters. Revision grows through stages, and here is a quick overview to help guide *general* expectations (add to this list based on your own observations):

✔ *Beginners* (about kindergarten to early grade 1): Adding pieces and parts—such as missing words, a name, a title, a cover page, a small detail.

FIGURE 5.16 *Revised draft.* Olivia (2)

As the feathery snow falls and chirping birds sing a song, the orange sky turns to celeste blue. The trees sway and my dogs are running all around in my snowy yard. Their feet push the soft pillow-like snow into the ground. I say this day was the best.

✔ *Experienced revisers* (at or about grades 1 and 2): Making true changes—such as selecting a new title from several possibilities, changing a lead or ending, changing a sentence beginning, adding sensory detail, or making a sentence show more than tell.

✔ *Advanced revisers* (at or about grades 2 and 3): Basing revision on the whole piece, not only individual parts—reworking the lead (or ending) once the piece is written, making sure the piece focuses on one story or theme, not two, changing a word or phrase, making sure details connect to a main idea, revising to add voice, combining sentences to heighten fluency, reading aloud for continuity.

Suggest, model, encourage, and applaud revision. Do not demand it from beginning writers. Opportunity for revision results in creative, spontaneous new thinking. Required revision often produces mechanical, forced change that has little to do with what the writer thinks or feels. Which do you want from your students?

Shea and Sheheryar are [first grade] writing buddies. They are sharing their writing so that they can both understand the writing better.

Photo and caption courtesy of Christine (Grade 4).

PUBLISHING

I once had a student ask me why "Being done" did not appear in my circular model of *The Writing Process*. "It's the best part," he said, and I thought of how often in my life I would have agreed with him (and not just about writing either). For a sense of closure, being done is tough to beat. Still, it is true that many students love publishing. They enjoy seeing their work in print and are pleased to have their efforts celebrated, whether publishing involves book making or simply posting work on a wall for everyone to see.

Publishing can take several different forms with children, and so it is important to clarify your own expectations in your mind before you set out to "publish." Some teachers publish only clean copy, and so everything must go through a final editing stage prior to publishing. This final editing usually involves the writer but is done with the help of the teacher or assistant or sometimes a parent or older student. Some teachers publish the draft just as the writer created it but may include a "book language" translation so that it will be readable to others as well as to the author (in the future).

Published "books" may be done on regular eight and a half by eleven inch sheets of paper or on other paper selected by the child. They may or may not be formally bound, may or may not be illustrated. Many teachers like to include features that model the way published books are put together by publishing houses, so students' books may include such features as

✔ A title page
✔ Credits for author, illustrator, and editor(s)
✔ A dedication page
✔ An "About the Author" section
✔ Illustrations or other graphics
✔ A cover

John (Grade 1) is writing a final draft. He makes sure that the final is all polished up. He makes sure that words are spelled right and that he really wants that sentence! A final draft is when he decides what he wants for sure.
Photo and caption courtesy of Natalie and Katie (Grade 4).

Including these features encourages student writers to notice the same things in the books they read and also parallels the way real-world publishing usually occurs.

As for editing, publishing houses are sticklers about it, and so I think it is realistic to ask for a higher standard of "correctness," plus attention to layout, when books are being prepared for this more formal sharing. Think of it this way: There is *functional editing*, which makes copy readable and reasonably correct for purposes of sharing it with a general audience. Then there is *editing for publication*, which makes copy as clean and correct as we can get it and also includes significant attention to layout—making pictures (or other graphics) and text look appealing on the page.

The *way* in which you choose to publish depends on two things:

✔ The ages and readiness of your students
✔ The frequency with which you publish students' writing

Clearly, younger students are less ready to take on many publishing and final editing tasks for themselves, and so if you want correct copy for their published work, you have just volunteered for extensive editorial duty (unless you are lucky enough to work with assistants or parents who are exceptionally good sports). Older students can do much of their own editing before the final run-through, and if they have access to word processors, they can even experiment with layout and use of different fonts (which most love). Spell-check programs and other computer aids make both revision and editing much easier and faster, but student writers of all ages and abilities still need some help, and almost all need a second pair of experienced eyes for final editing (just as we ourselves do).

Keeping It Manageable

Following are my suggestions for keeping the publishing process manageable:

1. *Do not publish everything.* In our zeal to include every stage of the writing process, we sometimes have felt compelled to publish everything our students write. This puts pressure on them as well as on us or else diminishes the significance of publishing by rendering it little more than a stapling together process. Neither extreme is desirable. Encourage the author to select a few pieces for formal publication, and give those the extra needed attention publication warrants.

2. *Review selections together to see what needs to be done.* Keep in mind the capabilities of the author. For a very young child, creating a cover and adding a name as author of the piece may be quite sufficient. For older writers, a more thorough revision/editing step may be quite appropriate, with help from an assigned, experienced editor (who may be you). Pictures also can be added, and if the document is word-processed, of course, the author may wish to choose an appropriate font—or fonts.

3. *Edit to suit the writer's skill level.* With older, more experienced writers, it may be quite sufficient to produce a final, edited draft. If the corrections are small and few, there is little to gain by saving the rough draft unless, of course, the author chooses to do so. On the other hand, for very young or less experienced writers, it may be helpful to do a "book language" translation that accompanies the original text. In this case, you may choose to save both copies so that the writer can read the text (from the book print version) but also track

his or her own growth by looking at the original. This honors the child's own writing while still preserving it in a form that allows everyone to read it later.

4. *Ask for students' permission to include editorial changes.* In real-world publishing, an editor sends the author edited copies and then galleys (corrected versions of the original) to review. This gives the author a chance to look over the changes—and to learn from them. Why not give students this same opportunity? Most young writers are eager to know the "right way" of doing things—yet it can be discouraging to be handed a paper full of corrections that you must then deal with yourself. On the other hand, when you act as the student's editor and then ask for his or her approval of your changes, you put the power right back in the writer's hands while still showing him or her what needs to be done differently. A simple initial on a Post-It gives the author's OK to proceed with corrections as marked.

5. *Give credit where credit is due.* Indicate the author, illustrator (who may be the same person), and editor(s), including yourself if you participate in this way. It is fair, and it parallels the world of publishing. You can then begin to point out to students (as you share books) the author, the illustrator, and even the editor, if you wish. Countless students who can name favorite authors have difficulty naming a single favorite illustrator. Yet the pictures speak to us as much as the text.

6. *Think beyond stories.* So many of the books we publish are stories. I love them, too. However, some children prefer to write expository pieces, how-to pieces, recipes, travel brochures, alphabet books, or any number of other things. Encourage this. A classroom with variety inspires everyone.

7. *Include basic features, such as a title page, cover, dedication, and so on.* Such features enrich the publishing process and make the book more fun to put together.

8. *Give reluctant or challenged writers a way of participating.* Some writers are intimidated by the thought of a whole sentence, much less a whole book. What about them? They can do several things:

   ✔ Serve as an illustrator for another author
   ✔ Write a wordless picture book
   ✔ Dictate a book
   ✔ Dictate a review of another author's book (which can then serve as a back cover)

Note: You may wish to encourage second-language students to work with native English speakers on a bilingual book and then share it aloud. Everyone benefits!

9. *Give highly skilled writers a challenge.* More skilled writers also can help in the publication process. They may write slightly longer books, even chapter books. They also may serve as editorial assistants (with credit) to other authors in the class. They may wish to be

   ✔ Copy editors, helping with corrections or layout
   ✔ Content editors, offering suggestions on detail, organization, or voice

Some Examples

The following samples show just a few of the many formats published works can take. "The Trip to Africa" (Figure 5.17), written by second grader Amity

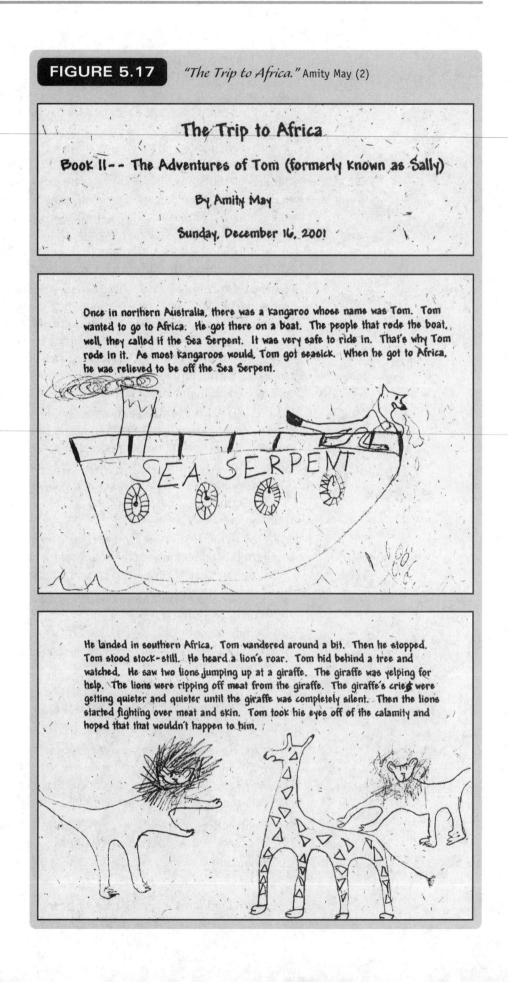

FIGURE 5.17   *"The Trip to Africa."* Amity May (2)

FIGURE 5.17 *Continued*

Then suddenly, he heard a scritch-scratch-scritch-scratch noise. He started twitching his ears. Something fishy was going on and he knew it. He turned around and saw a black leopard standing in front of him. Tom had no idea that this particular cat was a predator. So he just said, "So whaddaya think you're doing on a bright and sunny afternoon, huh?" The leopard stood quite still looking somewhat puzzled.

While the leopard was thinking about what he was going to do to Tom, Tom grabbed some saw grass. Tom blindfolded the leopard with the saw grass. Then Tom told the leopard he was going to take him to a place where the leopard could feast on a zebra in peace. The leopard licked his lips. Tom led the leopard off a cliff. The cliff was five miles high. You could hear the thump of the leopard for miles. Then Tom went home.

The End ☺

May, is exceptionally complete, with a wonderful sense of story. It is the tale of a clever kangaroo, Tom (formerly known as Sally, presumably in another story), who escapes a gruesome fate by tricking a crafty leopard. The text is thoroughly illustrated with expressive characters. This extended text surely would lend itself to book binding and also could include credits for writing, illustrating, and editing—all of which go to Amity May herself (with the exception of a little help in editing).

"The Chocolate Mouse" (Figure 5.18) is written and illustrated (the cover) by Nikki. She had some help with the editing, and as we can see, she dictated her "About the Author" page to the teacher, who wrote it in the third person. This delightful story of a chocolate-loving mouse who turns into a chocolate "artifact" has rich detail and word choice. It also has strong moments of fluency combined with numerous sentences that begin with "The doctor . . . ." Changing this one feature would bring out even more voice.

Kindergartner Jacque has created a very extended text for her age, "The Horse and The Duck" (Figure 5.19), the tale of an unusual friendship. Each page is illustrated, adding to the detail. Notice the very satisfying ending. Jacque also has included a cover page (word-processed) and a good bit of detail on her dictated author's page, which helps us to know her better. Her teacher includes a book version to help Jacque read her text in years to come.

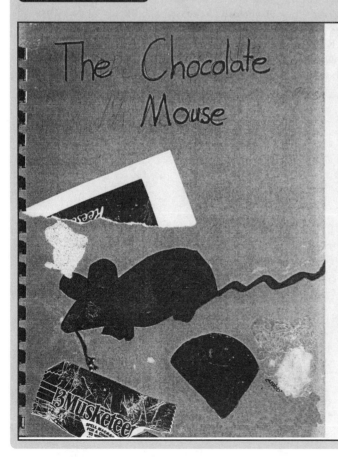

FIGURE 5.18   *"The Chocolate Mouse."* Nikki (3)

The Chocolate Mouse

Dedication
This book is dedicated to my Grandpa because he loves chocolate and I love him!

Once upon a time there was a greedy mouse named Scamper. Now, Scamper's favorite thing in the whole galaxy was CHOCOLATE! If he was with one of his friends and found a Cheerio, jelly bean, cheeseball, or especially CHOCOLATE, he would never share it.

One day Scamper woke up to find that he had brown spots and gold rings all over his back! He just thought it was mud until . . . . . he tried to wash it off! It wouldn't come off! All of his friends asked why he was so dirty, but he didn't reply because he didn't know himself.

The next morning Scamper found more spots all over his back. He was very puzzled! He called the doctor and asked what was wrong with him, but the doctor wasn't much help. All he did was think, put his hand on his chin, scratch his head, and think some more. Very puzzled, he said he didn't know either. He said he would come back tomorrow and bring his doctor bag.

The doctor came over the next morning to find the mouse still in bed. The doctor took out his stethoscope to listen to the mouse's heart beat, but there was none! The doctor was shocked and almost fainted.

The doctor put Scamper in the Museum so everyone could see him. He had to put Scamper in a very cool room so he wouldn't melt.

Inside the room was a sign that said, PLEASE DO NOT TOUCH!" And then, in smaller print it said, "Please do not eat either!" Mice and rats from around the world came to see this food artifact.

The doctor got a lot of cheese for bringing Scamper in the museum. The doctor thought about the mouse, whispered and said, "I didn't even know his name."

By Nikki
Grade 3

About the Author
Nikki lives at home with her mother, father, and little brother. She gives credit for her writing success to her mother, who also loves to write. Someday, Nikki thinks she may want to be a teacher! Nikki plans on writing more stories this year. Her friends (and her teacher) can't wait to read them.

FIGURE 5.19   *"The Horse and the Duck" (6 pages).* Jacque (K)

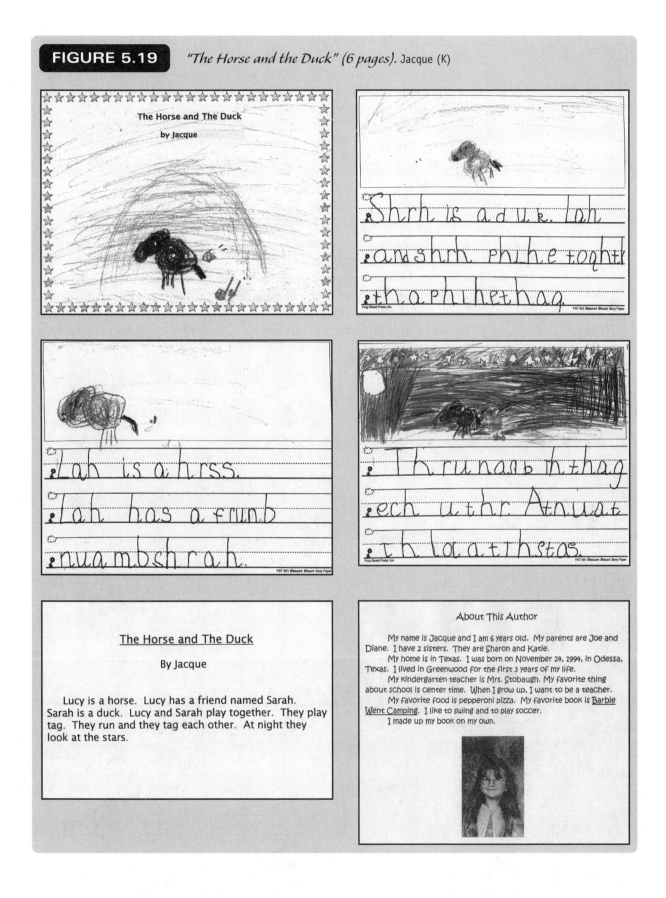

The Horse and The Duck
by Jacque

Shrh is a duk. lah
andshrh phlhe toqhtr
tha phlhe thag.

Lah is a hrss.
lah has a frunb
nua mbshrah.

Th ru naob th thag
ech uthr. Atnuat
th laa tih stas.

The Horse and The Duck

By Jacque

Lucy is a horse. Lucy has a friend named Sarah.
Sarah is a duck. Lucy and Sarah play together. They play
tag. They run and they tag each other. At night they
look at the stars.

About This Author

My name is Jacque and I am 6 years old. My parents are Joe and
Diane. I have 2 sisters. They are Sharon and Katie.
My home is in Texas. I was born on November 24, 1994, in Odessa,
Texas. I lived in Greenwood for the first 3 years of my life.
My kindergarten teacher is Mrs. Stobaugh. My favorite thing
about school is center time. When I grow up, I want to be a teacher.
My favorite food is pepperoni pizza. My favorite book is Barbie
Went Camping. I like to swing and to play soccer.
I made up my book on my own.

Brady, a first grader, has written an all-about book on insects (Figure 5.20). This organizational pattern is a favorite with young writers and gives them an opportunity to show off what they know or what they have observed. As you will notice, Brady's word choice is running well ahead of his conventional spelling, which is as it should be. In case you need a "book copy," here it is: "Insects, by Brady. Ladybugs pretend to die. Ants get food for their colony. Bees get nectar for their hive. Butterflies can be beautiful. Dragonflies can be big. Some can be small. Praying mantises can be camouflaged on the leaves."

One Last Thought

While publication is very gratifying, it is not the only reward for writing or writing well. Sometimes, as that student writer pointed out, just finishing is enough. Take your cue from students, however. If they feel the urge to publish fairly often, and if they are willing to give a little extra attention to a published piece (which is appropriate, I think), then go for it. If you (or they) are feeling some publishing burnout, do not feel guilty if you cut back. It is the writing itself that is most important, not the publishing per se. Other ways to celebrate writing include

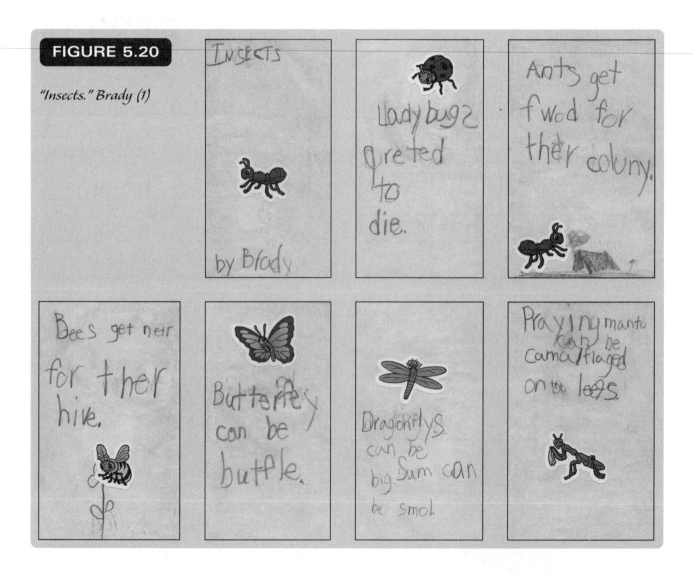

FIGURE 5.20

"Insects." Brady (1)

- ✔ Taking it home to be shared with parents (or others)
- ✔ Sharing in a response group
- ✔ Sharing writing from an author's chair
- ✔ Simply posting a writing sample for display, even if it isn't formally published
- ✔ Adding a piece to a personal portfolio
- ✔ Hosting a writer's workshop evening, which parents or other community members can attend to hear children read their work and to celebrate your writing community

FINAL REFLECTION

We so often think of reflections as being linked to specific pieces of writing. It is interesting, though, to ask student writers themselves what writers need. Figure 5.21 shows Andrew's answer.

Notice how many different things Andrew identifies: thinking time, an idea, pictures to prompt your thinking—and of course, good books. As it turns out, this is an insightful reflection, as the work of other student writers shows. In Figure 5.22, kindergartner Katie

FIGURE 5.21 *"What Does a Writer Need?"*

You need thinking time and an idea before you start writing. It helps to know what you want to write about before you start. Jonathan shows me some of his pictures he's drawn and that gives me a good idea. It helps if you've read some good books, too.

By Andrew, Grade 2

FIGURE 5.22

Portrait of her sister.
Katie (K)

shows off the thinking she has done about her older sister Sharon, who seems to have a talent for music as well as a love of butterflies and flowers. How much detail and voice she manages to work into her art. In Figure 5.23, Justin begins by painting a hammerhead shark, and the picture itself causes him to explode with ideas: the swishing of the seaweed, the hunger of the shark, and the hunt for crabs (notice the small one hiding on the ocean floor). First grader Kristen has been listening to stories of Orca whales and sharks and is inspired to create first a picture then a description that suggests a story to come (Figure 5.24). What an enticing last line. Questions make terrific endings—sometimes.

FIGURE 5.23

"Hammerhead Shark."
Justin (2)

The gray hammerhead shark is cruising in the cold Pacific Ocean. The seaweed is swishing against hammerhead and he is very hungry. He is swimming between rocks and seaweed to look for crabs.

FIGURE 5.24

"Orca Pup." Kris (2)

The rain makes the sun reflect off the aqua colored ocean near the Washington coast. Orca pup is shouting to his mom. He is too far away from her. A shark is nearby. Will orca pup escape or will he be breakfast for the shark?

CHAPTER 5 IN A NUTSHELL

- Growth is about change. Revising and publishing are ways of making significant changes in writing. Reflecting and keeping portfolios are ways of noticing, recording, and documenting change.
- Portfolios do not need to be huge and complex. They serve us—and our students—better if they are simple and manageable.
- The primary purpose of a portfolio is to encourage the student writer to look carefully within his or her writing and to notice signs of change, growth, and risk taking. In this way, the student traces the journey of himself or herself as a writer.
- Reflection (which often plays a significant role in completing a portfolio) is mostly about noticing change. Students who know the six traits of writing have specific elements to look for as they reflect on who they are, where they began as writers, and what they can do now.
- Revision is not about fixing but about *rethinking* a piece of writing.
- Students are ready for revision when they begin to think of their writing conceptually (Does this make sense?) rather than thinking (at a more elementary level) of how to form letters or spell simple words.
- Revision begins with a simple choice: Continue the writing, change the writing, or move on to a new piece?
- Revision skills progress in stages from simply adding an element (a name or title) to reworking sections or the whole piece, for example, redoing a lead, deleting a paragraph, changing the voice.
- Publishing occurs in many forms, from simply sharing a piece publicly to making a book.
- Formally published books require a slightly higher level of attention to detail and editing and may include such elements as a title page, credit page (for author, editor, and illustrator), dedication page, cover, illustrations, and so on.
- Publishing every piece of writing is not essential—and can even lead to burnout for both teacher and students. Many teachers find it makes sense to publish carefully selected pieces so that publishing remains special and celebrational.

EXTENSIONS

1. Do you keep a portfolio of your own? If you do, how did you go about choosing the pieces to go into it? If not, this is a good time to begin. Choose one piece right now and let that be a beginning. Continue to add your portfolio for the next six to eight months. Then write a reflection on who you have become as a writer/artist. Ideas for things to include: personal writing of any kind, reviews or covers from favorite books, letters (to you or from you), any commendations or reviews of your work, samples of art, lists of favorite artists, films or books, photographs—anything that is *you.*

2. This chapter recommends keeping folders/portfolios of students' work so that assessment can be based on a body of work rather than on individual samples. What are the advantages of this practice? Do you feel that it leads to more accurate assessment of what young student writers can do?

3. When, in your view, are student writers ready for revision? What expectations are realistic? What might be unrealistic? Could too much emphasis on revision too soon discourage students' enthusiasm for writing?

4. Consider Figures 5.13 through 5.16. If you are currently teaching, do your student writers revise more than this? Or less?

5. What sorts of things do you do—as a writer—when you revise? Are you a cautious reviser, or do you really plunge in? Many writers consider this the best part of the writing process—the part they enjoy most. Do you agree? Why?

6. Suppose that you had a colleague who made this statement: "No student writing should be published unless it is editorially flawless." What is your response to such a statement? Do you agree or disagree—or feel pulled both ways? Write a brief response.

7. In your view, is publication a vital step in the writing process? Is it essential for every child to publish writing in some form, in some way? Why do you feel this way?

8. Assume that publishing, in some form, will be part of your classroom instructional process in writing. List three things (or more) that you feel you personally could do to ensure that *all* your students could be part of this process.

9. Have you ever had a book (or any piece of writing) published? If so, think about sharing this experience with your students. Even if you have not, list some ways that instructional procedures in the classroom can parallel the world of publishing.

SOURCES CITED

Avery, Carol. 2002. *And with a Light Touch*, 2d ed. Portsmouth, NH: Heinemann.

Benson, Laura. "A Writer's Bill of Rights." In *Colorado Reading Council Journal*, Vol. 13 (Spring 2002), pp. 20–23.

Brodie, Deborah. 1997. *Writing Changes Everything*. New York: St. Martin's Press.

Cramer, Ronald C. 2001. *Creative Power: The Nature and Nurture of Children's Writing*. New York: Addison-Wesley Longman.

Graves, Donald, and Virginia Stuart. 1985. *Write from the Start*. New York: Signet Books.

Lane, Barry. 1993. *After THE END*. Portsmouth, NH: Heinemann.

Routman, Regie. 2001. *Conversations*. Portsmouth, NH: Heinemann.

Spandel, Vicki. 2001. *Creating Writers*, 3d ed. New York: Addison-Wesley Longman.

6 Modeling the Process

Mrs. Goodsky is asking her class for a word that ends in s.
Photo and caption courtesy of Natalie (Grade 4).

*N*othing, absolutely *nothing* you will ever do as a teacher will be more powerful than modeling writing in front of your students. It is vital to the successful teaching of writing, yet it does not happen nearly as often as it should. Do you recall ever seeing one of your own teachers write? Not lesson plans or comments on students' writing—but actual original writing? A story perhaps or a poem? If you do, you are among the lucky few, and odds are good it made a strong impression on you. I never saw a single teacher write, kindergarten through college. My teachers, for the most part, fit Nancie Slonim Aronie's (1998) vision: powerful figures dispensing knowledge from the front of the room.

Write in front of your students. Think aloud as you write. If you have never done this before, close your classroom door and risk it. It will get easier, I promise. When you write, you see firsthand the struggles, doubts, thoughts, and processes that writers (including your students) go through. When you write, you share not only your composing process but part of who you are and what matters to you. Your own insights as a writer will make you a more effective teacher of writing.

—Regie Routman
Conversations (2000, p. 232)

Your philosophy of writing is determined by your personal experience as a writer. That means your own life as a writer is ultimately reflected in your classroom. And it means if you want to change your classroom, you begin by changing you.

—Tommy Thomason
More Than a Writing Teacher (1993, p. 2)

If you had asked me, when I was a child, to give a generic description of a teacher, I would have said someone who wears nice clothes, stands in front of the room next to the chalkboard, and knows everything.

—Nancie Slonim Aronie
Writing from the Heart: Tapping the Power of Your Inner Voice (1998, p. 171)

Talking *about* writing only takes you so far as a writer, though. How much I would have loved to see exactly how to

✔ Choose a topic ✔ Come up with a good title
✔ Take notes ✔ Plan my organization
✔ Write a good lead (or ending) ✔ Put more voice into writing
✔ Get rid of unneeded detail

or, well, you name it.

My colleague, Jeff Hicks, who is one of my writing and teaching heroes, always writes with and in front of his students. "I really would not ask my students to write anything I don't attempt myself," he says. "And besides, it's hard enough to get across to kids what it is you really want from them—when they see it, it's like some kind of magical door opens in their heads, and they say, 'Oh, *I* get it.'"

Briefly, these are the advantages to modeling:

1. To learn more about writing process *as writers*.
2. To show students the process in action. How does it look as it is happening?
3. To show students how to deal with specific challenges and problems in writing.
4. To give students an opportunity to be coaches for us.

In this chapter we'll consider each of these individually.

BENEFIT 1: LEARNING ABOUT WRITING PROCESS AS A WRITER

Think back. When was the last time you observed another person write? You would be unusual if you could recall more than two incidents in a lifetime.

—Donald H. Graves
Writers: Teachers and Children at Work (1984, p. 43)

Most of us have read books about writing process. Most of us have been to seminars and workshops. We have *taught* writing as a process, allowing time for prewriting and drafting and encouraging students to revise and edit their work. None of these activities, however, provides the in-depth understanding of the writing process that comes with being writers ourselves. Doing it. Prewriting, drafting, sharing, revising, editing—all of it. Then doing it some more.

It does not really help me as a teacher, for instance, to know the importance of choosing personally significant topics if I do not select some topics that are personally significant to me—and then write about them. It does not help me to know about the power of revision if I do not experience it myself, revising work I care about, hoping an audience will like it, hoping it will be published. Here are just a few of the many things I have learned by modeling writing in front of students:

✔ On some days the writing does not come easily. Fortunately, you don't die of it.
✔ A lot of what I write is not as creative as things students come up with.
✔ The lead and the conclusion are usually the most difficult parts of any piece of writing.
✔ Titles are tough, too.

✔ Not all prewriting techniques work for everyone. I like the look of webbing, for instance, and I even like doing it. But I do not use webs when I write. Lists (mostly lists of questions) are more helpful to me.

✔ Conversation and drafting (just starting in) are my most effective prewriting tools.

✔ Reading certain writers influences my personal voice.

✔ The problems I experience most often as a writer are making the introduction too long, repeating words or phrases I've "fallen in love with" while writing, and going down a side road because I think of an anecdote I want to share even though it does not fit.

✔ You really should listen to the audience, even when you do not like what they say.

✔ Student writers usually do not want to criticize; they want to *help*—and they are good at it.

✔ You can tell more about an audience's reaction from how they sit and how they look at you than from what they say.

✔ Organization is, overall, my weakest trait.

✔ I like sentence fragments and will always use them in my writing, even though some people do not like them.

✔ I like to start sentences with *And*—even though *lots* of people do not like this either.

✔ *-able* and *-ible* words are very hard for me to spell.

✔ A lot of my writing takes a humorous turn, even when it does not start out that way.

✔ Almost nothing I write follows my original plan (including this book).

✔ Almost *all* my writing takes a lot longer than I thought it would (including this book).

✔ Leaving writing alone for a *long* time (two or three weeks or more) improves revision 1000 percent.

If you write with/for your students, you probably have made discoveries very much like these. It occurs to me that without the benefit of writing my way through the writing process, I might very well feel comfortable teaching writing by

✔ Assigning topics that are uninteresting or that make little or no sense to students

✔ Expecting students' writing to match some preconceived picture in my mind—without showing them what that might look like

✔ Having very unrealistic expectations regarding the amount of time it takes to write

✔ Having unrealistic expectations about the quality of student performance

✔ Imagining that students will do more than neaten up or fix spelling when they revise

✔ Imagining that titles and leads will offer genuine hints of what follows

✔ Assuming that students know such skills as cutting extra wording, making word choice more interesting, or listening for voice in their writing—when, in truth, it never occurs to them to do these things

The assumptions we make as teachers of writing often come from our sheer lack of experience as writers. Would you want to take a driver's test or be taught driving by someone who did not actually drive but only observed other drivers?

Mrs. Meyers is going step by step through buddy conferences to help her kids write better.

Photo and caption courtesy of Katie and Natalie (Grade 4).

BENEFIT 2: TO SHOW STUDENTS THE PROCESS IN ACTION

Many veteran teachers claim that the most important thing they do both to teach writing and to build a writer-friendly classroom is to write with their children.

—Tommy Thomason and Carol York

Write on Target: Preparing Young Writers to Succeed on State Writing Achievement Tests (2000, p. 3)

As teachers of writing, we can't just write. We have to write so that we come to understand what it is that we are teaching. We have to push ourselves to notice and to understand what's happening when we write, so that our writing becomes a powerful curriculum tool for our teaching.

—Katie Wood Ray

What You Know by Heart (2002, p. 6)

We can show students all the writing process wheels we want, and we can even walk them through the steps of the writing process one by one, but nothing is as powerful as an actual demonstration of how it looks *while it is happening.* Remember, we have two kinds of models to show students:

✔ The *products* (samples of writing from other students, professional writers, or ourselves)

✔ Writing as it is happening—in short, *process*

It is the difference between holding a baby and watching a birth. Of course, they are related experiences, but they are *not* the same.

In Santa Fe a year or so ago, I watched a painter at work on the square. Nothing he did matched what I would have imagined had I seen only the

FIGURE 6.1

My sketch of a woman's face.

finished painting. He was creating a woman's face, and I would have pictured him painting a sort of outline of the head and hair—because that is how I draw myself, so that is what I see. Instead, he worked from the eyes out. The eyes stared back at him the whole time he filled in the rest of the face—nose, then cheeks, then chin, then mouth. The hair, which I would have painted first, he did last. His strokes seemed bolder, more vigorous, more spontaneous than anything I had ever tried—and I wanted to imitate that approach. Although I am not an artist, I tried this eyes-first technique later in my hotel room, and the result startled me because it was so different from anything else I'd ever drawn (see Figure 6.1). I am still not an artist, but if I could watch that man paint every day, well, who knows?

BENEFIT 3: TO SHOW STUDENTS HOW TO DEAL WITH SPECIFIC WRITING CHALLENGES AND PROBLEMS

There are two kinds of challenges you can deal with: (1) the struggles and decisions all writers face and (2) the challenges your own writers are facing. Sometimes these are the same—but not always.

Challenges All Writers Face

Let's start with the first. All writers, regardless of experience or ability, must do certain things—choose a topic, for instance, or write a lead, or decide when a piece is finished. You will not have time or opportunity to model every single writer's decision, but the more of them you deal with, the more opportunities your writers have to grow.

Take finding good topics, for instance. In *Conversations*, Regie Routman tells of a second-year teacher, Neal Robinson, who said two things helped his students write well: seeing models of other students' work and "finding a topic that mattered to them" (2000, p. 221). Our students' lives are filled with possible writing topics—but often they do not know it. They see their lives as dull and lusterless, not worthy of Hollywood.

Remember our discussion of small topics in Chapter 4? One third grader wrote a charming piece about how to keep goldfish healthy. She had just purchased a goldfish and so had some expertise. A second grader who had been to a tea party wrote a how-to piece on proper behavior and etiquette at a formal gathering. Other small topics that have worked well for students include

✔ A letter to the tooth fairy about a lost tooth
✔ A story of a stray cat who stayed—and became a fine mom to four kittens

✔ Spending winter break having an appendectomy
✔ Having a grandfather as a best friend
✔ Moving—when your friends can't come with you
✔ Being afraid to get on an airplane

Writing is about passion. When our students moan, "I have nothing to write about," it's time to ask them, "Ever feel afraid? Anxious? Annoyed? Downright furious? So bored you thought you'd fall asleep? So worried that you couldn't sleep? So happy you wanted to scream out loud? Well, what made you feel that way? Those are the moments to write about." Teaching writing well requires knowing our students and knowing what touches their lives.

As I mentioned earlier, I also keep a running list of topics that are important to me personally, and I model this by writing them (or some of them, anyway) on an overhead projection and asking students to choose one they would like me to write about:

✔ An annoying neighbor who talks *so* loud on the phone that he doesn't need a phone
✔ Wearing someone else's glasses (I picked them up by accident!)
✔ Watching a very annoyed man in his pajamas trying to scare a female moose out of his petunia bed
✔ A scary teacher

I share my topics mainly to show students that I do not have trips to China or meetings with the President on my list either.

Most students love papers about teachers. Like most people, I have had several teachers who were worthy of whole books. My kindergarten teacher was a character. She loved to dress up and refused to sit on the floor (although we had to take naps "down there"—which was disturbing to me, so I never let my head touch the ground). I recall her saying that she was "sick and tired of putting our boots on for us and blowing our snotty little noses." I also recall that she wore very high heels and very red lipstick and smelled better than most of us. She liked schedules and hustled us off to the restroom right on time, whether we had to go or not. Since I virtually never had to go, this was a recurring problem for me in school (my nickname was "the camel"), especially since we had to "perform" before we could leave the restroom. I spent hours there.

My first and second grade teachers were saints and so are less interesting to write about. My third grade teacher was a wanna-be model who fell back on teaching because she had such trouble getting her weight under 100 pounds (we all found this fascinating and loved to see what she would bring for lunch—nothing, usually). She was so busy job hunting that she had a hard time focusing on us.

Then, in fourth grade, all hell broke loose. Of course, at the time, I wasn't thinking, "It's good I'm living this nightmare because later I'll have this to write about." But such events are often the stuff of good writing. When I tell students even a tiny detail about this blood-thirsty woman, my fourth grade teacher, who left sobbing and screaming children in her wake, they are eager for me to write something about her—and so I do. This is an ideal time for me to model two important things: how to write a good lead and how to choose a good title. I start with the lead and write several on the overhead, reading them aloud as I go. "I want you to help me choose the one you think is best," I tell them. Usually I will write at least one lead that I think is pretty weak, one that nearly everyone will recognize as weak. Often it is a lead that students are likely to use in their own writing—only it sounds worse when I write it. Here are some possibilities:

✔ "If I had known how bad fourth grade would be, I might have failed on purpose and stayed in third."
✔ "Have you ever known someone who was so mean that you could hardly stand to be around her? I have. In this paper I will tell you about her."
✔ "My fourth grade teacher was not the nicest person in the whole world. In this paper, I will explain why."
✔ "We could *feel* her coming before we heard her. Her big shoes hit the floor so hard, we couldn't tell for sure if it was vibrating, or if we just had the shakes."

I make the print big, and I read them more than once if students want to hear them. Then we talk about which one(s) they like best and why—and which ones do not work as well and why. Sometimes they have other suggestions—other things to try. Great. I record those, too. This is a lesson in how to write a good lead, but it teaches something equally important: The first lead you think of may not be the best one. It is good to try more than one way of saying something.

Wait a second, though. What about those kids who are only writing single sentences. Is this lesson lost on them? Absolutely not! Think of what they are internalizing about leads. Let them *hear* what you write—even if they cannot read it independently. Even if they are not writing leads themselves—yet. When they get to a level of fluency where they are writing two or three sentences, their leads will be stronger. Some will amaze you.

Possible titles? Let's see, I tell them, and I begin to brainstorm, and then I invite them to join in. I could start with her name:

Miss Sader

Or I could describe her:

The Meanest Teacher on Earth

Or I could describe the experience:

Grade Four—A Tough Year

"What about her shoes?" someone will say. "I like the part where you feel her coming. Use that!"

How about:

Battle Shoes

We settle on this one for now, but I mark it **WT** for *working title* and put a circle around it. This means, I explain, that after I finish my story, I will come back to the title to see if it still works. I may want to change it.

As I work on the draft about Miss Sader, and then later when I revise it, I can model many other things, including

✔ Putting voice into writing
✔ Choosing lively words
✔ Making sentences more fluent
✔ And so on

As I model these things, I will not write badly on purpose, but I will not create the all-time flat-out best writing I can either. In this way, I make room for stu-

Mrs. Meyers is using David as an example. It is always good to first do a model before you let kids do a buddy conference.
Photo and caption courtesy of Natalie (Grade 4).

dents to offer suggestions. For example, in describing Miss Sader, I might start out something like this (notice that this copy is double-spaced):

> We could feel her coming before we heard her. Were her shoes hitting the floor that hard, or did we have the shakes? She had a HUGE voice and used it like a weapon, especially when she caught us doing something wrong.

I will ask students what questions they have, and I will use their questions to add details—and usually, voice.

Note: It is not necessary to write voluminous drafts to model writing. Little snippets work fine. Do a bit now and more later. In this way, you do not feel overwhelmed, and neither do your students.

Challenges Your Writers Face

✔ "I have a student who will only write one sentence."
✔ "So many of my students start *all* their sentences the same way."
✔ "My students use the same words over and over and over—it's putting me to sleep!"
✔ "I have a student who *never* remembers to put a title on his paper."

Any of these sound familiar? You can probably make a list of your own. Do that. List everything you can think of that is a problem for your students—it may be a problem for *most* writers. The answer, in almost every case, is model the problem and its solution. Model it more than once if you need to. Attack it in slightly different ways, with different pieces of writing. Be creative. Here is just one example. You can easily invent more. The more you model, the more natural it feels, and the more relaxed you will be about tackling virtually any problem right on the spot. You won't even need to think about it.

One Example: The Single-Sentence Syndrome

Let's be clear. For some students, a single full sentence is a lot. So instead of despairing because there isn't more, we should be celebrating. It is also true, however, that some students will persist in writing just one sentence for a long, long time. It is almost as if they feel no special need to stretch. So start by writing a single sentence on an overhead projection:

> I visited Alaska.

Now say something like this: "Sometimes, when you write one sentence, it's enough. But this doesn't seem like much to say. I think I need more details. Help me out. What would you like to know?" Use students' questions to create a detail or two that will expand your writing:

> Last summer, I visited Alaska. There were so many mountains you could never count them. I ate Alaska king crab for the first time. It was cooked on an open campfire, and we dipped it in melted butter.

Now ask students, "What is different about this piece? How many sentences did I write? Let's count—OK, four. Did I give you a lot more information? What do you picture? Which piece of writing do you like better? This one? Me, too. You know what? When I read your writing, I like details, too. I need details to understand what you are trying to tell me. Let's try this: After you write, ask yourself if you could add just one or two more details. That might take three or four sentences."

Do not be afraid to give students your honest reader response to writing. You aren't throwing personal darts at anyone. You are just stating your preferences. Be opinionated. If you dislike violence in writing, say so. If you are bored hearing the same words over and over, tell them. And when you encounter a poor piece of writing (not one of your student's pieces, but a published work of any kind), bring it in and read it to them. Don't hem and haw. Say exactly what you think. You can be gentle and be honest at the same time, especially when you are showing them, time and again, that you find reasons to revise your *own* writing, too.

■ A Question

If you model ways to solve writing problems, won't your students quickly catch on to the fact you are writing badly (or not as well as you could, anyhow) on purpose? Yes—of course. But as long as you do not overdo it, it's fine. What you are modeling in this instance is how to solve a problem, not how to create one. You need to demonstrate the problem to do this. Writer/teacher Carol Avery talks about modeling haphazard placement of periods (just slamming them into the text in any old place), and her students laughingly telling her the text makes no sense that way. They know what she is up to. "I play the inexperienced writer, allowing them to be the experts who teach me," she explains (2002, p. 115).

In other instances, you *will* be doing your best. In that case, you are modeling for another purpose: to show your thinking in action. Do not be surprised, though, if you encounter an unanticipated problem or two on the way!

SPECIFICS (THINGS TO MODEL)

Here are a few suggestions for specific things you could model for students:

✔ Planning and developing a novel
✔ Researching the definitive autobiography
✔ Writing a screenplay for a video documentary

I'm *kidding*. See—that's the thing. Often, the reason we do not model is that we are thinking too big. Let's get real. Here are some down-to-earth, manageable things that you can readily model:

✔ Writing on just one side of the paper
✔ Putting spaces between words
✔ Writing on every other line to allow room for revision or editing
✔ Leaving margins
✔ Adding a title
✔ Changing the title when you finish—if it no longer fits
✔ Using an apostrophe
✔ Reading the lead aloud to see if it's a grabber
✔ Reading the ending aloud to see if the piece feels and sounds finished
✔ Combining two short, choppy sentences to make one smooth one
✔ Getting rid of too many *ands*
✔ Changing a sentence beginning or two to avoid monotony
✔ Including some sensory details—sounds, smells—to enrich the text
✔ Putting in some dialogue to add spice

Samantha and Mr. J look for ideas. What that means is they might find some new ideas or they might make sure ideas make sense. It's good to have someone read your work, even a grownup.
Photo and caption courtesy of Natalie (Grade 4).

✔ Saying something directly and honestly to boost voice
✔ Making sure questions end in question marks
✔ Using quotation marks to show speech
✔ Deciding where a new paragraph should begin
✔ Taking out a bit of information that is not needed
✔ Working effectively with a writing partner (writing buddy)
✔ Reading a whole piece aloud to see if it is clear and fluent

See? Small is good. Small is do-able.

SECRETS TO GOOD MODELING

1. Base *some* modeling activities on specific problems *you* see in your students' writing. This makes your examples relevant.

2. Base other modeling activities on personal pieces *you* are actually working on at the time. Let students see you struggle with work that is important to you.

3. Model *everything*—from choosing a title to editing spelling or wrapping text from line to line. No writer's question is too small for modeling.

4. Talk as you go, but do not make the mistake of thinking that explaining alone *is* modeling. It isn't. Explaining helps make modeling clear, but you must *write*.

5. Illustrate problems and struggles, but let students know that you are purposely modeling a problem many writers have. If you pretend that you do not know where a sentence ends, they will not believe you.

6. Get over being self-conscious. Modeling is good teaching. You are showing process, not award-winning text.

7. Read the text aloud as you go. Remember that some of your students may not be able to read what you write with ease, so read it for them (sometimes more than once), but also talk about changes as you make them.

Mrs. Meyers shows the class a student's work that was particularly good (and also shares a sample of her own writing). The importance of this is that people learn from the qualities in the writing.
Photo and caption courtesy of Lilly (Grade 4).

8. Keep examples short and very focused. Do not try to write five-page essays. Write a lead, a short description, a poem, an opinion.

9. Occasionally, give students choices: Which is the best lead? Which is the best title? How should I end this?

10. Keep it interactive. Constantly ask for students' opinions.

11. Use shortcuts. Use carets, arrows, deletion marks, or anything else that saves you time and effort.

12. Do not forget to read the final version aloud.

CHAPTER 6 IN A NUTSHELL

- Modeling is among the most powerful strategies we have for promoting strong writing among our students.
- Through modeling, students learn how to solve writers' problems and see thinking (writing and revising) in action.
- No part of the writing process is too small to model, from coming up with an idea to knowing where the periods or commas go.

- Base some of your modeling on personally important work so that your students can see you making decisions from topic selection through editing.
- Base some of your modeling on problems your students are having in their writing so that they can see how to work out those problems as they draft or revise or edit.

EXTENSIONS

1. What specific problems have you noticed in your own students' writing? Make a list of up to five. Now think of ways you could model a solution to each problem. Keep your examples short and focused.

2. Are you working on a personal piece of writing right now? If so, what decisions might you model using that piece? (If you are not working on something currently, consider starting something, or begin your modeling with topic selection—let your students help you get going.)

3. Have you done modeling in the past with your students? If so, list three advantages. Discuss these with colleagues, if possible.

4. List two ways you could improve your modeling. Discuss these also.

5. If you have never modeled writing with/for your students, think about why. What is blocking you? Is it time? Is it discomfort with writing? Is it lack of ideas on what to write about? See if you can pinpoint reasons—and ways you could overcome whatever is blocking you.

SOURCES CITED

Aronie, Nancy Slonim. 1998. *Writing from the Heart: Tapping the Power of Your Inner Voice.* New York: Hyperion.

Avery, Carol. 2002. *And with a Light Touch,* 2d ed. Portsmouth, NH: Heinemann.

Graves, Donald H. 1984. *Writers: Teachers and Children at Work.* Portsmouth, NH: Heinemann.

Ray, Katie Wood. 2002. *What You Know by Heart.* Portsmouth, NH: Heinemann.

Routman, Regie. 2000. *Conversations.* Portsmouth, NH: Heinemann.

Thomason, Tommy. 1993. *More than a Writing Teacher.* Commerce, TX: Bridge Press.

Thomason, Tommy, and Carol York. 2000. *Write on Target: Preparing Young Writers to Succeed on State Writing Achievement Tests.* Norwood, MA: Christopher-Gordon Publishers.

7 Loving Books

Exploring the world for ideas. Janet finds a pair of sunglasses that make her think of going to the beach—a favorite writing topic.

We also have to be readers to write well. To write using rich, compelling language, we need to hear and read rich, compelling literature. Only a love of reading will promote an understanding and awareness of imagery, tone, voice, and other nuances of good writing. There is no shortcut.

—Regie Routman
Conversations: Strategies for Teaching, Learning, and Evaluating (2000, p. 221)

When we first start trying to teach ourselves to read like teachers of writing, we often struggle because we've never really looked at texts this way. . . . We have to move forward and trust that once we train our eyes to look at how texts are written (in addition to what they're about), it will get easier and easier, and before long it will start to snowball. We'll know more about how to write well than we'll ever need.

—Katie Wood Ray
What You Know by Heart (2002, p. 109)

We need to be seen laughing over books, being unable to put books down, gasping over horror stories, and sighing over love stories—anything, in fact, that helps our students to realize that there is some reward, that there are many rewards, to be had from the act of reading.

—Mem Fox
Radical Reflections (1993, p. 63)

*I*f you love reading aloud to your students—and what teacher of writing does not—you already have in your hands one of the most powerful ways to teach writing, and to show the six traits of writing in action. Everything we have talked about—good details, enticing leads, voice, word choice, fluency—is right there, waiting, within the world of books. In this chapter I will review some of my favorites and suggest some ways to connect them to writing. You do *not* need to use these very books. The ones you already know and love will do nicely. I simply include this *very* short list to give you a sense of how I use literature to make connections to writing traits. To do this, you must look at writers *as writers*—modelers of good writing. Some books, you know, sing with voice. Some are rich with detail—or the fluency is so smooth that you just have to read them aloud. Some books present us with new words or words used in ways we would never have thought of. So much of reading aloud is done just for the sake of plot—not that that is an unworthy reason. It is fun finding out what happens next. Sometimes, though, I feel that we forget to notice writers *as writers*. We forget to appreciate their skill in touching our imaginations and hearts and shaping our thinking. So when you say to a child, "Listen to this passage—don't you love the sound of it?" you are not just sharing plot, but also the writer's craft. And this enriches your reading time together. (For additional ideas, see *Books, Lessons, Ideas for Teaching the Six Traits* in the "Sources Cited" list at the end of this chapter.)

A sidebar: As teachers, we can sometimes be too zealous about linking *everything* we read to a writing activity. Reading is a powerful stimulus for writing—and for many people, nothing works better. They read, and they get inspired. They see what works and what doesn't. They hear a voice that's appealing, and they want to write like that. Writing provides models. Reading is an end in and of itself, though. When you read, you *are* teaching writing—just by the act of reading. Your students learn by listening, whether they go on to write something as a follow-up or not. And if you read with passion, they are also learning to love books.

FAVORITES

All children need literature. Children who are authors need it even more.

—Donald H. Graves
Writing: Teachers and Children at Work (1984, p. 67)

The following sections list some of my favorite books for sharing and for modeling good writing. They are listed alphabetically by author under the trait where I feel the connection is strongest, but clearly, *any* book can be used to illustrate any trait. Just because a book is rich with detail is no sign that you cannot use it as a model of remarkable fluency. (*Note:* I have not included books for teaching conventions because virtually any print can be a model for conventions.)

We must immerse our students in outstanding literature every day, help them notice how the author has dealt with the topic, genre, organization, setting, mood, word choice, sentence construction, more.

—Regie Routman
Conversations: Strategies for Teaching, Learning, and Evaluating (2000, p. 221)

Books for Teaching Ideas

Baylor, Byrd. 1974. *Everybody Needs a Rock*. New York: Simon & Schuster.

Summary
In this lyrical, visually beautiful book, Byrd Baylor celebrates the joy of simple things—such as finding a rock that is special. What makes it special? Well, that is something each person must decide, but she gives us wonderful guidelines for finding just the right rock and knowing how special it is.

Writing Connections
✔ After reading the book, ask students to hunt for their own special rocks. Write descriptions that help students tune in to the details. Be sure they look, touch, smell—and reflect—before writing.

✔ Brainstorm details that make rocks special. Use the details to create poems celebrating the beauty of rocks.

✔ Make a rock display featuring poems, descriptions, or stories based on the rocks your students find.

✔ Ask students to imagine what it would be like if a rock could speak. What things has it seen in its "life" on earth? Where has it been? What would the rock write if it could tell its own history of sights, experiences, and travels?

 Collard, Sneed B., III. 2002. *Beaks!* Watertown, MA: Charlesbridge.

Summary

Sneed Collard is one of our finest nonfiction writers for young people. His books are filled with voice and precise word choice. In this inviting, highly readable text, he shows how birds eat, survive, and hunt using their beaks.

Writing Connections

✔ Point out the differences between the large-print main ideas and small-print details. Use this distinction to help your students develop their own definitions for the term *details.* As you read, invite your students to reflect and consider the illustrations. Then ask, "Would you like to hear the details?" If they say yes, share!

✔ Copy Collard's format in some writing you and your class do. Create a main idea (on any topic) in large print. Then, in smaller print, add details.

✔ Notice the striking illustrations by Robin Brickman. Not only are they beautifully done, but they are informative as well, adding meaning to the written text.

✔ Point out Collard's very focused approach. He does not try to tell "all about birds" but focuses instead on one detail—beaks! This kind of focus, you can tell students, makes big writing small and manageable.

✔ Bring everything together—main idea and detail plus art—creating some autobiographical sketches. Students might begin with a main idea about themselves, then add details in smaller print, and set it all off with a painting, sketch, paper collage, or any type of art.

 George, Twig C. 2000. *Jellies.* Brookfield, CT: Millbrook Press.

Summary

Text and illustrations (full-color underwater photos) balance beautifully in this fascinating look at the world of jellyfish. This book is everything good informational writing should be: informative, enticing, striking, memorable. On each page, readers learn something new, and the details the author has uncovered for us (jellies have no brains, they can only move up or down under their own power, some are as big as a blue whale) will leave young readers eager to share through writing or drawing of their own.

Writing Connections

✔ Invite students to do their own jellyfish illustrations, focusing on any of the fascinating facts Twig C. George shares.

✔ Make a brainstormed list of "Things We Learned" about jellyfish. Remind students that good writing often teaches readers.

✔ After reading/hearing this book, how do your students think it might feel to be a jellyfish? Write some short statements, stories, or poems from the jelly's point of view! These can be illustrated, too.

 Heide, Florence Parry. 2000. *Some Things Are Scary*. Cambridge, MA: Candlewick Press.

Summary

Pulitzer Prize–winning cartoonist Jules Feiffer lends his considerable talent and wacky view of life to Heide's honest and often funny exploration of the little things in life that frighten us all. This is not a book of horrors. Instead, it is a whirlwind review of the many small encounters with fear and trauma we all face daily—things like forgetting where you parked the car, watching as you get a bad haircut, holding onto the wrong person's hand, and so on. Author Florence Parry Heide says of herself, "What scared me as a child was that I'd never learn how to be a real live grown-up—and the fact is, I never did find out how it goes."

Writing Connections

✔ Make a list—with your students—of little things in life that you all find scary. Be sure to add your own fears to this list. Keep it light, though.
✔ Create a class book of "Things That Are Scary." Each person can add a page, using text, illustrations, or both.
✔ Talk about the pictures in this text. What kind of *voice* do they suggest? What kind of person draws pictures like these?

 Jenkins, Steve and Robin Page. 2003. *What Do You Do With a Tail Like This?* Boston: Houghton Mifflin Company.

Summary

Jenkins and Page pack an incredible amount of information into a small amount of text that is highly accessible to young readers. In this nonfiction book, readers have a chance to first guess whose nose, tail, feet, eyes (and so on) they might be peering at—and then, how that animal might make use of its unique features. For example, if you are a blue-footed booby, you use your feet to dance, but if you are a chimpanzee, you use your feet to feed yourself! Each well-researched section holds some surprises.

Writing Connections

✔ As you read the book, invite students to make their best guesses about whose foot, nose, or whatever they are looking at. Then, ask them to guess how it might be used. Why do they think so? The pictures offer good clues!
✔ Copy the book's ingenious format by asking students to sketch just one part of a favorite animal—a spider's leg, a frog's webbed foot, and so on—and to ask the reader a simple question: How would you use a tail (eye, nose, ear) like this? In Part 2 of this activity, they should sketch the whole animal (on a separate page) and answer the question, using the picture and words. This lesson builds attention to detail and expands knowledge.

✔ Notice the annotated index in the back of the book. It provides rich, expanded information on each topic the book covers. Invite students to tell *you* which animal body parts they wish to know more about (the elephant's trunk, perhaps), and share those aloud "by request." Talk about how this index provides "extra" information for readers who want it. Notice how we read it differently, though—not beginning to end, like a book, but looking up only what we want.

McPhail, David. 2002. *Edward in the Jungle*. Boston: Little, Brown and Company.

Summary

This book plays on the power of the imagination. What if your favorite book came to life just as you were reading? This is what happens to Edward as he is going through his favorite book about Tarzan, Lord of the Jungle. As Edward looks up from his reading, he finds that he is being stalked by a fairly large crocodile. Thus begins an adventure that takes him quite outside the realm of the book.

Writing Connections

✔ If one of their favorite books could come to life, which one would your students pick? Ask them to choose and make a list of their choices.

✔ Use the list as a springboard for writing/drawing. Ask students to do a sketch or short paragraph about one adventure involving a character from a book who springs out of the book and becomes part of their everyday life. Where might they go? What might they do?

✔ Write a come-to-life paper of your own and share it with students.

✔ Turn the tables. If your students could enter one book, which one would it be? Again, create pictures/writings to reflect their adventures.

Shannon, David. 2002. *David Gets in Trouble*. New York: Blue Sky Press.

Summary

This recent addition to the David series has the same whimsical style and laugh-out-loud humor of earlier texts. In this book, David is forever in trouble—but has a million excuses: "I didn't mean it, It was an accident, But she likes it. . . ." It's what we *all* do—and that's why we laugh.

Writing Connections

✔ We all do things we shouldn't—sometimes on purpose, sometimes by accident. What are some excuses we make? Brainstorm a list of excuses.

✔ Then invite students to use one of the excuses and write a short paragraph (with or without an illustration) showing how or when this excuse might be used.

✔ Compile a class book of the results.

✔ Interview others (older students, teachers) in your building about a time they have used an excuse for something said or done. Write the stories of what happened, using text and pictures. Create a schoolbook called "Our Excuses" or "We Didn't Mean It!" (Be sure that interviewees know their stories are going to press!)

Sís, Peter. 2002. *Madlenka's Dog.* New York: Farrar, Straus and Giroux.

Summary

In this imaginative, fanciful story, a young girl very much wants a dog—a wish with which many young students will identify. Creative formatting shows how to weave text and pictures together to create a story in which imagination plays a strong role. The pictures extend—and sometimes carry—the meaning. The book has two main ideas, really: First, Madlenka wants a dog more than anything she can dream of. Second, imagination sometimes makes wishes come true in a special way.

Writing Connections

✔ Ask students to identify the writer's main idea. What *is* the main idea of the story? How do they know?

✔ Peek behind the little pop-up pictures throughout the book. Ask students what they notice. In each picture, the "dog" that the person sees is a little different. Why?

✔ Extend this idea of differences by imitating the author's format. Ask students to create pictures of themselves (or anyone) with a pop-up portion that shows what the person is really thinking or picturing. Students will have fun with this format—a creative way to show what is going on in a character's mind.

✔ At the end of the story, Madlenka comes home with quite a troop of dogs. Are they real—or imagined? What do your students think? Ask them to write their responses and reasons.

✔ Ask several students to act out the story, playing the parts listed in the back of the book. You can narrate as they perform.

Zolotow, Charlotte. 2002. *Sleepy Book.* New York: HarperCollins.

Summary

This book is simply beautiful—in language, concept, format, and artwork. It is an easy-to-read informational text, ideal for showing young writers what good informational writing is. In text that reads almost like poetry, Zolotow skillfully explains the sleeping habits of a wide range of animals. It's a book to enjoy and to learn from.

Writing Connections

✔ Talk about the content of the book. Did your students learn anything new or surprising about animals' sleep habits?

✔ Try a piece of informational writing modeled on Zolotow's text, for example, what animals eat.

✔ Try a piece of informational writing that follows a different format, for example, a pamphlet on where you live, a how-to piece on any topic, a recipe, an advertisement, or a newspaper article on something that happened recently at your school or in your community. Share the writings.

Books for Teaching Organization

When you read informational books, not only are you helping children develop an ear for expository genre, but they are also learning facts about nature, science, history, social studies, cooking, art, music, books, sports, etc. Your reading aloud does double duty.

—Marcia S. Freeman
Teaching the Youngest Writers (1998, p. 95)

Brown, Margaret Wise. 1949 (Reprinted 1977). *The Important Book*. New York: Harper Trophy.

Summary

This little classic has stood the test of time; many teachers who use it (with delightful results and responses from their students) were not yet born when it was written. The book has a strong central theme: Each person, each thing on earth, has some important, special quality. We have only to look to see what it is. Because it pays homage to individuality, the book is also excellent for teaching this aspect of voice: the uniqueness of self. I have chosen it for organization because it is a pattern book with a readily recognizable format that is fun and easy to imitate. Almost as soon as you begin reading, your students will begin to anticipate what is coming.

Writing Connections

✔ As students begin to recognize the pattern in the book, ask them to fill in the blank as you go along: "The most important thing about _____ is that it's _____." (Most will find this both easy and fun.)

✔ As a class, create a "most important" chapter about anything in your lives—a sister, a mom, a pet. Write the section together.

✔ Next, ask students to do a "most important" piece about a friend. They will need to tell several things about the friend and then to choose the most important. Go over this format before they begin so that they can remember it and feel comfortable with the writing.

✔ Ask students to do a "most important" piece about themselves. In doing so, they should really think and reflect. A most important characteristic might be a special talent, something they value (or someone else values), or something not everyone knows about them—for example, "The most important thing about me is that I love turtles."

✔ Write your own "most important" piece about yourself—and share it with your students. They will love it.

Carle, Eric. 1997. *From Head to Toe*. New York: HarperCollins.

Summary

Writer and artist Eric Carle introduces us to a wide range of movements and dance steps in this lively and colorful pattern book. Big print and easy-to-read text make this a book even young readers can tackle on their own. Do not miss the dedication—it expresses Carle's love of art.

Writing Connections

✔ Brainstorm a list of other animals Carle might have written about, and talk about the special movements each one makes—for example, "I am a turtle, and I can pull inside my shell. Can you do it?"

✔ The pattern within the book is simple and easy to imitate. Let students try it with some writing and sketching of their own. Be sure to focus on animals Carle has not included.

✔ Act out the various portions of the book, with one child playing each animal part—or (a variation) everyone doing everything as you read the parts. This is a real on-your-feet kind of book.

✔ Talk about Eric Carle's special kind of art. It has a voice all its own. How does it make you feel? Write some responses (an early form of review).

✔ Provide some samples of cloth or colored paper from which students can cut pieces to make some art like that shown in the book. They can make animals—or anything at all. Write sentences, labels, or poems to go with the pictures.

✔ Use the art form shown in Carle's book to create illustrations for greeting cards. Send the cards to friends or parents.

Cuyler, Margery. 2002. *That's Good! That's Bad! In the Grand Canyon.* New York: Henry Holt and Company.

Summary

Hilarious, zany illustrations by David Catrow add voice and pizzazz to this pattern book about the adventures of a young visitor to the Grand Canyon who encounters more than his share of adventures with critters and wild rivers—but it all works out in the end, and that's good! Unfortunately, the book ends, and that's bad! Like its predecessor (Cuyler's original *That's Good! That's Bad!*), the story rings with strong verbs, sound-effects words kids love, and rollicking voice. It *must* be read aloud.

Writing Connections

✔ Identify some of the strong verbs from the book. Make a list, and add them to a word wall.

✔ Make a list of the sound-effect words from the story. Ask students to try one short piece of writing weaving in a sound-effect word. Why are these so much fun? (Hearing the story helps bring it to life.)

✔ Create "That's Good! That's Bad!" pattern writings based on any experience students have had. It is an easy pattern to imitate, a simple form of organization for stories or essays.

Fleming, Denise. 1997. *Time to Sleep.* New York: Henry Holt and Company.

Summary

In this delightful, simple story we peek in on several animals about to go to sleep for the winter. Bear begins the whole tale, sniffing winter in the air—and warning Snail, who in turn must speak to Skunk, and so it goes—finally coming full circle round to Bear again. Use the book to show this full-circle approach to organization. Event follows event until the end winds right back up where you began!

Writing Connections

✔ Brainstorm some other kinds of stories that could have full-circle connections (e.g., a trip that begins with packing and ends with unpacking the same suitcase; a message passed in a note or by e-mail or by phone that comes back to the original writer; a gift given to one person, then another, and then another until it returns to the original giver).

✔ Act the story out, with various children taking the parts of Snail, Bear, Woodchuck, Ladybug, Turtle, and so on. You can be the narrator.

French, Vivian. 2003 (paperback ed.). *Growing Frogs*. Cambridge, MA: Candlewick Press.

Summary

Children everywhere are fascinated with the transition of frog eggs to tadpoles to "almost frogs" to grown frogs! Vivian French thoughtfully lays out the process step by step, with easy to follow text and illustrations. Though presented as a story, the book is really informational in nature, and tells just what you need to know to hatch your own little frogs (and eventually release them).

Writing Connections

✔ Review the main stages of the frog's life with your students so they can picture each one: eggs, tiny tadpoles, tadpoles with small legs, and so on.

✔ Create sketches to go with each stage, and put them in order. Emphasize that pictures can have a logical order just as text does.

✔ If you're lucky enough to live where you can obtain frog eggs, you might try a hatching project right in your classroom. You need a fairly large aquarium and access to fresh pond water—not tap water! Follow the steps in the book, allowing students to be researchers who guide the setting up of this project.

✔ As the eggs hatch and the tadpoles mature, invite students to keep journals on your frogs' progress, documenting each step. Organization by time and growth are built right into this simple activity. Later, some students may wish to create stories, essays, poems, or how-to pieces (how to set up a frog aquarium) to extend their journal writing.

 Lane, Barry. 2002. *The Tortoise and the Hare Continued. . . .* Shoreham, VT: Discover Writing Press.

Summary

We have all heard Aesop's well-known fable of the "Tortoise and the Hare." But do you know what happened the next day? Or a week later? Or 30 years later? Let Barry Lane spin the tale for you with his own inimitable brand of humor. His "Continued . . ." version is a delightfully readable set of tales—for each story suggests yet another to come. And yes, each does have its own moral, too. Use this book to help students see that embedded in any good ending is the suggestion of another essay, another poem, another story down the road.

Writing Connections

✔ As you finish each of the six back-to-back fables, ask students to predict what might come next. This encourages them to use endings to launch new ideas.

✔ Guess what the moral might be, too. Morals are really one way of summing up the main idea.

✔ Pay attention to leads as you read. This book, with its unusual format, is full of leads. As you read each one, ask students, "What do you like about this lead?"

✔ Try Barry's format with another fable. You may wish to read several fables so that students can choose. Then ask them to write a "What happened the next day" paper extending the story. Each should have a moral, too.

✔ Create sketches to illustrate the "next day" papers.

St. George, Judith. 2002. *So You Want to Be an Inventor?* New York: Philomel Books.

Summary

History textbooks were never like this. Judith St. George creates a wonderfully captivating overview of amazing and hopelessly flawed inventions (such as goggles to protect chickens' eyes). But her organizational style is unexpected. Instead of going through them alphabetically or by date, she focuses on interesting questions a reader might like to know: What were the most helpful inventions? The most ridiculous? The most dangerous?

Writing Connections

✔ Which modern-day inventions are most appealing to your students? Brainstorm a list.

✔ Can anyone imagine a handy invention no one has come up with yet? It can be serious or silly—it doesn't matter (as the book shows, not all inventions have been sensible). Write about them or create pictures.

✔ Do some research. Ask students to choose *one* invention from any time in history. Stuck for ideas? Just look around! Everything from shoelaces to chalkboards is someone's invention! From the library or the Web, see if you can dig up a picture of the invention plus one interesting bit of information. Each child becomes a human "note card" with a picture, fact, or both. You can put these research tidbits together in a class book or share them orally.

✔ Write letters to a company (or companies) of your choice about a modern-day invention. Letters may commend the invention, ask questions, or comment on a problem. Save the letters and any responses you get.

Steig, William. 1982. *Dr. DeSoto.* New York: Farrar, Straus and Giroux.

Summary

Steig's much-loved story captivates readers of all ages and is wonderful for word choice and voice as well as organization. This book has a striking lead and conclusion—you may wish to capitalize on this as you share it. Notice too how Steig manages to tell a complex story in very few words.

Writing Connections

✔ After sharing the whole story, ask students to listen for *just* the lead—and *just* the conclusion. How would they rate each one? Excellent—so-so—or needs work?

✔ Try modeling some other possible leads for this same story, and ask students to make comparisons—for example, "This will be a book about a mouse, who is a dentist, and a fox, who is his patient."

✔ Imagine that following this story, Dr. DeSoto takes on another patient, a cat perhaps, or a snake. Write a picture or tell a story showing what might happen.

✔ After going home with his tooth pulled, the fox decides to eat the DeSotos. What if he wrote about this in his journal? What might he write?

✔ Ask your students, "How important are the pictures in this book? Do they tell or show things we do not learn from the words alone? Which picture is your favorite? Why?"

✔ Many parts of this book lend themselves to drama: the first encounter with the fox, the pulling of the tooth, the DeSotos lying awake wondering how to outfox the fox, and the fox having his teeth glued together. Choose one or more for your students to act out.

Wallace, Karen. 1993. *Think of an Eel*. Cambridge, MA: Candlewick Press.

Summary

Lavishly illustrated (by Mike Bostock), this nonfiction book is packed with information about eels, but reads like a story. The organization is so smooth the reader hardly notices it unfolding. Wallace uses the life cycle of the eel as her organizational pattern, and it works beautifully; the result is a seamless education in how eels are born and where they grow to maturity, live, return to lay their eggs, then die. Use the book to show the importance of having a pattern in writing—like a map to follow.

Writing Connections

✔ Once you have read the book, see how many events in the eel's life your students can recall. List them, and then see if you (and your students) can put them in order.

✔ Although this book is strong in organization, it is a good model of fluency, too. As you read, use your voice inflection to bring out the rhythm. Ask your students if they hear the rhythm as you read.

✔ The lead is very simple: "Think of an eel." Do your students like it? Why?

✔ Do some research on another creature—let students decide which one(s) you'll work on. Assemble facts. Then see if you can follow Karen Wallace's design for organization by writing a short report that touches on four to six steps in the creature's life cycle. You can write individually or make a class book.

✔ Invite students to do a visual map of their own life cycles, focusing on important events: being born, learning to walk, making a friend, getting a pet, starting school, moving, riding a bike, and so on. Pictures can mark key points.

Books for Teaching Voice

Walsh, Melanie. 2002. *My Beak, Your Beak*. Boston: Houghton Mifflin Company.

Summary

Here's an example of comparison that even the youngest writers/readers will find accessible and easy to imitate. The text is very simple, but teaches an important lesson: A writer can share more information through a comparison than through a simple statement. For example, we learn that "lions are big and have hairy manes," while "kittens are small and fluffy." What do they have in common? "They both have scratchy claws."

Writing Connections

✔ Talk about some easy comparisons from your classroom or your students' everyday experience: a bus and a car, for example. A bus is big and holds lots of kids, a car is smaller and only holds a few—but they both have wheels. Try to follow the format of the book in setting up your comparisons.

✔ Invite students to try *writing* one or two comparisons, based on any topic— foods, buildings, insects, pets, and so on. Again, follow the format of the book to give students practice with the comparison structure. Read results aloud. Create illustrations to go with your comparisons.

Carman, William. 2002. *What's That Noise?* New York: Random House.

Summary

Here's a book that will give you the chills (and some laughs) without being too scary. It is a book of contrasts. When we hear sounds at night, we imagine one thing—but in reality, it is usually something quite different! Used with care, this book can help students to see that most "scary" sounds come from something harmless.

Writing Connections

✔ Brainstorm some "scary" sounds you might hear at night that turn out to be something else. What could a scratching sound be? (The cat.) What could a thud be? (Someone knocking a book on the floor on the way to the fridge.) Draw pictures and/or write stories to go with the "What I thought" and "What it turned out to be" parts of the story.

✔ Talk about the pictures in the book. How do they contribute to the scary feeling? What things do artists do to make a picture scary? Once you know some of the tricks (playing with sizes, for example), the pictures aren't quite so scary anymore!

✔ This book really lends itself to drama because of the sound effects. Perform some parts, sounds and all. Students can use their imaginations and have fun—but also come to realize that most sounds we hear are nothing to fear once we know the truth.

Curtis, Jamie Lee. 2002. *I'm Gonna Like Me*. New York: HarperCollins.

Summary

Sometimes it can be hard to like yourself. Those are the very moments when self-esteem is so important to carry you through. This gentle but powerful little book is all about learning to like yourself so that you can share the wealth and like others too.

Writing Connections

✔ Are there ever moments when it is hard to like yourself? Brainstorm a few. Then write or draw pictures to show what these times are like. (The point: Everyone has moments like these!)

✔ What do your students like about themselves *especially*? Brainstorm some of your best qualities—it's OK to love little things: not losing your cool when your shoelace breaks, being kind to animals, having a sense of humor, making your mom (or someone) laugh, being willing to spend time with a small brother or sister. If you share a few small things you like about yourself, it will be easier for your students to think of some, too. Write or draw about your thoughts.

Falconer, Ian. 2000. *Olivia Saves the Circus*. New York: Atheneum Books.

Summary

If you loved Falconer's earlier book, *Olivia*, you'll love this one, too. Olivia is an independent spirit, and her voice shines through in everything she says and does. In this adventure, she arrives at the circus only to discover that everyone is suffering from ear infections—and cannot perform! Olivia to the rescue! She is more than willing to play all the parts, from lion tamer to acrobat, and even more willing to share her story with her classmates later. Use the book to show that individuality is an important ingredient in voice.

Writing Connections
✔ Have you ever "saved the day" in a large or small way? Write a story about it, and share it with your students.
✔ Invite students to share stories (or pictures or both) of how they saved the day. (It can be very small—for example, doing an errand, saving the cookies from burning while mom is on the phone.)
✔ Put Olivia in another adventure. What if she got lost shopping? Got left at the zoo by mistake? Went home with the wrong family? Or let your students invent a "what if" situation of their own. Draw sketches or write a story to get Olivia out of her predicament.

 Fox, Mem. 1988. *Koala Lou.* San Diego: Harcourt Brace.

Summary
Deep feelings of love, fear, anxiety, and insecurity underlie this deceptively simple tale of a beautiful koala baby who worries that she will lose her mother's love if she does not perform at her best in the Bush Olympics. The message is powerful but never overstated.

Writing Connections
✔ *Koala Lou*, according to author Mem Fox, was inspired by two experiences in her own life: losing an award and wondering (as one of three children) whether her parents loved her as much as she hoped they did. You may wish to share Mem's anxieties with your students, who sometimes wonder where writers get their ideas. Here are two quotations from *Dear Mem Fox* (1992) to share with your students:

> Koala Lou . . . , *which is a story about a koala who comes in second in the Bush Olympics, developed subconsciously out of my disappointment at* Possum Magic *not winning Picture Book of the Year award, an event that hadn't been a disaster in world terms although I had bawled like a baby at the time. Coming in second with "highly commended" hadn't been enough. I wanted to hide for a while, to live through my failure alone (p. 149).*

> *Is my father pleased with the way I've turned out? Is my mother proud of me? Do they think I'm absolutely and utterly terrific, or not? In my heart of hearts I believe that they do, but I had to write* Koala Lou *just to be sure (p. 151).*

✔ Ask students to brainstorm, as a class, some of the things people can feel disappointed about. Would any of these make good writing topics?
✔ Ask students if they think that Mem's own feelings of rejection (not winning the award) or uncertainty (not being sure if her parents really loved her) helped make her voice stronger. (Yes!)
✔ How would your students describe the voice in *Koala Lou*? What are some words that go with this voice? (It's a powerful story, but not humorous. It's loving, tender, dramatic, tense—and from the heart.)
✔ Look at the pictures in *Koala Lou*. What kind of "voice" do they show?

Haseley, Dennis. 2002. *A Story for Bear*. San Diego: Harcourt.

Summary

For a curl-up-and-listen kind of book, it is hard to beat this heart-warming tale of a bear who is enchanted with books and loves being read to. As he listens to the woman who gently shares stories with him, he falls in love with the very sound of her voice, with the whole peaceful feeling that engulfs him. Although not a word is intelligible to him, he nevertheless derives meaning from the very way she speaks the words.

Writing Connections

✔ Ask students about their personal responses to the experience of having someone read to them. Write in journals about this.

✔ Talk about specific things the woman says or does that enchant the bear. Why does he love his time with her so much? Make a list.

✔ How does the bear feel at different points in the story? What are the clues in the text or in the pictures that let you know?

✔ If the bear could speak to the woman in words, what would he say? Write it down.

Huneck, Stephen. 2001. *Sally Goes to the Mountains*. New York: Harry N. Abrams.

Summary

This simple but charming tale of Sally the dog, who visits the mountains with her family, is told completely from the dog's point of view, in both pictures and text. It has easy print that even beginning readers can tackle with success. Use this book to show how perspective affects voice.

Writing Connections

✔ In this story, a dog goes on a mountain adventure. Ask students to imagine themselves in the role of a pet or any animal having a similar adventure—to the mountains, beach, forest, river, lake, or even a local store. Write or draw a picture showing the adventure from the animal's point of view.

✔ Usually we hear stories from a *person's* point of view. This one is different. How do your students like that? Share comments.

✔ Stephen Huneck has an interesting artistic style in this book. Can you find some words to describe it?

Polacco, Patricia. 1994. *My Rotten Redheaded Older Brother*. New York: Simon & Schuster.

Summary

Treesha is troubled with an obnoxious older brother, Richie, who does everything better than she can—runs faster, throws harder, swims farther. Treesha miserably wonders when her turn to shine will come, and the wisdom of her grandmother helps her through. Use the book to illustrate striking, true-to-life voice but also to show that when we have bad feelings, such as anger or jealousy, one good thing to do with them is to write them out.

Writing Connections

✔ Ask students to define how Treesha feels. How do they know?

✔ Ask how many of your students have ever had feelings like Treesha's. Explain that this association is called *identifying* with a character. When voice is strong, it is often because we identify with the character.

✔ Ask students if Treesha and her brother seem like real people. (They do!) Realism enhances voice.

✔ Create a dialogue between Treesha and Richie that does not appear in the book. Act it out.

✔ We know Treesha feels wounded; she always seems to come out second best! How does *Richie* feel, though? (Expect students to have different opinions about this.)

 Schulman, Janet, compiler. 2001. *You Read to Me and I'll Read to You: 20th Century Stories to Share*. New York: Alfred A. Knopf.

Summary

One of the best ways to teach voice is to enable students to hear a wide range of voices. In this collection assembled by Janet Schulman you will find some of the best stories around, each a little different in flavor and tone. Here are just a *few* of the outstanding examples (twenty-six in all) from this collection: "Amos and Boris," by William Steig; "The Magic Finger," by Roald Dahl; "The Tenth Good Thing About Barney," by Judith Viorst; "Cloudy with a Chance of Meatballs," by Judi Barrett; and "Catwings," by Ursula K. LeGuin.

Writing Connections

✔ Read a variety of samples from the book, each time asking students, "Do you hear voice in this piece? What kind of voice?"

✔ Try imitating one or more of your favorite writers from the book in your own short writing samples. Imitation is also a good way to learn voice.

✔ While not all the authors in this book are still living, most are. Invite students to draft a note to any of the authors talking about something in the writing that impressed them.

✔ Some of the writings—for example, "The Magic Finger," by Roald Dahl—also lend themselves to drama. Ask students (with coaching) to act out one scene from a given story.

✔ Have an "awards day." Invite students to present awards to various stories/authors from the book—for example, Best Illustration, Funniest Story, Story with the Best Character, Story with the Most Voice. It is OK to have more than one winner—it isn't really the Oscars, after all! Have students design the awards: certificates, buttons, etc.

 Seskin, Steve, and Allen Shamblin. 2002. *Don't Laugh At Me*. Berkeley: Tricycle Press.

Summary

This is a book that stands right up to bullying, and that's a good thing—because it hurts! Illustrations and text will tug at your heart and make you think about an issue that hits close to home for many young students.

Writing Connections

✔ Talk about bullying. What is it? Have your students experienced it? Have they ever done it themselves? Why?

✔ Write some stories about bullying—students can write about a time they bullied someone or a time they were bullied. How did it feel? How did they get over it? Use pictures to extend the voice and detail.

✔ This book includes a song about bullying. Try singing it together.

✔ Write a note to one of the characters in the book expressing reactions or opinions. Notes and letters are a great way to build voice.

 Teague, Mark. 2002. *Dear Mrs. LaRue: Letters from Obedience School.* New York: Scholastic.

Summary

Poor Ike. Just because he ate the chicken pie, disturbed the peace, and chased the neighbor's cats (who were a pain anyway), he has been hustled off to obedience school to learn manners. The main thing Ike seems to be learning is loneliness, which he conveys in his plaintive letters to his owner and friend, Mrs. LaRue. This wonderful read-aloud offers humor, warmth and irony—as well as incredible models for letter writing.

Writing Connections

✔ Compare the black and white pictures to the colored versions. Which ones tell the *true* tale of Ike's adventures?

✔ Throughout this book, Mrs. LaRue does not write back. But what if she did? What might she say? Invite students to adopt Mrs. LaRue's voice and write a note to Ike in response to one or more of his. Read these aloud. Does Mrs. LaRue tell the truth about *her* life—or does she exaggerate, too?

✔ Ike exaggerates just a little. See if your students can identify some examples. Does exaggerating sometimes build voice? Yes! Talk about exaggeration as a way of stretching the truth in writing. Writers do this for effect: "It rained buckets!" Ask students to write an exaggerated piece about a good or bad experience.

 Viorst, Judith. 1997. *Absolutely, Positively Alexander: The Complete Stories.* New York: Atheneum Books for Young Readers.

Summary

Everything goes wrong for Alexander—or so it seems! And don't we all feel like that sometimes? In this complete collection we learn that it is OK to complain now and then, really, just as long as you do not do it all the time.

Writing Connections

✔ Brainstorm a "frustration list"—little things that have gone wrong today or this week or this month. You can start—stepped in a puddle, dropped something that broke, spilled toothpaste on my favorite shirt, and so on.

✔ Now write about one or more of these events. You can write paragraphs or poems about one event or a whole series.

✔ What would happen on a really perfect day—if everything went right (like hitting all the green lights)? Turn things around, and write about the three, four, or more things that would happen on the "Absolutely, Positively Perfect Day." Read results aloud.

Waber, Bernard. 2002. *Courage*. Boston: Houghton Mifflin.

Summary

Waber takes the stuff of everyday life—making up with a friend after an argument, jumping from a diving board, getting your haircut, breaking a bad habit—to show that any person can be a hero. You may not get medals, but you and your students are likely to finish this book feeling pretty good about yourselves and gaining some insight into the everyday heroism of others.

Writing Connections

✔ Ask students to think about the heroes in their lives—humans and animals too. Who has done something brave? Discuss this.

✔ Draw pictures or write about everyday heroes who have done small, brave things that do not make the news, but are still important.

✔ Create a class book or poem celebrating "Heroes." It is OK to write about yourself if you have done something brave.

Wiesner, David. 2001. *The Three Pigs*. New York: Houghton Mifflin (Clarion Books).

Summary

What if characters could move right out of a story—and into another one? That's just what happens in this imaginative retelling of an old favorite. Just as the wolf is about to consume poor little piggy number 1, whoosh, his huffing and puffing blows the pigs clear out of the book and off to adventure. They wind up making a paper airplane out of the book pages and sailing off to seek their fortune (wasn't that the idea?). Along the way, they encounter a dragon, who finds his way back into the original story. Who says you have to tell a tale the same way every time? This intermingling adds a *lot* to voice!

Writing Connections

✔ Start with what happens. In this book the pictures tell much of the story. Readers must pay close attention to put the pieces together. Make sure that your students know what is going on.

✔ Ask your students to retell the story once you have read it and looked at the pictures. They can do this orally. It helps develop their sense of sequencing.

✔ What might the pigs, the dragon, or the wolf have to say about this adventure? Create a one-day-later picture and/or journal entry from any one of the characters.

Books for Teaching Word Choice

In picture books, particularly, the choice of words is as crucial as the choice of notes in a fugue. I constantly read aloud what I've written in order to feel and hear the rightness of phrases or sentences. I know from experience that a rhythm that seems fine on the silent page often turns out to be clumsy or unwieldy when it's spoken.

—Mem Fox

Dear Mem Fox (1992, p. 165)

Child, Lauren. 2000. *I Will Never Not Ever Eat a Tomato*. Cambridge, MA: Candlewick Press.

Summary

Lola has more than her share of things she simply will not eat—carrots, peas, potatoes, mushrooms, cheese, and of course, tomatoes. What if some of these foods were known by more exotic names, though? Could simple revision in word choice transform a "never not ever" food into something delectable and appealing?

Writing Connections

✔ Brainstorm a list of your students' own "never not ever" foods. Add one or two of your own to the list—be honest!

✔ Now, following the format of the book, ask each student to choose one item from the list and give it some more appeal (as Charlie does) by describing it in different words. Remind students of the book's delightful examples to get their imaginations going.

✔ If students enjoy this activity, take it a step further and create a class menu. It does not have to include just the less appealing foods. Any menu item can be enhanced in the reader's mind with the right description. Menus are all about word choice, after all!

Cronin, Doreen. 2000. *Click, Clack, Moo/Cows That Type*. New York: Simon & Schuster.

Summary

You and your students will laugh at this delightful story of a stubborn farmer and the persistent cows and hens who threaten to go on strike if they are not given electric blankets. At length, they resort to writing to get their way, using an old typewriter. This simple book contains some surprisingly sophisticated language you can easily overlook if you aren't on the lookout for it: for example, *typewriter, sincerely, go on strike, background, impatient, demand, furious, ultimatum, snoop,* and *neutral*. What if your students knew all these words well enough to use them in their own writing? They could, you know!

Writing Connections

✔ Pass out words ahead of time, and ask students to guess at meanings.

✔ Share the story and invite students to listen for the words that you have passed out. Do they recognize them? Can they tell the meanings from the way words are used in the story?

✔ Add favorite words to your word wall or to personal dictionaries.

✔ See if you can find a typewriter and bring it into your classroom—especially for students who have not seen one. Talk about differences between a typewriter and a computer in word processing.

✔ Talk about what it means to "go on strike." Can your students think of anyone they know or anyone from the news who has gone on strike? What are some reasons for students, teachers, or parents to go on strike? Make a list.

✔ Ask students to think about the story and Farmer Brown's side of things. Is it fair for the cows and chickens to go on strike if they need blankets? What about Farmer Brown needing eggs and milk? Ask them to take a side and write a short reflection on how they feel. It can be as short as a sentence or as long as several paragraphs. This is good practice in persuasive writing.

dePaola, Tomie. 2002. *Adelita: A Mexican Cinderella Story*. New York: G. P. Putnam's Sons.

Summary

Pictures and text blend beautifully in this twist on the well-loved fairy tale. Look for strong verbs, simple language used with grace and style, and a delightful, effortless blend of Spanish and English that makes this a true bilingual text.

Writing Connections

✔ After reading the book, see how many Spanish words your non-Spanish speakers can remember. If you have native Spanish speakers in your class, let them do a little coaching here if non-Spanish speakers get stuck.

✔ Talk about the glossary at the close of the book. What *is* a glossary? How does it help a reader?

✔ Write a piece that includes a glossary—one word will do (or two or three for those students who feel ready). You do not have to get too elaborate. The word could be a second-language word or a math or science term. Be creative.

✔ Next time you read something in which some of the vocabulary is difficult, create a class glossary. First, ask students to identify which words should go into the glossary. Then ask them to help you alphabetize. Work together to create definitions that would be helpful to a reader.

Facklam, Margery. 2001. *Spiders and Their Websites*. Boston: Little, Brown and Company.

Summary

This is the fourth in Margery Facklam's impressive and acclaimed natural history picture book series. It is a model of what good informational writing should be: clear, educational, and filled with voice. This text is well beyond the independent reading skills of most primary students, but as a read-aloud book, it's a winner: Facklam's words are simple but precise. She creates images and takes us right into the world of the spider: "All the 4,000 different jumping spiders stalk their prey like cats. When they leap, they push off with strong hind legs, like a swimmer taking off from a starting block."

Writing Connections

✔ Draw any of the spiders Facklam describes in her book. This is great practice in noticing detail.

✔ Invite students to label spider drawings. Ask them to watch for labeled drawings in other informational writing. (Not all writing is done in sentences.)

✔ After reading/hearing one chapter—say, on the black widow spider—ask students to recall information first and then to try writing it in another form: a story, news article, or poem on the same topic.

✔ Each time you finish a chapter, see if students can list (independently) four things they have learned. Emphasize that good informational writing teaches the reader something new.

✔ Keep a pet spider in your classroom for a time. Watch its habits. Compare your pet spider to the description in Facklam's book. Ask students to write a comparison paper drawing one or more comparisons between the book and the real thing. Explain that comparing is one important way to document information.

✔ Create a glossary of spider terms. Ask for students' help as you finish a chapter in identifying important terms to remember. Create a spider word wall. Use the terms later in writing about spiders.

Frasier, Debra. 2000. *Miss Alaineus*. San Diego: Harcourt.

Summary

In this highly original book the hero, Sage, catches a cold and has to miss Vocabulary Day. When her friend gives her the list over the phone, she mistakes *miscellaneous* for *Miss Alaineus*—with very funny (but also mortifying, for Sage) results.

Writing Connections

✔ So many new words are introduced in this book that you may wish to read it more than once so that your students can "take in" a few more each time. As you go through, identify favorites, and add them to a word wall or to personal dictionaries.

✔ Create an alphabet book of the kind modeled in *Miss Alaineus*. Ask each student to write one sentence about himself or herself using three words that all begin with the same letter.

✔ To bring in some drama, ask students to dress up as favorite words—the book provides some pictures to inspire them.

Lionni, Leo. 1967. *Frederick*. New York: Alfred A. Knopf.

Summary

This one's a classic. Your students will delight in the story of Frederick, the little poet mouse, who—while his friends are gathering grain and other staples for winter—gathers ideas, memories, and *words*. As winter howls outside their den, the food diminishes, and the chill sets in, Frederick warms his friends with stories, recollections, images—and words they love. *Frederick* is a delightful book for showing the power of language to sustain us in less cheery times.

Writing Connections

✔ Frederick gathers favorite colors and images to take with him into their winter den—things he does not want to forget. What if your students hibernated for the winter. What would they take to cheer themselves up and share? Draw or write your answers.

✔ The "Fun Facts" in the beginning of the book tell us that *mouse* comes from a Sanskrit word meaning "thief." Why would this be? Invite students to write or talk about this.

✔ We also learn from the "Fun Facts" that a mouse's teeth grow all its life. That could be a problem, couldn't it? Ask your students to write about how they might solve this problem if they were mice.

✔ We learn from the story that deep inside their winter hideout, the mice told one another stories of "foolish foxes" and "happy cats." Invite students to write one of the stories the mice might have told. Share these aloud.

Laden, Nina. 2000. *Roberto the Insect Architect*. San Francisco: Chronicle Books.

Summary

Though he's a termite, Roberto does not want to destroy buildings; he wants to build! The entire book is a wonderful celebration of creativity, with Roberto (aka author Nina Laden) designing some fantastic buildings out of "things around the house." The pictures are as witty as the text, with Roberto inventing one extraordinary design after another and finally realizing his dream.

Writing Connections

✔ Ask your students to listen for and comment on favorite words and phrases.

✔ Talk about Roberto. What sort of termite is he, anyway? What words could you use to describe him?

✔ Look carefully at the buildings Roberto designs. Which ones do your students find most creative? What are they made of? Collect scraps of this and that, and have a Roberto Celebration Day, during which your students unleash their own creativity and come up with their own architectural designs.

✔ How does Roberto feel when at first it seems he will not find success? Ask students to do some role playing, writing home as Roberto and expressing their feelings.

✔ Suppose that there were an architectural award known as the Roberto? Who in your community would win? Ask students to write their nominations.

Marcellino, Fred. 1999. *I, Crocodile*. New York: HarperCollins.

Summary

This tongue-in-cheek tale uses colorful language to tell the tale of a happy crocodile who is captured by Napoleon and hauled off to France—where he becomes quite the tourist attraction for a time. Then, when his popularity diminishes, it is time to make crocodile pie with onions! Of course, our friend the croc has other ideas.

Writing Connections

✔ Savor the language—for example, "I had the perfect diet. An endless variety of delectable fish, all sorts of succulent water birds, plus a few reptiles on the side—distant cousins only." Add favorite words to word walls or personal dictionaries.

✔ Our crocodile friend has no name, except "Crocodile." Should he? Brainstorm some possibilities with your students.

✔ The illustrations in this book are particularly expressive. Talk about the "voice" or mood that some of the illustrations project. How is the crocodile feeling? Explore different words to describe the moods shown in the pictures.

✔ Napoleon never does get to make that crocodile pie! What do you suppose his recipe was? Create some recipes of your own with colorful word choice (they do not have to include "crocodile" as an ingredient, but they can).

✔ The ending of the book is told mostly in pictures rather than text. What happens? How do your students like this ending? Does it add to the voice?

Mora, Pat. 1997. *Tomás and the Library Lady*. New York: Alfred A. Knopf.

Summary

This account of a young Mexican-American boy who loved books and the librarian who encouraged him is based on a true story. The young boy, Tomás Rivera, grew up to be a writer, professor, and university administrator. The campus library at the University of California, Riverside, now bears his name. In her story of his early encounters with books, author Pat Mora gently weaves in a few Spanish words and phrases, which non-Spanish speakers will pick up with ease. Students also enjoy the author's depiction of Tomás teaching the librarian Spanish words—his first experience as a teacher.

Writing Connections

✔ Review the Spanish words from the story. See how many your students can recall.

✔ If you have Spanish speakers among your students, invite them to be the teachers—to translate a few more words from the story into Spanish and teach them to the class.

✔ If none of your students are Spanish speakers, see if you can find a Spanish-speaking visitor who will translate a portion of the book and teach it to your class.

✔ Use Spanish and English words to create a bilingual piece of writing: a poem, a story, a personal reflection, a memoir.

✔ Create a short glossary of Spanish words for another book your children love. Let them choose the words. Then seek consultation from a Spanish speaker or use a Spanish-English dictionary to create your glossary.

Pinkney, Sandra. 2002. *Shades of Black: A Celebration of Our Children*. New York: Scholastic.

Remember that you do not need to read an entire book to make a point about detail or voice or whatever. Bits and pieces can be magical—and sufficient.

—Vicki Spandel
Books, Lessons, Ideas for Teaching the Six Traits (2001, p. viii).

Writing enhances all the concepts a child needs to become a skilled reader. . . . The child who writes first will actually read earlier because writing furnishes practice using word forms and sentence patterns.

—Bea Johnson
Never Too Early to Write (1999, p. 10)

Summary

Rich in text and presentational style, this collage of photographs and poetic text is a visual feast that celebrates the uniqueness of each child. The children pictured are not just "black," but "the creamy white frost in vanilla ice cream" or "the velvety orange in a peach." If ever there was a book to teach precision in word choice (and in thinking), this is it.

Writing Connections

✔ Use this book for description. Leaves are green, the sky is blue—but what *shade* of green, what *shade* of blue? Explore shades of meaning by expanding ideas about and definitions of color.

✔ What makes each person unique? This book explores unique colors—but of course, this is only part of the story. Use drawings or photographs to capture the uniqueness of each child. Then using poetry or prose, write about the unique qualities that make each person special. Students can write about themselves or about each other—or both.

Books for Teaching Sentence Fluency

Aylesworth, Jim. 2001. *The Burger and the Hot Dog.* New York: Atheneum.

Summary

Stephen Gammell's wonderfully wacky pictures provide the perfect complement to this collection of delightful poems for young students. All the characters portrayed are food—Hamburger and Hotdog, the country band Veggie Soup, Yack and Yimmy (two eggs), the Bacon Buddies, the Forlorn Gum left beneath the stool—and so on. It is a perfect read-aloud book, and it's perfect for dramatizing poetry as well.

Writing Connections

✔ Talk about illustrator Stephen Gammell's humorous style. How would your students describe it?

✔ Have some fun imitating Gammell by drawing some food characters of your own.

✔ Make up poems to go with the characters. They do not have to rhyme!

✔ Act out some of Aylesworth's poems. You can be the narrator—or, if you prefer, join in the fun and be one of the characters while one of your students narrates. Encourage expressiveness!

Cannon, Janell. 2000. *Crickwing.* San Diego: Harcourt.

Summary

Like Cannon's other beloved books (*Verdi, Stellaluna*), *Crickwing* is a model of outstanding word choice: "The next morning the ants found Crickwing fussing with his latest ant trap. He had no chance for escape as thousands of leafcutters swarmed over him, dragged him back to the anthill, and marched him down its dark, winding corridors." It is the tale of a cockroach with a damaged wing (hence the nickname) who is plagued by a barrage of predators and ultimately captured by an army of ants, whom he eventually saves from a fearsome anteater. You can use this book to teach any trait. The ideas are imaginative, the organization is easy to follow, and the voice is lively and irresistible. It is also a fine example of fluency, with carefully crafted, flowing sentences. Be *sure* you read it with flair and feeling!

Writing Connections

✔ Cannon begins sentences in many different ways. After reading the book once just for fun, let a few days go by and read it again, this time focusing on sentence beginnings. How many different ones do you hear? List some.

✔ Many portions of the book contain speech. Read one or more aloud—for example, "Can we trust this yahoo?" yelped Gravel. "Do we have much choice?" snapped Terra.

✔ Ask your students, "Does this dialogue sound real? Is it the way real characters would speak?" (Yes! This is why it increases the voice and the fluency.)

✔ What things do your students learn about cockroaches from this book? Make a list. Do not forget to check out the nonfiction summaries "Cockroach Notes" and "Ant Notes" at the end of the book. Help students make the connection between this research information and the book Cannon wrote.

✔ Bring an actual cockroach into class for your students to study. How does the real thing resemble Cannon's drawings? How is it different?

✔ Make some cockroach sketches of your own. Encourage students to incorporate as many details as they can.

✔ Many people do not like cockroaches at all. How do your students feel after reading Janell Cannon's book? Share feelings in writing—for example, a personal response to the book, a poem about cockroaches, a note to Crickwing.

✔ Brainstorm a list of creatures most people are not fond of: ants, snakes, slugs, flies, and so on. Then, ask students to choose one creature and to write a note—"Dear World"—from that creature's point of view. Role playing builds fluency and voice.

 Florian, Douglas. 2001. *In the Swim*. San Diego: Harcourt.

Summary

Like Douglas' previous books (*Mammalabilia*, *Insectlopedia*), this book is a masterpiece of word choice presented in fluent, playful poetry. It features highly original use of fresh language—and certainly should be used in teaching that trait as well. I have put it in the fluency section simply because the poems are so rhythmic and delightful to read aloud that it would be a true shame not to use it in this way. It is ideal for choral reading.

Writing Connections

✔ Read the poems aloud first—then teach one or two to your students. Invite them to read or recite with the same inflection. Really bring out the fluency.

✔ Perform some of the poems as choral readings—complete with gestures, dance, movement, or drama of all kinds. Let loose! Let your imaginations soar!

✔ Encourage students to write poems of their own. Choose a common theme for the class if you like: insects, trees, flowers, the outdoors, school, people, or whatever. Or let students choose any topic at all. Create sketches or paintings to accompany what you create. If you have an art teacher to guide your work (or if you teach art yourself), you may wish to imitate Florian's watercolor technique.

✔ Notice Florian's fanciful presentation of text—with the poem on salmon and swordfish, for example. If students like this, they may wish to try using the shape or design of text to reflect the topic, as Florian does.

✔ Talk about the paintings as you share the poems. How would your students describe this writer's artistic voice? Does it match his writing voice?

 Grimes, Nikki. 2002. *A Pocketful of Poems*. Boston: Houghton Mifflin.

Summary

Here is a charming, creative collection of haiku poetry (seventeen syllables) that brims with the personality and spontaneity for which Grimes is famous.

Best of all, each poem is inspired by just one important word in the poet's life—what could be simpler? Have fun reading this one aloud.

Writing Connections
✔ Explain what haiku poetry is—a poem with seventeen syllables that explores just one idea. As you read some poems aloud, ask students to clap hands at each syllable until they start to get the feeling for what a syllable is. Read slowly, and clap with them to help them get the idea. This also helps them build a sense of rhythm. (Ask one student to count the syllables as you go.

✔ Brainstorm a list of "important words" for your students. Explain that this could be a collection on which to build poems.

✔ Ask students to take just one of those words and create a haiku poem. The object is seventeen syllables, but if your students have trouble with this, don't worry! Ability to count syllables will improve with time. Meanwhile, focus on the main priority: to create a short poem on one important subject.

Marshall, James. 1972. *George and Martha*. Boston: Houghton Mifflin.

Summary
Like all the "George and Martha" books, this one is an excellent example of both fluency and voice. George and Martha clearly care for each other deeply, but they have their share of disagreements and small troubles to overcome—nothing too heavy-duty. They love teasing each other in a kind and friendly way, but with a touch of humor. Use the book to illustrate effective use of dialogue, a major component of strong sentence fluency.

Writing Connections
✔ Ask students to try writing a small sample of dialogue, using *George and Martha* as a model.

✔ Ask students to act out one of the *George and Martha* stories. Other students can assume the roles for different stories. Encourage students to make the most of the dialogue, speaking with lots of expressiveness and letting their faces show their feelings.

✔ If students are ready, ask them to create a new story, putting George and Martha in a different situation—for example, arguing over which movie to see, deciding what to buy at the grocery store, deciding whose turn it is to drive or to cook, or shopping together for something like a couch or a pet.

Milne, A. A. 1950 (first edition 1926). *Winnie the Pooh*. New York: E. P. Dutton.

Summary
Revisit an old favorite, as wonderfully lyrical and fluent as ever. "Here is Edward Bear, coming downstairs now, bump, bump, bump, on the back of his head, behind Christopher Robin. It is, as far as he knows, the only way of coming downstairs, but sometimes he feels that there really is another way, if only he could stop bumping for a moment and think of it. And then he feels that perhaps there isn't" (p. 1). Distinctive. The one, the only.

Writing Connections

✔ Try imitating a short passage, perhaps a sentence that reflects Pooh thinking or speaking. Read the results aloud. Can you (and your students) capture a bit of A. A. Milne's style and flavor?

✔ Read some of the dialogue aloud more than once. Ask students to think about whether the dialogue sounds real (it is highly individual!). What makes it work?

✔ Suppose that one of the characters from Winnie the Pooh were to visit your classroom for the day. Write a bit of what might happen. Pooh having lunch with you perhaps. Eeyore on the playground. Owl teaching a spelling lesson. Use your imagination.

 Simmons, Jane. 2001. *Little Fern's First Winter*. Boston: Little, Brown and Company.

Summary

In this delightful story, Fern (a rabbit) experiences snow for the first time. A little event—playing hide and seek—turns into a big adventure. The book has a wonderful lead—use that feature when talking about organization. For fluency, focus on the gentle rhythms of the language and the excellent dialogue. Notice how the print changes to match Fern's voice when she has lost her friend. Also, notice wonderfully inviting illustrations.

Writing Connections

✔ Read just the lead. Talk about it. Also talk about other ways the writer could have begun the story.

✔ Brainstorm some "first" memories your students have: first snowfall, first day at school, first time swimming, first time holding a baby, first time skiing, first time cooking alone, first bike ride, first book, or whatever. Ask them to choose one and to write about it.

✔ Write some dialogue on an overhead projector. Play one character and write what you would say, then ask students to fill in what the *other* character would say. As you work, model the way to punctuate dialogue.

✔ One subtheme of the book is how it feels to be "lost" in the sense of being alone. Have any of your students ever been lost? Use pictures, writing, oral storytelling, or all three to explore this theme.

 # LOCATION, LOCATION, LOCATION

Becoming a writer can also profoundly change your life as a reader. One reads with a deeper appreciation and concentration, knowing now how hard writing is, especially how hard it is to make it look effortless. You begin to read with a writer's eyes. You focus in a new way.

—Anne Lamott
Bird by Bird (1994, p. 233)

I better understand now that reading aloud to children is teaching and that how I read and the talk surrounding that reading has a direct influence on children's growth as readers and writers. Daily read-aloud time cannot be shortchanged for it helps children understand the fundamental purpose of the written word.

—Carol Avery
And With a Light Touch (2002, p. 5)

I am lucky to work across the street from one of the world's great bookstores, Paulina Springs (accessible at *paulinasprings.com*). The owner and staff welcome their customers by name. They actually read the books on their shelves, and they can always direct you, it seems, to just the right book. They serve iced tea and ice water in the summer—hot tea or cocoa in the winter. Music is always playing, and the lighting is soft. "Reading feels good" is the message.

As I sat there one day looking through a stack of books I had assembled and trying to select the "keepers" (You can't buy them all—I know because I've tried), in came a slightly younger shopper (she was three) with her dad. Her eyes lit up as she looked at the book covers, and she touched them reverently as if they held magic. I said hello to her, and her dad asked her if she wanted to say hi. "No," she said. "Not today." Sara's mind was elsewhere. She pulled a book from the shelf for Dad to read, and he plunked himself right down on the carpet; clearly, this was a routine for them. He read book after book, letting Sara turn the pages, so she could pace it. He asked her questions about the pictures, and she responded: "How does the boy look in this picture?" "Sad."

After three or four books, I thought Sarah would be ready for something else, but she was just warming up. Dad said, "OK, it's time for you to read to me—so I get to choose the book." He did. He picked *Olivia* by Ian Falconer. Sara read this time (she knew it pretty well), and Dad turned the pages. She asked him questions, just as he had done with her: "What is Olivia doing in this picture?" He answered them all, just as she had answered his. At the end, she asked him if he liked the book, and he said it was one of his favorites.

When it was time to go, dad said, "I hate leaving the bookstore. Let's decide when we're coming back."

"Tomorrow?" Sara suggested.

"Good!" Dad responded, not missing a beat. "I was hoping you'd say that. Let's get a snack—reading makes me hungry."

Me, too. And I bet Sarah will always think of reading as something that lifts your spirit and brings you home.

If we don't laugh, gasp, block our ears, sigh, vomit, giggle, curl our toes, empathize, sympathize, feel pain, weep, or shiver during the reading of a picture book, then surely the writer has wasted our time, our money, and our precious, precious trees.

—Mem Fox

Dear Mem Fox (1992, p. 149)

Christophe, a fourth grader, with his first-grade buddy Ammon, review Ammon's African Book together.

Photo and caption courtesy of Natalie (Grade 4).

CHAPTER 7 IN A NUTSHELL

- Reading aloud is among the most important things we do in teaching writing, for it offers invaluable models, and even more important, underscores the joy of reading and the power of books.
- Reading aloud *is* teaching writing, even if no writing activity follows the reading.
- *Reading as writers* helps us to be better teachers of writing.
- Every book has a lesson (or lessons) to teach.
- We can—and should—select books for specific features; however, a book chosen to illustrate powerful word choice, for example, may be equally wonderful for fluency or voice or ideas.
- It is not necessary to use the specific books listed here, or *anywhere*, to teach writing traits. Use your own favorite books to guide your young writers to a deeper understanding of ideas, organization, voice, fluency, and other key concepts that define writing.
- Love what you read. Read with passion. Hold nothing back. Know that the most important lesson you teach is the love of books.

EXTENSIONS

1. Think of your favorite read-aloud books. Are they on this short list? Perhaps you have several favorites that are not. List some here:

   Book 1: _____

   Book 2: _____

   Book 3: _____

   Book 4: _____

2. Try to think of one or two writing connections you *could* make with each of your favorite books. Remember that reading for its own sake is important and does not always have to lead into a writing activity.

3. Thinking of your list of favorite books, do you see a pattern? Is there one special trait you love to teach? In other words, do you choose books mostly for detail (ideas), mostly for tone and flavor (voice), or mostly for the wonderful wording (word choice)? Or is it a combination?

4. How would you rate yourself as a reader?

   ____ Outrageously expressive—over the top, really!

   ____ Quite expressive, with a flair for drama where it's needed.

   ____ Timid, actually—I don't put enough oomph into it.

   Try to think why you have rated yourself as you have. Do you think that you are putting enough expression into the reading to bring out the voice? The fluency?

5. Think of the books you love most as an *adult* reader. List three or four here, and ask yourself, "Which traits are especially strong in each book I love?"

   Book 1: _____ Strength: _____

   Book 2: _____ Strength: _____

   Book 3: _____ Strength: _____

   Book 4: _____ Strength: _____

6. It is possible to assemble hundreds of quotations to support the importance of the reading-writing connection. It is virtually undisputed! But can you think of a way it is personally important to you—as a writer, a reader, or both?

7. In *Books, Lessons, Ideas for Teaching the Six Traits* (listed under "Sources Cited"), I review numerous additional books that can be used to teach traits. Check a copy of this book for additional options—and add some of your own to the list.

SOURCES CITED

Avery, Carol. 2002. *And With a Light Touch*. Portsmouth, NH: Heinemann.

Fox, Mem. 1992. *Dear Mem Fox I Have Read All of Your Books Even the Pathetic Ones*. New York: Harcourt Brace Jovanovich.

Fox, Mem. 1993. *Radical Reflections*. New York: Harcourt, Brace.

Freeman, Marcia S. 1998. *Teaching the Youngest Writers*. Gainesville, FL: Maupin House Publishing, Inc.

Graves, Donald H. 1984. *Writing: Teachers and Children at Work*. Portsmouth, NH: Heinemann.

Johnson, Bea. 1999. *Never Too Early to Write: Adventures in the K–1 Writing Workshop*. Gainesville, FL: Maupin House Publishing, Inc.

Lamott, Anne. 1994. *Bird by Bird*. New York: Doubleday.

Ray, Katie Wood. 2002. *What You Know by Heart*. Portsmouth, NH: Heinemann.

Routman, Regie. 2000. *Conversations: Strategies for Teaching, Learning, and Evaluating*. Portsmouth, NH: Heinemann.

Spandel, Vicki. 2001. *Books, Lessons, Ideas for Teaching the Six Traits* (primary/elementary edition). Wilmington, MA: Great Source Education Group.

Casey and Will (Grade 1) work on revising Will's story. Will reads his writing while Casey takes notes about positive things that can be changed.

Photo and caption courtesy of Lilly (Grade 4).

Assessment must promote learning, not just measure it. When learners are well served, assessment becomes a learning experience that supports and improves instruction. The learners are not just the students but also the teachers, who learn something about their students.

—Regie Routman
Conversations (2001, p. 559)

If children can't talk easily about texts, they will have a hard time being critical readers of their own or anyone else's writing.

—Lucy Calkins
The Art of Teaching Writing
(1994, p. 326)

Kindergartners, you know, are often just handed a pencil the minute they walk in the door. We're so worried about getting something to hang on the wall. It's not all about product. We should think about process.

—Minnie Hutchison
Teacher, Thurgood Marshall School,
Newark, Delaware

Maximum anxiety does not lead to maximum learning. Rather, confidence in one's self as a learner leads to student success and school effectiveness.

—Rick Stiggins
Student-Involved Classroom Assessment (2001, p. 3)

*A*ssessment is not about making judgments—not really. It's about discovery and learning. In this case, it is about learning what it means to write well and what writing well looks like for us and for our students. As Barry Lane points out in the Foreword, the word *assessment* comes from the Latin word *assidere*, which means "to sit beside." Good assessment should be a companion to learning, not a threat, but a help—to the teacher *and* to the student. It should be a way of answering, "How am I doing?" It should provide an opportunity for students to demonstrate all that they *can* do.

The best assessor a *beginning* writer can have is a coach who not only *sits* beside but also *works* alongside the learner, showing the writing process in action, pointing out what that learner is doing especially well (especially things the learner might not otherwise notice), and asking questions that encourage a beginning writer to make good choices and to move forward. A good coach models—continuously. Along with suggestions, he or she finds something to support and celebrate in every performance because even on the worst of days we learn something that can take us to the next level.

The best assessor an *experienced* learner can have is himself or herself. We do not teach children to assess their own work just so that the Monday grade will not come as a surprise. We teach them so that they can review what they have done, take pride in their achievements, revise with purpose, and improve on their efforts next time around—with or without an instructor as a guide. Good assessment pushes the learner toward independence always.

THREE LEVELS OF ASSESSMENT

Assessment of young writers generally occurs at three levels: large-scale, classroom, and personal.

Large-Scale, Formal Assessment

Large-scale assessment happens at district or state level usually; occasionally, though, individual schools do their own assessments across grade levels. In large-scale writing assessment, more than one rater reads each paper, and if the two readers do not agree, it may go to a third reader for resolution. The readers are usually, but not always, teachers. When papers are sent to a test company for professional evaluation, the readers may include trained teachers, student teachers, journalists, writers, editors, or other persons with a strong language arts background. At this level, students may be assessed analytically, on key components of performance (the kind of assessment described in this book), or holistically, with a single score summing up overall performance. Holistic assessment provides a broad-brushstroke point of view, whereas analytical assessment provides more of a performance profile, helping students and educators identify strengths and problems in students' writing. Scores may be used for reviewing or modifying curriculum, judging how well students meet established standards, or placing/promoting students.

Classroom Assessment

Classroom assessment differs from large-scale assessment in a number of ways, the most striking being that it has the potential to look at performance over time and to consider a body of work versus a single performance. Individual performances may be assessed, it's true, but the summative assessment for a grading period generally takes several performances into account, along with other factors, such as growth. It seems almost a cliché to say that multiple assessments tell a truer story than any single assessment can hope to tell: "One test cannot give an accurate picture of what [a] child knows, how the child is doing, and what the child needs to learn next" (Routman, 2001, p. 561). It is like the difference between a snapshot and a full-blown video. (In all fairness, single-test scores *can* provide important information, provided the test is carefully and thoughtfully constructed; they simply do not provide *all* the information.)

In addition to looking at a body of work, classroom assessment usually mixes spontaneous and "best possible" performances, sometimes looking at what students do in their daily work and sometimes focusing on long-term, multiday projects, publishing projects, and so on. Because it is teacher-directed, classroom assessment is based on the observations and perceptions of someone who knows and works with each student, so it is by nature more personal. This often means that it is more insightful than large-scale assessment, but it does introduce an increased potential for some types of bias. Bias occurs when a grade is based on something other than performance itself—such as a child's general classroom behavior, quality of work in previous classes, or how a particular performance compares with the child's usual efforts (e.g., "John is really having an off-day"). Large-scale assessment is certainly not bias-free, of course; such factors as neatness, handwriting, selection of topic, general tone of the writing, and many others (even crossouts, size of margins, or ink color!) can influence scores unduly—and unfairly. Nevertheless, in large-scale assessment, readers rarely know the writer personally and so have no preset expectations regarding performance or general attitude or ability, and this does give them a small edge in overcoming many common causes of reader bias.

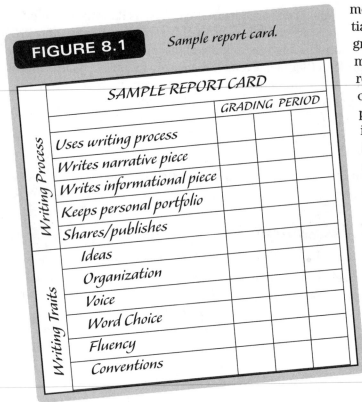

FIGURE 8.1 *Sample report card.*

SAMPLE REPORT CARD		GRADING PERIOD			
Writing Process	Uses writing process				
	Writes narrative piece				
	Writes informational piece				
	Keeps personal portfolio				
	Shares/publishes				
Writing Traits	Ideas				
	Organization				
	Voice				
	Word Choice				
	Fluency				
	Conventions				

Classroom assessment (and grades, for that matter) can be based on any or all of the following: performance on individual writing samples (possibly across modes), growth over time, participation in the writing process, skill in revising or editing text, and the student "story" told by a portfolio. An increasing number of district report cards now incorporate the six traits or an amended version thereof. (See Figure 8.1 for a sample of how such a report card might look).

Personal Assessment

Students who keep portfolios, who are taught to use rubrics, and who are taught to make reading-writing connections can also become skilled assessors of their own work. They learn to "look within." The result is not a score or grade but a personal reflection that may be written and may become part of a portfolio. Personal assessment—especially with practice—also becomes the most fundamental and trustworthy basis for revision, as well as for improvement in future writing.

IMPORTANCE = IMPACT

Of these three forms of assessment, the third is most significant, yet it receives (usually) the least attention. After all, personal assessment generally has no grades or paperwork attached to it. Results are all in the students' heads—or sometimes recorded in written reflections. It is significant *not* because it is data-based with elaborate statistics to illustrate growth and *not* because it makes headlines (which it never, ever does) but because it has the most potential to truly influence how students think, write, revise, and edit—and how they will do so throughout their lives. Unless student self-assessment is firmly entrenched as a major goal of our writing curriculum, all other assessments will pale both in importance and in impact. This is so because *only* self-assessment gives students an internal compass to guide their development as writers. They must know whether their work is good not because we tell them or a state test tells them but because they can judge their performance for themselves.

Next in importance, of course, is classroom assessment. Unlike most large-scale assessments, classroom assessment can take into account *both* process and product and can look at students' performance over time and across various forms of writing—informational writing, narratives, personal essays, reflections, and so on. The teacher who is a writer himself or herself is acutely aware of a student's participation in and comfort with the process of writing and is able to pose important questions such as these:

Does the student

- ✔ Have strategies (conversing, sketching, listing) to draw on for prewriting?
- ✔ Try new things?
- ✔ Borrow ideas from others?
- ✔ Borrow print from the environment?
- ✔ Come up with personally important topics (see Jared's spontaneous piece, Figure 8.2)?
- ✔ Show a willingness to try new forms of writing?
- ✔ Enjoy writing?
- ✔ Extend individual pieces through use of detail?
- ✔ Imitate favorite books, poems, or other pieces?
- ✔ Love reading?
- ✔ Choose books for himself or herself?
- ✔ Listen with expectation and appreciation to both professional writing and the writing of peers?
- ✔ See himself or herself as a writer and reader?

| FIGURE 8.2 | *"Dear New York."* Jared (2) |

> Jared
> Deer New York i've herd
> wot hapin I hop the
> police finds them. I hope
> all the engerd git biter. I hope
> all the bad peopel fined a
> beter heart. I hope people bil
> d the bildings back agen.

Questions such as these are vital to creating a true and accurate portrait of who a student really is as a writer, but they are far beyond the scope of what large-scale assessment can measure. This does not mean that large-scale assessment does not provide important information; it simply means that we should be realistic about its capabilities and its limitations. Our reaction to large-scale assessment scores in recent years has grown into a virtual frenzy, sometimes out of all proportion to the substance and completeness of the information this kind of testing can possibly provide. It is like responding to newspaper headlines without bothering to read the stories behind them. Classroom assessment tells a bigger story; it fills in the details—in part because we know the writer behind the words and also because we witness tiny nuances of change and risk up close. Personal assessment, in the hands of an experienced student writer, helps complete the tale.

In the past decade, increasing numbers of teachers have asked whether, given its inherent limitations, large-scale assessment is appropriate for primary students. There is no simple answer to this question (although opinions abound). Let's explore some of the issues at stake.

LARGE-SCALE ASSESSMENT: IS IT RIGHT FOR PRIMARY STUDENTS?

Used properly, large-scale assessment (which typically focuses on just one performance by each student) can give us valuable information on how students *as a group* are performing in an area such as writing, and can offer *one indicator of performance* for an individual student who is tested.

Such data are useful in determining whether a school or district ought to devote more time to writing instruction or in identifying the general kinds of problems (or strengths) student writers are having. It can also be *helpful* in determining whether individual students need additional instruction, though, of course (as noted earlier), it is a "single-dip approach" and so necessarily provides *indicators* as opposed to definitive, satisfying, complete answers. Regie Routman notes that "Combined with other assessments, formal, standardized measures are appropriate for accountability, monitoring, selection, and placement *as long as* [emphasis in original] they are supplemented with other assessments." She also notes the importance of specific feedback, stating that the language of any criteria used "must be clear and jargon free" (2001, p. 560). I would add that both prompts and rubrics must be grade-level-appropriate and reasonably appealing in order to elicit anything resembling a typical response. Many times, especially with assessments of younger students, this is far from the case.

"I don't get it."

Often, primary students do not understand writing prompts, and this seemingly simple problem can greatly influence both how the student writes and how his or her paper is scored. Many things can get in the way of comprehending a prompt: reading skill, knowledge of or familiarity with the topic, and misunderstanding of a particular word or phrase—to name just a few. Sometimes students simply have no experience with the situation that is the focus of the prompt (e.g., "Explain how to care for a pet"). Or they may find the topic so dull that they are not stimulated to write much or to write with flair (e.g., "Describe a time you were surprised").

In a classroom, misunderstanding or disinterest is less likely to create a problem because the teacher can explain the prompt, come up with a different prompt altogether, or (best of all) give students freedom to come up with their own personally important topics. Students in a large-scale writing context, by contrast, generally are expected to interpret a prompt for themselves, and to respond to that prompt, and that prompt *only*. This means not only understanding what the prompt literally says but also knowing what *kind* of writing is called for—a story, an essay, a description, and so forth. Making such distinctions is a challenge even for older students (sometimes even for adults). It is next to impossible for many young students, even when the teacher reads the prompt aloud. There may be unfamiliar words, or just the way the prompt is written can create confusion—for example, "Describe what happened." *Describe* suggests that the prompt writer is looking for a descriptive piece, but the words *what happened* suggest a story. Prompt writers seldom take time to write to their own prompts (assigning is always easier than writing yourself), and so they seldom discover how confusing their own directions often are.

A simple touch sparks Ashlee's imagination: "My favorite part is the nose because it is soft and weird. It has big holes. It is not the same color as my nose."

A student who misunderstands such directions may write a description instead of a story or may give up trying to figure out a poorly written prompt and simply write on a different topic altogether. Such responses often lead to lower scores (scores, by the way, that reflect more the student's ability to follow directions or interpret someone *else's* fuzzy writing than the student's writing ability per se). They may even lead to outright dismissal of the paper. Poorly worded prompts plague writers of *all* ages and abilities, but clearly, primary writers are the most susceptible because of their lack of experience in reading, writing, and responding to prompts.

"I didn't have enough time!"

Few primary students are accustomed to being handed a sheet of paper and timed in their writing. Writing in a classroom is a little warmer and friendlier. There's a warm-up period during which students draw or listen to a story or make a list. Sometimes they have a chance to converse with a classmate. Sometimes they write in response to a project or an event that occurs right there in the classroom—a visiting baby or pet, for instance. Usually, there is an opportunity to ask questions, and the teacher may roam the room during writing to offer helpful tips or answer more questions. Some teachers post a word bank on the wall or chalkboard.

None of these things is likely to be part of large-scale assessment. Some primary students take this difference in stride; others find it traumatic. Some are even reduced to tears because, after all, it *is* a test, and you don't have to be very old to learn that school is a place where you are expected to succeed. Were this not the case, surely you wouldn't be tested so rigorously or so often.

American students are the most tested students in the world, and it doesn't look like that distinction is going to change any time soon. Our testing mania is ironic, because if testing were the means to higher achievement, we'd be the top-achieving country. Since we live in a culture where testing is highly valued, we need to be proactive and vocal in being sure that the tests being used are good ones.

—**Regie Routman**
Conversations (2001, p. 590)

"I can't write this much."

What about those students who are not yet fluent writers—fluent in the sense of generating *lots* of text? For them, writing assessment can spell panic. Even adults who do not write skillfully or frequently get shaky when handed a blank piece of paper, especially if someone else is going to review what they put on it. (Maybe you feel this way yourself.) Some students simply freeze and turn in a blank page. Others strategize to find ways of filling the page at all costs—writing extra big or repeating familiar words endlessly or filling most of the page with a picture. Such strategies also translate into lower writing scores—or no scores at all. What's more, anxiety itself affects performance, inhibiting some young writers who normally enjoy writing. Young writers who might otherwise delight us with their originality and voice become so afraid of incorporating *any* errors into the text that they write drivel—ridiculously simple sentences with three- and four-letter words that they feel confident they can spell. Ironically, some reviewers are actually pleased with these results, especially if they are relatively error-free. This is unfortunate, for it reinforces in students' minds the restrictive and misguided notion that good writing is *correct* writing—and little more.

Correctness is a worthy goal, but it is not enough. Not even close. You can have the shiniest shoes in the world, but if they are all you are wearing, it is unlikely that you will be viewed as well dressed. To make a reader shout, clap, laugh out loud, gasp in surprise, tear up with nostalgia, or reach to turn the page—now *those* are goals worth the effort of writing. We must not settle for less—or teach our students to settle for less. We want our students to experience the thrill of writing something, *sometime* that moves a reader—don't we? We steal this opportunity from our student writers when we use assessment to terrify them or when we do not respect personally important topics as sufficiently worthy.

In Summary

Large-scale assessment is an expedient method of gathering "writing at a glance" information from writers who are old enough and experienced enough to deal with the logistics. This generally occurs around midyear of third grade or later. At this point, students are generating sufficient text that the

FIGURE 8.3   *"My Sister."* Taylor (1)

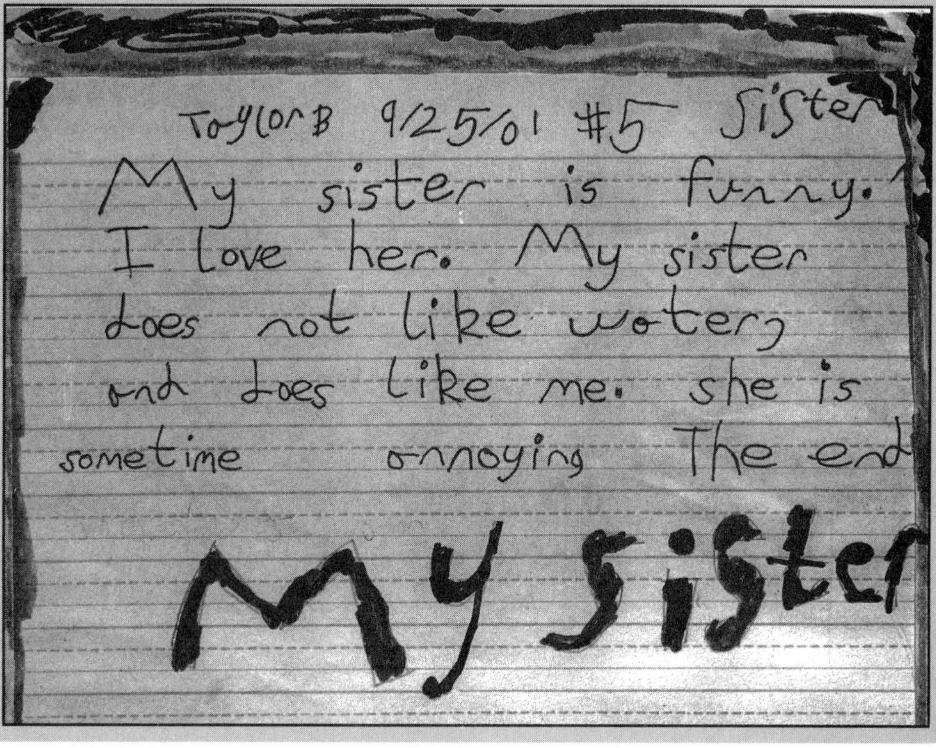

challenge of filling half a page to a page with writing is no longer intimidating. They may have had some practice in the classroom reading and responding orally to various prompts—trying them on for size, if you will. A wise teacher provides this kind of practice. It is a lifeline for students who will be tested. Students may also have had some practice writing quickly, under a prescribed time limit. They are beginning to put conventions into perspective, as tools for showcasing ideas and voice, not an end in themselves. Further, writing to a prompt feels far more comfortable once you have done it a few times, and it becomes easier to judge how long it will really take you to plan and write a paragraph. This does take practice. If we asked many prompt writers to actually write in response to their own prompts, it is unlikely that they could guess the actual time it would take with any accuracy (and many would complain when time was up).

Despite (and in some ways, because of) its efficiencies, large-scale assessment is not ideally suited to the needs of most primary students. It is clearly very much at odds with the kind of writing most young writers are accustomed to doing within the classroom, and the demands are simply beyond the reach of many students—not all, but many. In addition, many of the rubrics customarily used to assess older students (see Appendix for an example) are simply not suited to the assessment of younger writers. They are developmentally at a much higher level, demanding skills beginning writers have not yet acquired and (more important still) ignoring totally many of those things (e.g., left-to-right orientation, sentence sense, spacing between words, use of letter strings to form a first complete sentence) that primary students have mastered so brilliantly but for which they receive no credit because *it is not in the rubric.*

To this let me add that we are still, I believe, in the early stages of designing first-rate rubrics with which to assess very young writers, and we need a good deal more field testing at the classroom level before we should dare to embark on a high-stakes assessment venture with primary students. We need to know, with far more certainty than we now do, that we are looking for the right things in our students' work and that we are capable of spotting them. I am not persuaded that all raters of primary-level work see beyond conventions to the detail or voice or even fluency (in letter strings, for instance) that hides within first writing efforts. Nor am I persuaded that artistic expression receives its just due in our assessment of meaning. Such things are far more likely to be addressed well at the classroom level.

Assessment of very young students is also tricky because many of them write very little or write in ways that we cannot comprehend speedily and often lack (or will not take) time to interpret. Or to put it another way, we are not sure what we are looking at. If we wait until students develop a certain level of

FIGURE 8.4   *Self-portrait.* Jacque (K)

FIGURE 8.5   *"It is the end"* (K).

It is the end. Summer is almost here,
But I won't ever forget Mrs. Stobaugh
[my teacher]. Kindergarten.

fluency and comfort with writing (for most students, around late grade 3 or early grade 4 or its equivalent in English-language learners), we are more likely to gain meaningful results from our large-scale assessments. It is not so much that young students have suddenly learned how to write. Very young students may not have mastered conventional text, but they *do write*. They *do* create meaning. It is we, the assessors, who improve in our ability to review performance accurately as students grow older and more capable of creating the sort of text with which *we feel comfortable*.

Here's the thing: In the bad old days, when conventions reigned supreme, we looked mostly for spelling and punctuation errors. Admittedly, this is a pathetically limited approach to assessing writing if we buy into the belief that writing is the verbal expression of thought. But it has one overriding, huge advantage that is so appealing that some people cling to it even now: It is easy. When we got elaborate and began to talk about development of ideas, organization, incorporation and support of a thesis, use of transitions, expression of personal voice, and fluent sentence construction, we didn't just raise the bar for students. We raised it for ourselves as well. We agreed to become very, *very* good assessors. When we commit to an assessment as inherently complex as judging performance in writing, a pledge goes with it: "If you meet these standards I have set for you, I will know it. If you express clear ideas, I will understand them. If you organize your writing well, I will follow where you lead. If you write with voice, I will hear you."

If we are to assess primary writers accurately and equitably, it is *ourselves* we must teach first—and I do not believe that we are there yet. In the context of a *classroom*, though, we have a fighting chance. We see the children and hear them. We speak to them and observe their responses. We see many samples of writing, not just one. We know what is typical and what is exceptional. We know what is born of understanding and what is more likely to be fortuitous. And we see change and growth.

My Recommendations

Let's keep large-scale assessment at grade 3 and higher. Assess beginning writers at the classroom level. Continue to improve our writing rubrics for young writers based on what we teach ourselves about primary writing. Keep looking. Keep learning. And as we go, bring students along. Make them partners in the assessment process, not just targets for our critique. Teach them writers' language and model, through our own work and the writings of others, what we want to see. Recognize their successes, and let them know what they do well. Above all, do not cave into the temptation to make curriculum and teaching strategies "match the test." Rather, continue the conversation about good testing practice so that our assessment methods truly reflect and honor what it is we wish to teach—namely, writing as thinking.

> *Because of the time needed to assess the samples, and because teachers do not receive the samples back, prompt-driven assessments have little value as tools for instructional improvement for individual students—this is still best achieved by ongoing assessment of student writing in the classroom.*

—Tommy Thomason and Carol York
Write on Target: Preparing Young Writers to Succeed on State Writing Achievement Tests (2000, p. 75)

MEANWHILE—SOME LIFELINES

I know—large-scale primary level testing is not going to go away despite my recommendations. Ours is a society of numbers. We love them. Height, weight, blood pressure, Social Security Number, Scholastic Aptitude Test (SAT) scores—and all the rest. So—what can you do in the meantime, just to cope?

Teach

Most important of all, teach writing the best way you know how. Do not fall into the trap of thinking that you must abandon the best part of your curriculum in order to teach formulaic writing that will be of no help to students in any situation outside of formal assessment. Remember that the biggest problem with formulaic writing is not that it creates poor writing (dull though the result may often be) but that it encourages formulaic thinking—thinking that lacks depth, insight, originality, or perspective. Stick with writing process. Allow time for writing. Encourage free exchange of ideas and sharing. Model. Model. Model. Read—and show how much you love it. It fills your students' heads with ideas—content, that is—plus strategies for writing. Help students make connections between what you (or they) read and the writing you all do.

> *Formula approaches are most useful in boosting the scores of non-fluent writers, whose work may jump a score point. . . . But the same cookie-cutter approach will also prevent those scores from going higher because the writing samples are obviously poured from the same mold. You certainly won't find the formulas in the "real world" of good writing.*
>
> **—Tommy Thomason and Carol York**
> *Write on Target: Preparing Young Writers to Succeed on State Writing Achievement Tests* (2000, p. 67)

> *If states really want student writing to improve, they need to insure that teachers have adequate time to teach writing well. Effective teaching means planning for instruction and responding to student writing.*
>
> **—George Hillocks, Jr.**
> *The Testing Trap: How State Writing Assessments Control Learning* (2002, p. 205)

Increase Students' Comfort

Because it is so different from what usually happens in the classroom, large-scale testing makes many students uncomfortable. Indeed, stressed. It is helpful to explain to students that this kind of writing *is* different and to give them practice in trying it out. "How does it feel to write for just a certain length of time? Let's try it and see" (and you do it, too). Have students time themselves when the stakes are low: "How long did it take you to fill half a page? Did that surprise you? Could you write faster if you needed to? Another day we'll try it and see. This is how much I wrote." And so on. Practice together.

Have a "Prompt Day"

It is also helpful to share a few prompts with students and to talk about what kind of writing you would do in response to each prompt. You do not have to *do* the writing—just talk about it. Talk about whether a prompt is asking for a story or for information. Talk about the very first thing you would write (the first sentence is always the hardest). Talk about whether a picture should be included (sometimes, sometimes not). Talk about how long a response needs to be—or *can* be. In some large-scale assessments, responses shorter than four sentences are unlikely to receive scores, so "Four or more" is a good rule of thumb for writers in grades 1 and 2 until they reach a level of fluency where longer pieces are much easier to generate. Teach them some coping skills, such as including the first letter of a word followed by a blank for words they simply do not know—for example, s_____ (for *soccer*). This allows them to get text on the page. If time permits, they can return to these "simplified" words and try to fill in the blanks, if possible. If not, at least they have written more copy than they likely would have had if they allowed themselves to be blocked by spelling.

> *Teachers need to take what they know about teaching reading and use it to help students learn to read these tests. Teachers can help put tests in perspective by reading stories like Miriam Cohen's First Grade Takes a Test and by discussing with students what tests can do and what they can't.*
>
> **—Kathleen Strickland and James Strickland**
> *Making Assessment Elementary* (2000, p. 121)

Practice Individual Prewriting

Some students get the wheels turning by talking. Usually, in large-scale assessments, they will need to fall back on some other form of prewriting because talking may not be allowed. You can suggest a picture, a word web, or a short list. Model these forms of prewriting, and make sure that students practice them.

Put Things in Perspective

I know—the stakes *are* high. The media stand ever-ready to pounce on the slightest hint of poor performance (never mind that their own commentators make numerous grammatical errors and their print makes a scrupulous editor's red pen quiver). Districts are held accountable and may lose funding or teachers. Their reputations for "poor performance" can affect real estate prices as parents scramble to find the schools that will magically make writers and readers of their children. These are serious consequences indeed, especially when so much still needs to be done to make state testing a fair and clear measure of student performance.

We must remain clear-headed through the stress, however, even though at times that feels next to impossible. Primary students, after all, cannot take on responsibility for declining real estate values or withheld funding. They must focus on what a child can focus on: *How am I doing today with this piece of paper and this pencil in my hand? Does anyone believe in me?*

Believe. Write with your children. Read to them. Help them feel that writing is a joyful thing to do, not a stressful chore to be done for the approval of a state or a stranger the child cannot picture. Give them practice reading prompts and responding to them—then discussing what was difficult to understand. Participate too so that you can share your perspective. Then, when the day of testing comes, have confidence. Your confidence will be contagious.

And tell your students this: A large-scale writing assessment is important because it provides information—like having your temperature taken by the doctor. It does not tell *everything* about you. No single writing test can tell whether you are a good writer. How you write on another day or on another topic may be different. Relax. Write as if you love it. Write as if you were writing a special note to your best friend in the whole world. And remember—there will be more tests and more opportunities.

> *Every time I thought I was smart enough to write, WHAM, I'd get smacked across the side of the head. And the more I whaled on myself, the dumber I felt, and the more it paralyzed me. I hadn't written the first word, but I hadn't given up hope.*

—Jack Gantos
Jack's Black Book (1998, p. 5)

Don't *you* give up hope either.

MAKING THINGS BETTER

Improving Tests

Large-scale assessment is an easy target because it creates so much stress. It can, however, under the best of circumstances, provide one important indicator of success. In addition, large-scale assessment draws attention to writing (or to any content area being assessed) in a way almost nothing else can do. It is doubtful that so many districts would have committed so passionately to the task of teaching students to write if assessments did not exist. So in this regard large-scale assessment works to our benefit.

The question always arises, of course, "Is it good to teach to the test?" Really, this is the wrong question. Our question should be, "If we teach students to be strong writers, will they do well on the performance test we're giving them?" The answer *should be yes*. When students do not achieve high scores, we almost always look to the curriculum—or to the teachers and students. That may not be where the answer lies at all. If we are allowing time for students to write, if we are reading to them extensively and from a wide range of sources, if we are inviting them to become evaluators, if we are sharing our expectations openly (through rubrics and other means), if we are teaching them writers' language, and if we are responding to their writing with unbridled enthusiasm and marked insight, then we are doing what needs to be done. And if the scores are still low, we must look elsewhere.

We must look to the test itself. Are we measuring *important writing skills*—or ability to follow directions? Are the prompts clear? Are they interesting? Could we write on them *ourselves* and do well? As well as we expect our students to do? Do we train those who assess our students well and teach them to look for what is significant (e.g., thoughtful creation of meaning)? Our tests can get better. And when (if) they do, large-scale assessment scores will reflect more clearly whether students can write.

Continually Reviewing Performance Standards

Setting standards for performance encourages us to set high expectations for our students, and it encourages conversations about what student writers should be achieving. At the same time, many educators agree that we have a long way to go in setting standards that truly promote academic improvement. In her analysis of current standards, Regie Routman notes that some critics find standards inequitable, "punishing many schools and students by holding them accountable for higher standards while failing to support them" (2001, p. 586). In addition, she notes, standards may be hard for some teachers to interpret or to teach from, and many consider them insufficiently rigorous, focusing too heavily on specific content, especially isolated facts, rather than on "the knowledge and understanding that is important in each discipline" (2001, p. 586).

Teacher and researcher George Hillocks, Jr., agrees with this, concluding from his extensive research on state writing assessments that writing standards in general are too low—for political reasons: "When the standards are low, it is easier to boast of more and more students reaching the same low standard" (2002, p. 204). Ironically, standards that do demand complex thinking may not be backed by classroom curriculum that supports inquiry or in-depth understanding. Tucker and Codding (1998) suggest that what is needed is greater clarity in the standards themselves, coupled with a closer match between expectations and curriculum. In fact, they recommend using samples of actual student work to make expectations clear not only to educators but also to students themselves: "Any student should be able to look at a performance standard and say, 'I understand now. I can do that'" (2002, p. 56).

FIGURE 8.6 *"If I could change one thing."* Jacob (2)

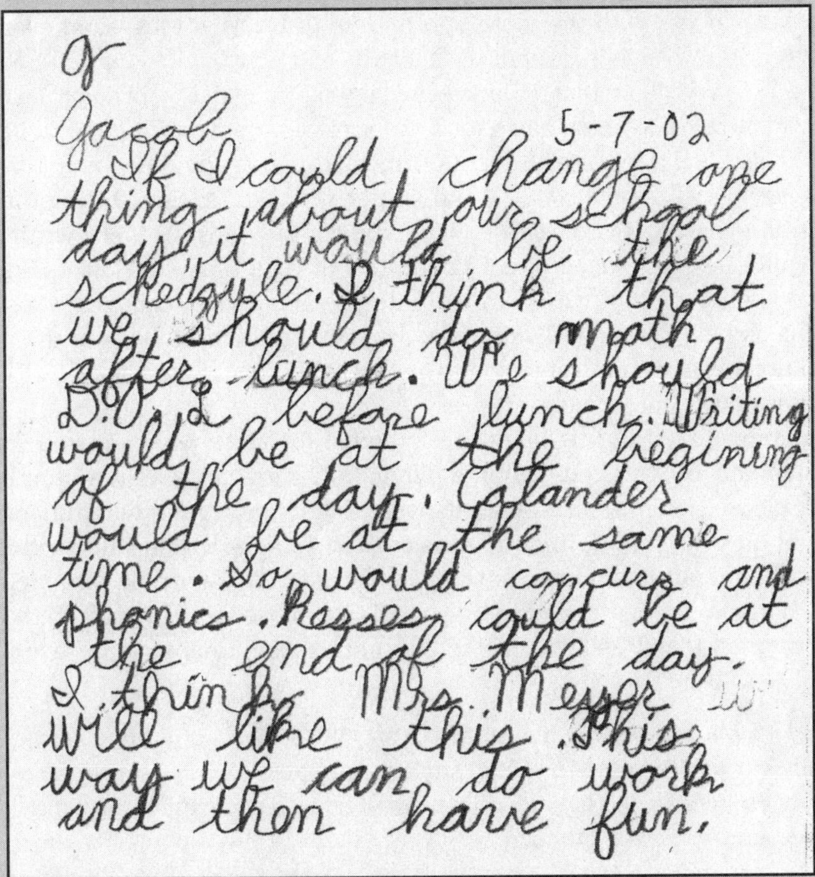
gr
Jacob 5-7-02
If I could change one thing about our school day, it would be the schedgule. I think that we should do math after lunch. We should D.O.L. before lunch. Writing would be at the begining of the day. Calander would be at the same time. So would concurs and phonics. Resses could be at the end of the day. I think Mrs. Meyer will like this. This way we can do work and then have fun.

Should we have performance standards for writing? Yes. We should continually review and improve them, however—even as we have with our rubrics that describe student performance. Assessment specialist Richard Stiggins suggests that "we should never regard performance criteria as 'finished.' Rather, always see them as works in progress" (2001, p. 207).

All good assessment, regardless of level, begins with a vision of success. What does it mean to be successful—in a particular classroom, a particular state, a particular writing situation? Until this is crystal clear, so that clear students can express it in their own words, we have not defined our target well enough. As Richard Stiggins reminds us, "The quality of any assessment depends first and foremost on how clearly and appropriately we define achievement the achievement target we are assessing. . . . If your job is to teach students to become better writers, you had better start with a highly refined vision of what good writing looks like" (2001, p. 19).

USING RUBRICS TO CREATE A VISION OF SUCCESS

Rubrics make expectations public and visible. They take the mystery away—and they require us to become more honest, open, and consistent in our assessment. I believe in rubrics because in developing them, we teach ourselves important truths about any content area (writing, reading, math, or whatever). And what we learn for ourselves guides our teaching forever after. So whether you use the rubrics in this book is less important by far than whether you use rubrics period. Have guidelines. Design them yourself if you wish. However, do not fool yourself that you know what you expect if you have not put it into writing. If you can't write it, you don't know it—not yet.

In developing their original six-trait rubrics, the Beaverton teachers carefully studied thousands of samples of student writing, *grades 3 through 12. No primary samples were included* because the Beaverton School District (which developed that first model) had no intention of assessing primary students on a large-scale basis. Therefore, to use those original rubrics with primary students is risky at best and unlikely to yield valid results. A few primary students, admittedly, are quite ready for assessment at that higher level, but such performance levels are not typical. Therefore, a classroom teacher can selectively apply the rubrics with students who are ready, easing other students into trait-based writing process with the more appropriate primary rubrics—and eventually moving on to a higher level of difficulty.

Let me be very clear that it is *not* my intention that the primary-level rubrics in this book become a basis for large-scale assessment. Much of what is portrayed here is the result of students' original thinking combined with time to explore, draw, talk, write, revisit, and confer with the teacher (or another trusted writing coach). It is unreasonable to expect that most of these writing samples would be reproduced under conditions of rigid time constraints and imposed prompts (some of which are not interpretable by the children whose performance is being measured). Further, the writing that *does* emerge under such conditions is often not representative of what students are capable of in typical classroom circumstances.

The rubrics shared in this book are intended *for classroom use* and for tracking students' progress across time. While they show progression in writing ability, please notice that they focus, very deliberately, on what students *can* do—not on what they *cannot* do. It is easy to think of a thousand writing skills most kindergarten students have not yet mastered. The trick is to identify those things young writers *are* doing—and to capture them in print so that we will not forget them. I suggest using the rubrics from Chapter 8 in several ways:

✔ As part of a portfolio, attaching rubrics to specific samples of writing incrementally through the year, to record students' progress.
✔ In parent conferences to help identify in an organized and explicit way the skills a young writer has attained.

✔ As a reminder so that in our comments to student writers we can be not only encouraging but also precise about the skills and accomplishments we see. Then, we teach students to see these things in their writing, too.

In the Appendix you will find a copy of the original six-trait rubrics used as the basis for *Creating Writers* (Spandel, 2001). Those originals were developed for use by children in third grade (about February of that year) on up and are *not* intended for use with primary students. However, there are exceptions; if you have students whose writing is *consistently* at the "Experienced Writer" level on the primary rubric, across traits and across various samples of writing, they are most likely ready for assessment on the original, more advanced rubrics that appear in the Appendix.

FEATURES OF SIX-TRAIT PRIMARY RUBRICS

1. Inclusion of Art

Like most writing rubrics, our original six-trait rubric does not deal with picture writing or even with the use of art as a form of prewriting. This feature has been added to the primary rubrics—for some significant reasons.

For many students (not only those at the primary level), picture writing is an essential form of expression. They need to use art to communicate. It does not just make the writing pretty. It *is* the writing. Much of the detail and most of the voice within early writing appears in picture form. To exclude this is like assessing Picasso's art by asking him to write an essay about form.

As Bob Steele notes, "Children use graphic units (schemata) much as we use vocabulary, and the thought processes that go into drawing—raw materials organized into meaningful and expressive forms—are syntactical in nature." He also comments that children "intuitively use the medium most likely to satisfy their [communication] needs: words for practical communication, drawings for expressing more subtle and complex thoughts" (1998, p. 7). In short, when we overlook drawing (or other art forms) in children's work, we may be missing the deepest and most important part of their thinking. This has two implications: First, we miss a vital opportunity to enhance thinking skills using children's natural inclination toward art as one means of doing so. In addition, we diminish the true value of any assessment that fails to recognize art as a legitimate means of communication. Art is "the unrecognized language," and language is the way children make sense of their world and, in doing so, develop their minds" (Steele, 1998, p. 7).

2. Focus on Descriptors, Not Numbers

The primary rubrics included in this book do not have numbers because I feel that the descriptors are more informative and more useful. I encourage educators to use them primarily *within the classroom*, preferably in the context of a writing collection, folder, or portfolio (a body of work), attaching rubrics to three, four, or more selected samples of work created at various times throughout the year.

FIGURE 8.7 *"My very worst boo-boo" (text and picture, grade 1).*

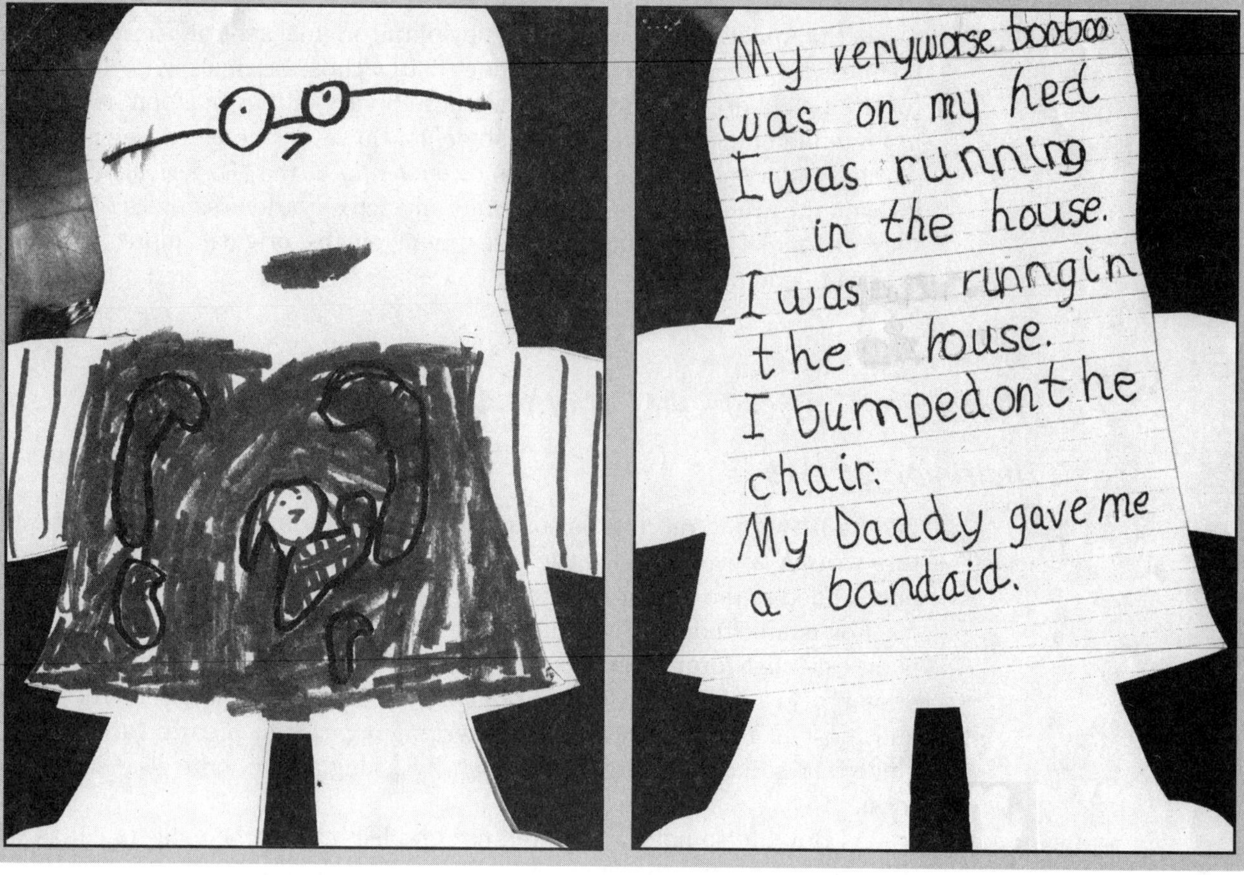

My verywarse booboo was on my hed I was running in the house. I was runngin the house. I bumpedonthe chair. My Daddy gave me a bandaid.

For each trait, the range of skills runs from "Beginner" (a writer who is just starting to make marks on paper) through "Experienced Writer" (a writer who is in control of many writing elements, creating full paragraphs and, to an extent, managing his or her own writing process). Again, let me emphasize that the rubrics focus on things the writer *can* do rather than on skills that are missing.

3. Inclusion of Behaviors

Some of the indicators within the rubrics are behavioral (such as editing own text or listening for voice or detail). Thus the rubric is much easier to use if you are assessing your own students in the classroom than if you are looking at writing by anonymous writers. Behavior is significant because (to use one simple example) it is more important for Meghan to know how to correct her spelling using a spell checker than for her to know how to spell a few words correctly; the first skill will serve her well in all situations. At the same time, much of each rubric relates specifically to what you will see in the writing, so classroom observation of behavior is not essential to using these rubrics.

FIGURE 8.8 *Primary rubric for ideas.*

Ideas

Beginner	Borrower	Experimenter	Meaning Maker	Experienced Writer
☐ Makes marks on paper.	☐ Uses "words" and pictures to express ideas.	☐ Uses text/art to create interpretable messages.	☐ Creates clear message via text or text plus art.	☐ Creates a clear, detailed message through text/art.
☐ "Reads" own writing, invents meaning.	☐ Uses imitative/borrowed print to create signs, lists, rules, notes, etc. (not always interpretable without help).	☐ Has clear main message/idea expressed in one or more sentences.	☐ Expresses complex, extended thoughts.	☐ Uses multiple sentences to enrich ideas or extend story.
☐ Dictates a clear message/story.	☐ Likes to come up with personal ideas for writing.	☐ Can "reread" text shortly after writing.	☐ Uses multiple sentences to add detail.	☐ Incorporates significant detail to enhance meaning.
☐ Uses art to convey message/story.	☐ Notices detail in read-aloud text and in pictures.	☐ Creates decodable lists, labels, notes, statements, short summaries, "all about" or "how-to" pieces and/or poems.	☐ Connects images/text to main idea.	☐ Creates writing that explains, gives directions, tells a story, expresses an opinion, describes.
☐ Recognizes that print has meaning/significance.		☐ Can talk about main ideas and details.	☐ Creates images that show detail: eyes, expressive faces, fingers and toes, leaves and grass, etc.	☐ Creates informational and narrative text; may write persuasive paragraphs or poems.
☐ Hears detail in stories read aloud.			☐ Creates writing that is fully decodable by independent reader.	☐ Can summarize own text.
			☐ Can "reread" text after several days.	☐ Can recognize and comment on detail in text of others.
			☐ Adds stories to repertoire.	☐ Chooses personally important topics.
			☐ Can think about and choose personal writing topic from several choices.	☐ May revise by adding a detail.

FIGURE 8.9 Primary rubric for organization.

Organization

Beginner	Borrower	Experimenter	MeaningMaker	Experienced Writer
☐ Fills space randomly.	☐ Can create picture and text that go together.	☐ Creates text/art with balanced look.	☐ Creates balanced, pleasing layout.	☐ Connects all text/art to main message.
☐ Can dictate sequential story or how-to piece.	☐ Creates layout with more purpose/balance.	☐ Consistently creates image and text that complement each other.	☐ Writes multiple sentences or images that suggest development/sequencing.	☐ Uses thoughtful titles.
☐ Can point to illustrations that go with text.	☐ May use two or more pictures to express story or message.	☐ May use title or THE END to signify beginning/ ending.	☐ Sometimes uses art to express sequence of events.	☐ Writes a true lead (usually, the opening sentence).
☐ Can "hear" beginnings/ endings in stories read aloud.		☐ Stays focused on message.	☐ Uses connecting words: *first, next, then, once, after, and, but, or, so, because.*	☐ Provides closure (usually, with final sentence).
		☐ Often creates labels/lists.	☐ Uses identifiable beginning and ending.	☐ Follows logical order/sequence.
		☐ Can organize recipes, all about and how-to-pieces, directions, and simple stories.	☐ Stays focused on message.	☐ Creates easy-to-follow text.
			☐ Creates organized summaries, stories, descriptions, short essays.	☐ Uses elaborate transitions: *After a while, The next day, Because of this, The first thing, Finally.*
				☐ Can structure stories, how-to pieces, short essays, and other forms.
				☐ Can use variety of organizational patterns: e.g., step by step, chronological, comparison, problem-solution, main idea + detail.

FIGURE 8.10   *Primary rubric for voice.*

Voice

Beginner	Borrower	Experimenter	Meaning Maker	Experienced Writer
☐ Creates bold lines.	☐ Incorporates voice into art through color, images, facial features, etc.	☐ Uses expressive language.	☐ Creates some text recognizable as "this child's piece."	☐ Creates lively, engaging, personal text/art.
☐ Uses colors.		☐ Often incorporates definite tone/flavor.		☐ Creates writing that is FUN to read aloud.
☐ Expresses voice in dictation.	☐ Uses exclamation points/underlining to show emphasis.	☐ Creates expressive pictures.	☐ Writes/draws with personal style.	☐ Is able to sustain voice.
☐ Responds to voice in text read aloud.	☐ Uses BIG LETTERS to show importance, strong feelings.	☐ Creates tone that reflects feelings.	☐ Creates individual text, art.	☐ Provokes strong reader response.
	☐ Shows preference for text/art with voice.	☐ Puts moments of voice throughout most text.	☐ Elicits emotional response in reader.	☐ Uses voice to influence meaning.
		☐ Recognizes voice in text of others, and can describe personal response: e.g., "I liked it," "It was very funny."	☐ May use conventional devices (exclamation points, underlining) to enhance voice.	☐ "Speaks" to audience.
			☐ Shows beginning awareness of audience: use of *you*, conversational tone, direct questions: *Do you like cats?*	☐ Creates voice that is easy to describe: *Joyful* *Funny* *Moody* *Sarcastic* *Fearful* *Angry* *Wistful*
			☐ Shows preference for certain types of voice in read-aloud pieces.	☐ Shows growing awareness of own voice and is beginning to control quality and strength of voice.
			☐ Often comments on voice in others' text/art: e.g., "That has voice," or "I want to hear that again."	☐ Can rate extent of voice in others' text/art.

FIGURE 8.11

Primary rubric for word choice.

Word Choice

Beginner	Borrower	Experimenter	Meaning Maker	Experienced Writer
☐ Scribbles.	☐ Borrows recognizable letter shapes from environment.	☐ Writes easy-to-read letters/numbers.	☐ Writes easy-to-read words.	☐ Uses vivid, expressive language.
☐ Creates letter "shapes."	☐ Labels pictures.	☐ Writes words with consonant sounds and some vowels.	☐ Writes with variety—dares to try new, less familiar words.	☐ Writes with vocabulary that may extend well beyond spelling ability.
☐ Uses favorite words in dictation.	☐ Uses titles on text.	☐ Writes decodable words/sentences.	☐ Loves descriptive words and phrases.	☐ Sometimes uses striking, unexpected phrases: *"I felt like a once contented and proud swan who lost its feathers."*
	☐ Creates letter strings that contain one- or two-letter words: *lk* (like), *dg* (dog), *hs* (house), *m* (my).	☐ Uses many simple, familiar words.	☐ Uses some strong verbs.	
		☐ Uses sight words frequently.	☐ Uses words to create images or add clarity, detail.	☐ Uses many strong verbs.
	☐ Chooses favorite words from read-aloud text.	☐ Has personal bank of favorite words.	☐ Keeps growing personal dictionary of meaningful words.	☐ Keeps extensive personal dictionary.
	☐ Repeats "comfort" (familiar) words in own text.	☐ Enjoys adding new words to text.	☐ Selects some "just right" words to express meaning.	☐ Repeats words only for emphasis/effect.
		☐ Adds new words to personal dictionary.	☐ Usually avoids repetition.	☐ Occasionally changes (revises) words to reflect preference.
		☐ Repeats some words.		

FIGURE 8.12 *Primary rubric for sentence fluency.* *Sentence Fluency*

Beginner	Borrower	Experimenter	Meaning Maker	Experienced Writer
☐ Dictates sentences. ☐ Enjoys poetry, rhythmic language.	☐ Creates letter strings that suggest sentences: **nohtipdin.** ☐ Writes text with a "sentence look" that may not be translatable. ☐ Dictates multiple sentences. ☐ Can hear rhythm, rhyme, and variety in read-aloud text. ☐ Can hear patterns—and may try imitating them.	☐ Writes letter strings that form readable sentences: **I lik skl.** (I like school.) **I HA DOG.** (I have a dog.) ☐ Writes more than one sentence. ☐ Usually writes sentences that complete a thought. ☐ Dictates a whole story or essay. ☐ Favors patterns: **I can pla. I can rid my bik. I can red.** (I can play. I can ride my bike. I can read.) ☐ Likes to repeat text read aloud with inflection.	☐ Consistently writes multiple sentences. ☐ Writes complete sentences. ☐ Creates easy-to-read text. ☐ Begins to show variety in sentence lengths, patterns, beginnings. ☐ May experiment with poetry—rhyming or free verse. ☐ May experiment with dialogue. ☐ Reads aloud with inflection.	☐ Can write two paragraphs or more. ☐ Consistently writes complete sentences. ☐ Creates text that sounds fluent read aloud. ☐ May use fragments for effect. **Wow! Crunch!** ☐ Creates text that is easy to read with expression. ☐ Often experiments with poetry/dialogue. ☐ Can read own/others' text aloud with inflection. ☐ Can combine sentences. ☐ May revise by changing word order or sentence length.

FIGURE 8.13 Primary rubric for conventions.

Conventions

Beginner	Borrower	Experimenter	Meaning Maker	Experienced Writer
☐ Does not use recognizable conventions in own text. ☐ Can point to conventions in print. ☐ Plays with letter or number shapes.	☐ Imitates print: letters, "cursive flow (eee)," punctuation marks. ☐ Writes own name. ☐ Writes one to several sight words. ☐ Loves to copy environmental print. ☐ Creates letters that face the right way. ☐ Can name/describe many conventions: e.g., period, capital, comma, question mark. ☐ Asks about conventions. ☐ Often writes left to right.	☐ Uses capitals and lower case—not ALWAYS correctly. ☐ Uses periods, question marks, commas, and exclamation points (often correctly). ☐ Puts spaces between words. ☐ Spells many sight words. ☐ Creates readable, phonetic versions of harder words. ☐ "Plays" with more difficult conventions: dashes, ellipses, quotation marks. ☐ Can name/describe numerous conventions. ☐ Shows concern for correctness in own text. ☐ Writes left to right.	☐ Uses capitals and lower case with fair consistency. ☐ Uses periods, commas, exclamation points, question marks correctly. ☐ Correctly spells ever-growing range of sight words and some challenging words. ☐ Uses some difficult conventions correctly: e.g., quotation marks, ellipses, dashes, parentheses. ☐ Gives some attention to correct format. ☐ Sometimes uses paragraphs. ☐ Makes corrections in own text. ☐ Writes left to right, notices margins.	☐ Uses wide range of conventions skillfully and accurately. ☐ Creates easy-to-read text with few errors. ☐ Uses paragraphs, often in the right places. ☐ Spells most sight words and many challenging words correctly. ☐ Uses conventions to reinforce voice/meaning. ☐ Is careful with layout and formatting. ☐ Consistently checks/edits own text for many conventions. ☐ Writes left to right and respects margins.

Meghan (Grade 2) checks for conventions with a spell checker. If she didn't, it might look something like this: "the berd flew awa" instead of "The bird flew away."
Photo and caption courtesy of Matthew (Grade 4).

4. Performance Over Time

Please note the blanks for checkmarks to the left of each performance indicator. You can use these to check any skill or observed behavior. There is no expectation that a child's writing will fall *fully* into one of the five performance levels described here—for example, "Beginner," "Borrower," "Experimenter," and so on. It is much more likely that a child will be quite high on the scale in some areas (perhaps ideas and voice) and not so high in others (perhaps conventions or fluency). Further, the levels are only approximations and cannot be more. Most writers will reflect some characteristics of one level and some of another. The purpose of the level descriptors is not to label children but to provide a convenient way of charting growth.

CLASSROOM ASSESSMENT: KEEPING IT SIMPLE

Not everything a child writes needs to be formally assessed. Sometimes a checkmark or a simple comment ("You did it!") is all that is needed. You certainly do not need to put yourself (or your students) through the task of assessing each piece of writing on each trait. You will all go crazy if you try it—guaranteed. And your first step to recovery will be to cut down on the amount of writing you do, and that benefits no one. So, instead, make a plan (it might look something like this):

✔ Assess a large portion of students' writing somewhat *informally*, using personal comments or a simple star (or other mark) to show completion of the task. You do not need a rubric for this.
✔ Teach *yourself* the traits so that you can spot them in your students' work.
✔ Use trait-related language to make your comments substantive and specific: "What remarkable word choice! Your voice is very clear in this piece!" and so on. If you know the traits, such comments will come easily to you.

✔ Help your student writers to identify strengths in their own work by showing them what to look for and by sharing literature that sharpens their listening skills.

✔ Encourage students to keep a file (call it a folder, collection, or portfolio) of written work and to select some pieces for inclusion throughout the year. Make sure that they are dated so that when you compare them, you can see growth.

✔ On three or four of those pieces, do a formal assessment using some or all of the six-trait rubrics for primary students. As you review each piece, check each of the indicators that seems to apply. Attach the rubrics to the sample and include it in the student's portfolio/writing collection.

✔ During parent conferences, invite parents to review their child's work and to look at the indicators you have marked. As the year goes on, invite parents to make comparisons and to see how many new skills their child has acquired. Using rubrics for this kind of comparison allows you to be specific instead of simply saying, "Notice how much Aisha has improved." If you cannot articulate the nature of the improvement, you need to look deeper.

✔ If you can make time, have an end-of-year conference with each of your young writers, reviewing one or more pieces of writing in light of the traits. You do not need to laboriously comment on every single skill the child is demonstrating but pick out four or five outstanding accomplishments, and let the child know what he or she is doing well as a writer. Also comment on specific areas of growth.

✔ Encourage students to create personal reflections commenting on their own views of themselves as writers. This reflection can take the form of a picture, picture and text, text alone, dictation, recording—or some combination of these.

✔ Present writing collections to children as important keepsakes, and encourage them to add future writings to those collections.

✔ Modify the rubrics as you identify potential strengths not yet noted.

THE DREADED GRADES!

Let's admit our feelings: We do not like grades much, especially when we are the ones receiving or giving them. No one I talk to—*ever*—likes grades. Everyone has the same comment: "I hate grades myself, but we have to have them because the _____ [fill in the blank to suit yourself—parents, administrators, students, school board members, businesspeople, employers, colleges, teachers at the next level] insist on them, so we have no choice." No choice? Well, this is not precisely correct. What we lack is a better alternative—for now.

Rubrics are a partial answer (and if done well, they provide infinitely more information than grades), but they only work if everyone uses them, understands them, and believes in them. Grades have an almost universal appeal (even among people who profess to hate them) because they are simple, deceptively so. They seem to tell so much—like fortune cookies. They are mysterious—and powerful. They appear to tell "the truth." In actuality, grades are overrated as authentic indicators of performance and frequently overvalued both by those who receive them and by those who hand them out. The danger lies in attaching *so* much weight to grades that we literally allow them to define who we are—as writers, learners, teachers, and people.

It takes a strong person to overcome this sort of labeling. As Strickland and Strickland remind us, "Grades don't define people in the real world outside of school. We could list several famous school failures who became successes—Einstein, Lincoln, Rockefeller.... We all know 'regular' people who are bright and overcame the odds, achieving more than their grades would predict. Unfortunately, not all [students] overcome such odds. Many believe what grades tell them and adjust their lives accordingly, giving up on themselves and their dreams" (2000, p. 125).

Despite their limitations and risks, though, grades carry with them the illusion of accuracy and thus are likely to be around for a while. Therefore, we must ask ourselves on what basis we should assign grades. No one can make this choice for you, but here are some suggestions you may find helpful for primary writers. Let me add that my recommendations would be decidedly different for older students. College-level writing is mostly about performance; primary-level writing is largely about participation, exploration, and growth. So the basis for grading must be different also, in my view.

Without suggesting percentages (i.e., 50 percent of the grade should be based on this or that), here are some factors to keep in mind in assigning grades:

- ✔ Actual performance
- ✔ Completion of work
- ✔ Participation in writing process
- ✔ Growth as a writer
- ✔ Willingness to branch out
- ✔ Coaching

Here's a quick look at each one; as you read through this section, ask yourself whether you do—or should—base a portion of your students' grades on each of these six factors.

1. Actual Performance

Look at some pieces in light of the traits, focusing particularly on strengths. *Kindergartners* write from the first day but may not (at first) create text (or pictures) that can be interpreted independently without the assistance of the writer. The early kindergarten writer may "read" his or her text immediately following completion but is often not able to do so a short time later. Nevertheless, even these very young writers have full understanding that marks on paper have meaning and significance. Many can create individual letters and connect some letters to sounds, yet much of the writing is likely to be random. Many can write their own names, names of family members or friends, and a few words of personal significance. They are likely to rely heavily on art to convey meaning. By the end of the kindergarten year, many are creating letter strings, moving into more phonemic spelling and including some sight words, and generating quite a lot of print that is meaningful to others.

First graders typically write numerous letters and some sight words. Many use letter-string sentences and, by the end of the year, may incorporate spacing and make enough letter-sound connections to spell or "create" most of the words they need to communicate. Most can write their names and words of personal significance: *mom, dog, cat, house, love, friend, school.* Spelling (except on simple sight words) may not be conventionally correct, but it is often phonetically close enough to allow most readers to make sense of the text without the writer's help. Many writers can read their work after writing, even when some time has passed. Some, however, cannot—or will place a slightly different spin on it. A close text-picture connection is common, and many first graders still rely heavily on pictures to create meaning. They are beginning to develop a sense of topic (as message) and of sequence. A few are attuned to their own personal voice—and most are highly attuned to voice in the work of others. Writing is expanding in terms of both actual length and depth of detail. First graders who write single sentences early in the year may well be writing multiple sentences and short paragraphs by year's end. Pictures are marked by increased attention to detail as well.

Second graders are moving toward independence, creating complete sentences, sometimes multiple sentences, and by the end of the year, full paragraphs (sometimes several paragraphs). They are gaining an increasing sense of topic or main idea, as well as an understanding of how details expand a main idea. They are beginning to make choices about how to write rather than writing "first thoughts." They choose words deliberately and have favorite words or phrases. They also like to choose topics. Most of their spelling is correct on familiar words and sight words or phonetically close enough to make for fairly

FIGURE 8.14   *Holiday pictures.* Taylor (1)

easy reading. Some are stretching constantly (especially with encouragement through reading) to include more difficult words. They still rely on pictures to express meaning, but their text is expanding in both length and complexity. Many are experimenting with dialogue and with poetry. Some have pronounced voice and write with a highly individual style. Attention to audience is increasing. Awareness of conventions is growing rapidly, and many are experimenting with an ever-growing range of punctuation marks.

Thirds graders write stand-alone text. That is, the writer does not need to interpret for the reader. Most can easily return to a previously written text and read it aloud. Many write multiple paragraphs. If it has been encouraged, personal voice may be quite strong. Vocabulary often runs well ahead of spelling skills unless spelling is overemphasized, and so expressiveness has grown markedly. Third graders also have a strong sense of topic and a deepened understanding of detail. Text is less repetitive, more informative. Expository writing may still be the favorite form for some, although many now have a sense of story (from text read aloud) and can create stories with beginnings, development of plot, and endings. Poetry is also a favorite form, especially among students with a strong sense of fluency or well-developed vocabulary. Many enjoy the free-verse form of poetry. Simple spelling and punctuation are well under control for many, and some experiment with sophisticated conventions: dashes, ellipses, parentheses, semicolons, and so on. Confident third grade writers will attempt spelling of difficult words and will not let spelling block expression. If use of art has been encouraged, third graders can create complex, highly detailed art that is not only expressive but also shows a strong attention to detail.

Use rubrics and your own checklists to capture these and other strengths important in your classroom.

■ *Differences*

These are simply guidelines, not hard and fast rules. Students do not necessarily move forward in the same way or at the same rate. Further, some children are highly imaginative or verbal; some are natural editors. We should allow for differences and expect them.

2. Completion of Work

At primary level, just completing the work—participating—is also important. You may wish to base a certain percentage of the grade on a student's simply writing, regardless of what that writing looks like.

FIGURE 8.15 *"If I Were a Flower."* Ellie (2)

If I Were A Flower

I was scared when I first bloomed. There were no other flowers. I can see a little bit of sky but all around me is snow. The snow was glittering like a diamond. It was very quiet. I was starting to feel sad and lonely because there are no other flowers and no friend or people to take care of me. Then I hear some thing. I do not know what it is. I look up and see someone who was moving the snow off of me. "Good Morning, Spring!"

3. Participation in Writing Process

Participation in writing process is a different consideration from the quality of the work per se. Participation is something you can only assess through careful observation and only over time. Overall, you are looking for such things as prewriting (through conversation, drawing, listing, thinking, reading/listening), sharing writing, offering or receiving suggestions, participating in a conference (with you or a peer), revising (even if it is just adding one detail to a picture or putting in one new word—this counts!), editing (even if it is only adding a forgotten name or date to a paper), or participating in group writing activities. Listening is a form of participation, too. Children are not all noisy, and reflective learners need to be rewarded along with the talkers. In addition, growing awareness that writing is developed through a process should be honored.

4. Growth as a Writer

This will be simple to measure if you keep writing folders/portfolios. It will be very difficult if you do not. Do *not* rely on your memory, no matter how well you think you know your students and their work. You need multiple samples, dated, and you need to look at them *with rubrics in front of you*. When you identify specific differences, you have documented growth, and at this level, when growth is the fundamental goal we want for our students, we certainly should allow it to influence our grading. Be careful, though! Do not base the whole grade on *how much* growth you see. For some students, the rate of growth will be phenomenal, whereas for others, little victories must make us rejoice. So, while amount of growth is significant, do not be afraid to reward the *presence* of growth as well. For some students, a little step forward (e.g., putting spaces between words) *is* big.

5. Willingness to Branch Out

In the real world of writers, risk taking is usually rewarded. Safe, functional, voice-free writing may win a polite nod of approval, but it will not get you published (except, perhaps, in government reports, where voiceless writing, like dead seaweed on the beach, is so common that no one thinks about it). It is never too early to teach this important lesson. Risk taking—in the sense of trying something new—takes many forms. A student may be experimenting with a different kind of writing (poetry or directions or a brochure or news article), trying out new words, or new kinds of punctuation, using multiple pictures to illustrate a story or expository piece, writing a first letter, or whatever. To some extent, this experimentation is reflected in the rubrics, but if you feel that the rubric does not go far enough, give more credit.

6. Coaching

Students learn much about writing from coaching others. A good coach does not have to be an expert writer. Above all, a good coach only needs to be a good listener and an enthusiastic responder. If you routinely pair students for writing activities, you make it easy for them to fulfill this role, and you provide another means for them to gain writing skills even when they are not actually writing themselves.

In Summary

My preference is to focus heavily on participation and growth for young writers versus performance per se. Performance changes so rapidly and so much at this age that it is hard to get hold of what we are assessing. It is like mercury. We need to pay attention to it, but not so much for the purpose of grading as to help students see what they are doing *well*. Your comments at this age are much more important than grades.

WHAT YOU CAN DO

Assessment discussions always seem to focus on the people being assessed. What about you, the assessor, though? What can you do to improve assessment within your classroom? Many things. Here's a beginning list:

1. Make *sure* that you have a very clear vision of success for your classroom. If you were a student writer in your own class, would you know *exactly* what you had to do to be successful? Could you express it in your own words? Can your students do so? If they can't, you haven't made the vision clear yet. Start right there.

2. Use rubrics to share your vision of success and to keep your own assessment consistent. Start with the rubrics in this book, but if they do not cover everything you value or if you need to reword something, by all means make the necessary changes. Rubrics are tools, not holy writ. Revise. A word of caution, though: A rubric with vague language is like mindless advice—"Be cool," "Stay out of trouble," "Take care." It says nothing. Make sure that your rubric says something. Picture a puzzled student reading (or hearing) your rubric and saying, "Oh, I get it." Picture a parent doing the same. If you can picture this, odds are that your rubric is clear and complete.

3. Share your vision of success with parents and with children. Use a common language to talk about writing performance so that everyone knows what the target is and can aim for it.

4. Make your writing curriculum clearly and indisputably connected to everything you assess so that your students have every chance to perform successfully. Do not assess what you do not teach.

5. Check for significance. Is everything you assess truly valuable? In other words, are you targeting significant skills, such as including details or organizing information, versus more superficial qualities, such as centering a title on the page or making margins wide enough?

6. Become very familiar with the performance standards for writing (and other content areas, of course) in your state. Look for the links to the six traits described in this book. You will find some because, as I point out in every workshop, the traits are just descriptors of basic good writing, nothing more. Do not be misguided by shifting terminology: *wording* is still word choice, *style* is often a mix of voice and fluency, *mechanics* are conventions, *design and structure* are organization, and so on. Do not expect precise parallels, but look for connections. They will give you confidence that your trait-based instruction is standards-based, too.

7. Do not assess *everything* your students write. It is not necessary or productive. In fact, it is a misuse of rubrics, in my view. Rubrics offer guidance.

Once they are internalized, your students will think—always—of voice, detail, leads, and the rest. You do not need to reinforce this writer's way of thinking with a constant barrage of scores. My friend Ann is a Scottish folk dancer, and she dances competitively—sometimes. And now and then she turns the Celtic music up so high that it rocks the timbers, and she dances for the sheer joy it puts in her soul. Writing needs to be like that, too.

8. Remember that a rubric, in the sense of a guide, really has three parts:
   - ✔ The written rubric that defines performance
   - ✔ Models of writing (including your own writing, of course) that show what performance looks like at those levels
   - ✔ Your own good teacher judgment and experience, the filter through which criteria work

   Use all the parts. Do not rely just on a written document.

9. Practice assessing your students' work. Practice until you feel confident that you are hearing moments of voice and fluency that you might have overlooked before. Practice until you know with *certainty* that you can offer the kinds of comments that will let your students know what they have done well and what they need to work on. Be a good responder. Make your comments respectful, insightful, and interesting.

10. Make self-assessment the goal of your writing program, thereby making students partners in the assessment process. Do not expect to get there in a week or even a month. But do expect that by the end of their time with you, your students will be able to look at a piece of their own work and say something like, "I really put a lot of voice in this." Expect that they will, eventually, apply such self-assessments with confidence and insight *regardless of your response to the writing.*

11. Keep portfolios/folders/collections of writing. Call them what you will. Keep them as small and manageable as you need to. But do keep samples of performance from throughout the year so that you can record growth. Nothing helps a parent or a student writer develop perspective better than to see where the journey began and how far the writer has come.

12. Keep your expectations high. As Mem Fox says, "If you don't have the highest expectations, how do you know you're not underestimating what your students can do? If you don't reach for the stars, you might be killing potential" (1993, p. 165). At the same time, though—

13. Allow students to screw up now and then. A welcoming, nurturing, successful classroom does not demand perfection from student writers at all times. I once knew a principal who would allow no work to be hung on the walls until it was conventionally perfect. (He did not mention voice or ideas, though.) Odd as it seems to some people, demanding perfection can squelch success. Why? Because it stifles effort. It rewards sameness, not growth. Growth requires trial efforts and a few misses. When students live and write in an environment that encourages effort, they dare to stretch—they dare to risk failure. Eventually, those who dare take off and soar.

14. Voice your view. Be heard. Write to or visit your state department of education, your district administrators, your school board, or legislature. Discuss ways of assessing students well and equitably. Bring samples of writing with you. Express what you value. Ask them to state clearly what it is they are looking for—and to offer their own samples of what that should look like.

Express clearly how vital it is to back standards or rubrics with models of performance so that expectations are clear and more achievable.

15. Provide practice. Most of the time, our classroom focus should be on helping students become lifelong writers and readers, yes. But so long as state testing is a reality (and for most of us, this might as well be forever), we need to offer students a lifeline. It is OK to explain that this is *a special situation.* "Writing for the test" is a genre unto itself. And because large-scale assessment is kind of a hurry-up process, you need to think fast, and you need to react. This is why you have to practice. Let your students know that you want them to feel ready so that the day of the test will be more comfortable. You might even try teacher Andrea Dabbs' very slick idea of making test day celebrational. She cooks breakfast for her students.

16. Be part of a writing community. Participate. Let students hear, read, and assess your work, too. Hear, read, and assess the work of other writers outside your classroom as well. Assessment never falls so heavy as when it falls only on you (the student). Let your students know that all writers are assessed, one way or another, whether by a state test or by a publishing house. It is part of the process. It does not feel so scary when you are not alone.

17. Think beyond conventions. Don't be afraid to display your students' work under a banner that reads "A Celebration of Our Voices" or "Listen to Our Fluency." Like Katie (Figure 8.16), let the flowers bloom.

FIGURE 8.16   *Katie's flowers (K).*

CHAPTER 8 IN A NUTSHELL

- Assessment is not about making judgments; it is about discovery and learning. In the case of writing assessment, we assess to discover who our students are and to learn what makes writing work so that we can teach more effectively.

- Assessment occurs on three levels: large-scale, classroom, and personal (self-assessment). Of these three, large-scale assessment receives the most attention, but personal assessment has the most impact when it comes to shaping writers.

- Large-scale assessment has definite limitations and poses a number of risks for use with primary students. It is important for us to question whether the results we receive from such assessments yield an accurate picture of primary students' performance.

- At the same time, large-scale writing assessment, when well constructed, can provide useful information about older writers, those with sufficient fluency and comfort with writing to create extended, meaningful, detailed text under time constraints.

- In cases where large-scale assessment is a given, we can offer students lifelines: teaching for lifelong learning, diminishing stress as much as possible, having a "prompt day" for practice, encouraging personal forms of prewriting, practicing timed writing.

- Like large-scale assessment, use of performance standards offers some real benefits when applied carefully and reviewed often. Standards keep us focused on what we hope our students will achieve and also encourage discussion about writing.

- Student performance in writing (or any area) is highly dependent on a clear vision of success. Rubrics help support such a vision. They cause us to be consistent and honest about our expectations.

- The primary-level rubrics included in this book are intended for classroom use and have several features specific to primary writing: inclusion of art, focus on descriptors rather than numbers, inclusion of behaviors (not just products), and focus on performance over time.

- Assessment looks a little different in each classroom, but some key indicators can help determine whether assessment is working as it should; for example, much of students' work is assessed informally (completion versus a grade), trait language (writers' language) is used by both teacher and students, assessment is based on a body of work and includes consideration of growth over time.

- Grades can be misleading and can be overvalued as indicators of performance. Unlike criteria on a rubric, they are seldom backed by language that defines meaning. Grades used as rewards encourage students to work for the grade, not for the joy of performing well.

- Given that grades are often a required part of the educational process, we must carefully consider what to base them on. Possibilities include actual performance, completion of work, participation in the writing process, growth as a writer, willingness to try new things, and willingness to serve as a writing coach for others.

EXTENSIONS

1. Compare the primary-level rubrics in this chapter with those developed for older students (in the Appendix). What similarities and differences do you see? What would happen if primary students were assessed using the rubrics designed for older writers? What are the implications for assessment data gathered through such practice?

2. Do you have a clear vision of success for your classroom? Write it out—as a paragraph, bulleted list, or whatever. If you can include student samples with it, so much the better.

3. Rate yourself, right now, on how well your students know your vision of success:

   ✔ _____ Extremely well. They could express it in their own words.

   ✔ _____ Somewhat. They have a general idea what I'm looking for.

   ✔ _____ Not at all. Grades are a surprise. They do not know what I expect.

   If either of the second two bullets describes your classroom, list some things you could do to clarify your vision.

4. Is your vision of success clear to parents as well? If not, what could you do to improve this situation?

5. What, in your view, are the most important elements to include in grading primary writers? Make a list. Compare your list with the one recommended in this chapter. Would you eliminate some of the recommendations listed here? Would you add other things? What are your reasons for doing so?

6. This chapter recommends keeping folders/portfolios of student work so that assessment can be based on a body of work rather than on individual samples. What are the advantages of this practice? Do you feel that it leads to more accurate assessment of what young student writers can do?

7. Make a list comparing assessment practices within the classroom to those used in large-scale writing assessment. What similarities or differences do you see? What specific features of each could help us to do a better job of assessing in the other context?

8. This chapter makes an argument that large-scale assessment may not be appropriate at primary level—for several reasons. Do you agree or disagree? Put your thoughts on paper and/or hold a discussion of this issue with colleagues. What particular concerns emerge? Are there ways of making large-scale primary-level writing assessment more effective, accurate, or less threatening to students? If not, should the practice be discontinued?

9. Teacher Minnie Hutchison suggests that, as educators, we are often so concerned with "having something to post on the wall" that we forget to focus on the *process* of writing. Do you agree with the practice of including writing process in grading the writing of primary students? Discuss this issue with one or more colleagues, and list some advantages/disadvantages of focusing on process as well as product when assigning grades.

10. Assessment specialist Rick Stiggins emphasizes (in *Student-Involved Classroom Assessment*) how much stress alone can influence student performance. Has this ever happened to you? Share assessment stress stories with colleagues. Then list some ways of minimizing stress in your classroom.

11. It is now a given in most teachers' minds that state-level assessments will, at least to some degree, influence classroom curriculum and practice. Should they? What are the potential benefits (if any)? What are the potential risks (if any)?

SOURCES CITED

Calkins, Lucy McCormick. 1994. *The Art of Teaching Writing*, revised edition. Portsmouth, NH: Heinemann.

Fox, Mem. 1993. *Radical Reflections*. New York: Harcourt Brace.

Gantos, Jack. 1998. *Jack's Black Book*. New York: Farrar, Straus and Giroux.

Hillocks, George, Jr. 2002. *The Testing Trap: How State Writing Assessments Control Learning*. New York: Teachers College Press.

Hutchison, Minnie. Personal interview with a teacher at the Thurgood Marshall School, Newark, DE, April 23, 2002.

Routman, Regie. 2001. *Conversations*. Portsmouth, NH: Heinemann.

Spandel, Vicki. 2001. *Creating Writers*, 3d edition. New York: Addison Wesley Longman.

Steele, Bob. 1998. *Draw Me a Story*. Winnipeg, Manitoba, Canada: Peguis Publishers.

Stiggins, Richard J. 2001. *Student-Involved Classroom Assessment*, 3d edition. Upper Saddle River, NJ: Merrill/Prentice-Hall.

Strickland, Kathleen and James Strickland. 2000. *Making Assessment Elementary*. Portsmouth, NH: Heinemann.

Thomason, Tommy, and Carol York. 2000. *Write on Target: Preparing Young Writers to Succeed on State Writing Achievement Tests*. Norwood, MA: Christopher-Gordon Publishers.

Tucker, Marc, and Judy B. Codding. 1998. "Commentary: Raising Our Standards for the Standards Movement." *Education Week* (February 18):56.

Making Magic Happen

Ana loves the softness of the donkey and the way he responds to her: "I like the ears because they move back and forth."

HOW DO YOU SEE IT?

What would a successful writing classroom look like—in your vision of things? Would the room be very neat and orderly—or a little chaotic? Would it be quiet or a bit on the noisy side? What would you be doing? Sitting at a desk, roaming the room, modeling at the overhead, curling up in a corner reading aloud to students gathered around you on the floor—or all these things at different times? Would students be at individual desks, in groups, or at tables? Picture your walls. What's on them? Picture your book shelves or book racks. Do you have a few books? A lot? Are they displayed with the covers showing? Is there artwork on display? Does student work mingle with the work of professionals—or do you keep them distinct? What's the lighting like? If I walked in spontaneously one day, what would I hear? Music? Your voice? A tape of an author reading? Students talking? One student sharing writing?

The golden rule of writing is to write what you care about.

—Jerry Spinelli
As quoted in Laura Benson, "A Writer's Bill of Rights" (2002, p. 17)

If you don't have clear expectations, how can your students know what to aim for? If you don't have the highest expectations, how do you know you're not underestimating what your students can do? If you don't reach for the stars, you might be killing potential.

—Mem Fox
Radical Reflections (1993, p. 165)

Writing is predominantly learned rather than taught.

—Janet Emig
In Tommy Thomason and Carol York, *Write on Target: Preparing Young Writers to Succeed on State Writing Achievement Tests* (2000, p. 1)

Children will remember only a fraction of what they learn in your classroom. However, when you empower them to express their views through writing, they continually will seek out new knowledge and have the tools for lifelong learning.

—Melissa Forney
Dynamite Writing Ideas (1996, p. 6)

There are no right answers to these questions, of course. Teachers work in a wide variety of ways, and the magic of teaching is a highly personal thing. One thing is for certain, though: The magic comes from within, from who you are. This is why I begin this chapter by asking you to visualize the environment within which you teach because it is an extension of yourself. The way you arrange your room, where you put your desk (if you have one), how you group students, how you schedule activities, whether your teaching is meticulously planned or pretty spontaneous or a mix of the two—it is all *you*. And when you enter a classroom, you get a feeling for whether things are clicking. Although every classroom has its own look and feel, there are some commonalities among those where students are truly becoming writers. In *Teaching the Youngest Writers*, Marcia Freeman (1998, p. xvii) talks about some of the things she looks for, among them—an "environment conducive to writing," writer's workshop at a regular time each day so that children expect it, teachers and students (even the youngest) using "writer's vocabulary," targeted lessons designed to teach specific skills, an evaluation process owned and understood by teachers and students, a place to keep portfolios, and parent involvement.

This is a pretty good list. To this I would add just some small things I have noticed in those classrooms where it seems to be working—by which I mean children are writing and loving it, and children are sensing and seeing their own growth as writers. The first is that student writers' work is celebrated and honored either through portfolios or through displays of some kind. Those displays might include less-than-perfect work; they feature art, voice, ideas—the more personal side of writing. Second, the room is filled with books. Maybe I care about this so much because when I was a young writer, our classrooms held mostly basals, dictionaries, and encyclopedias—and a book you'd read for fun was a treasure. Third, if you just popped in unannounced, you likely would see and hear children talking. Not that there isn't time for silence (or something approaching it), but writers need to share and ask for help. They also need to read their work aloud; it gets noisy sometimes. You can tell the difference between a productive hum and chaos, though. Fourth, when I visit a classroom, students who are writers and readers themselves usually assume that I am a writer and a reader, too. They ask me to share writing, even before I suggest it; they ask if I have brought books with me; and they show me things they are working on. The significance of this kind of behavior is that it shows they consider themselves part of a writing community. And fifth—this is most important—they do not have automatic reactions. If I share a student paper or piece of my own writing or a book they do not think is particularly good, they say so—in a polite way, of course. As one student said to me, "The last part of your paper just wasn't quite as good as the first." I value this kind of honesty, and hope you do too, because it shows how good evaluation skills take students off autopilot and make them critical thinkers. Six-trait writing is, above all, a model for encouraging thinking skills.

There is one more thing to keep in mind as you put your own vision for success together: A nurturing writing environment always encourages risk. As Linda Crafton says, "Playing it safe is a dead end when it comes to language and learning" (Crafton in Thomason and York, 2000, p. 3). If your students do not feel safe trying new topics and new forms of writing and writing in a way no one else has before, they can—make no mistake—still plod along at a functional level. But nothing truly exciting will happen. Comfort with risk has a side benefit, too: "Students whose workshop environment has made them comfortable with risk-taking and comfortable with writing and unafraid of failure have a definite advantage when they sit down to respond to the state's writing prompt" (Thomason and York, 2000, p. 3). Confidence is half the battle.

Although there is no one path to success, it's always helpful, I think, to see what other successful teachers of writing are doing to make magic happen in their classrooms. It is impossible, of course, to capture everything in a book. But in these few vignettes I will try to give you a glimpse of successful teaching in some different and highly original forms. Maybe you will see a glimmer of yourself, or maybe you have your own way of making the magic happen.

IN ARLENE'S CLASSROOM

Arlene Moore, who has been my friend, colleague, and inspiration for many years, teaches a K–1 class at Lincoln Elementary in Mt. Vernon, Washington. Arlene tells every child that he or she is a writer right from the first day. Some children do not believe it—at first. Arlene shows them how to make simple writing-like marks on paper and asks them to imitate her. She invites them to write any letters or numbers they know, and she also asks them to create pictures. Many are surprised that this is accepted as a form of writing. But, as Arlene says, "I am interested to see what they *can* do. We build confidence first."

FIGURE 9.1   *"Dog" (K).*

This is where we begin—with the belief that all children can write.

—Arlene Moore

In Spandel, *Creating Writers* (2001, p. 266)

Like virtually all teachers, Arlene gets some students who do not want to write. As one young writer told her, "I can't write, and I won't." Arlene squatted close to the ground, very near, and whispered, "In this class, everyone writes. We all write. Me, too." His eyes widened. His excitement at having a teacher who would also write eclipsed his own fears, and from that day, he did write. Not much at first, but he wrote.

Arlene writes almost daily with her students, and she asks for their help as coaches. They suggest words, details, beginnings and endings, and titles. As she reads her writing, she listens for their suggestions. During this kind of activity, she is the one making the marks on paper, but they are doing much of the thinking. This prepares them for the personal writing they do, which for many is a word or two, a letter string, or a single sentence. But in their minds, through Arlene's voice and her pen, they compose volumes. Gradually, the words and the sentences on their papers grow, too.

FIGURE 9.2 *"Friends" (K).*

The magic in Arlene is easy to spot. She loves, truly loves, *lives* in fact, to hear what her students will write next. She is unfailingly energetic and enthusiastic about their writing. She listens with her whole body, her whole face, her whole being. She responds with her body language, her voice, her expression, and her comments. Her students write because they have an audience who never tires of their writing and who finds wonder in their words, their expressiveness, their willingness to try. Moreover, she is one of them. She is a writer. Nothing impresses a student so much as a teacher who will do what she or he is asking: "To be a teacher of writing, first and foremost, write. Engage in the journey you ask your students to take every day" (Laura Benson, 2002, p. 24).

Arlene is an ardent believer in teaching trait language to even the youngest students, who, she maintains, pick it up "much faster than we do ourselves." She loves to tell the story of one of her 6-year-old students who was listening to her mother read and, totally caught up in the book, turned to her mother and said, "Do you *hear* the voice? Don't you *love* the voice in this book?" No worksheet in the world can take a child to this level of understanding.

 ## IN PENNY'S CLASSROOM

Penny Claire teaches second grade, and effectively, gracefully blends art with writing to maximize her students' creativity and expressiveness. The magic in Penny's classroom comes from her ingenious ability to use art both as a strategy for stimulating thinking and as a complement to writing—an extension of students' writing, really. As Penny's students draw, they begin to visualize, and

FIGURE 9.3   *"Yesterday we went tide pooling."* Brian (2)

> Brian.
>
> Yesterday we went tide pooling.
> I cot a crab. when I pict it up
> it scuteld on my hand. I fuawnd a
> shrimp. I trided to catch it but it
> swam away. After that we had lunch.
> Then we went to the touch tank. I picke
> d up a sea urchen.

FIGURE 9.4   *"On the gentle coast of Africa."* Kevin (2)

On the gentle coast of Africa all is quiet.
Nothing but the drifting waves is heard. The sun
is rising. It looks like a piece of gold is lifting
above the turquoise sea. Crabs scurry from their
tiny holes.

through that visualization, they expand their sense of meaning and the details that might not otherwise have appeared in their text. As they write, they think of more ways to enrich the art. And so it goes, each form feeding the other.

When she speaks of the importance of students' engaging in art, Penny becomes quite passionate, noting that art is not always given the credibility and respect of text-based writing: "[So many] teachers are not doing [original writing] with their children as much and are doing more prompts. Kids need art to pre-plan, organize, elicit details, sequence, allow plot to build and unfold, develop confidence, and . . . well, I could go on and on!"

In one of Penny's lessons on Africa (her approach to teaching is quite consistently thematic), students read and hear about life on the Serengeti Plains and use their facts and the mental images those readings conjure up to begin drawing. "They begin to understand and picture what animals in that biome look like—prey and predator—and a story between two animals at a waterhole emerges. Based on facts, the child fictionalizes characters and does a storyboard. Not a word has been written, but the story is planned, researched, and bursting to come out!" Art, Penny maintains, results in excitement—students "bursting" to write and to tell stories. "This, I believe, is how social studies and science can be taught well." Writing reinforces understanding of content areas (see Figures 9.3, 9.4, and 9.5); it is the foundation for thinking and making sense of the content. It also gives young writers information to inform their writing. As Melissa Forney notes, "Written communication is the key to self expression and the platform for knowledge. If you teach good writing skills first, those skills will benefit kids in every content area. Teachers who tack writing on last are robbing kids of their most valuable tool" (1996, p. 6).

FIGURE 9.5 *"On the rockey beche."* Kevin (2)

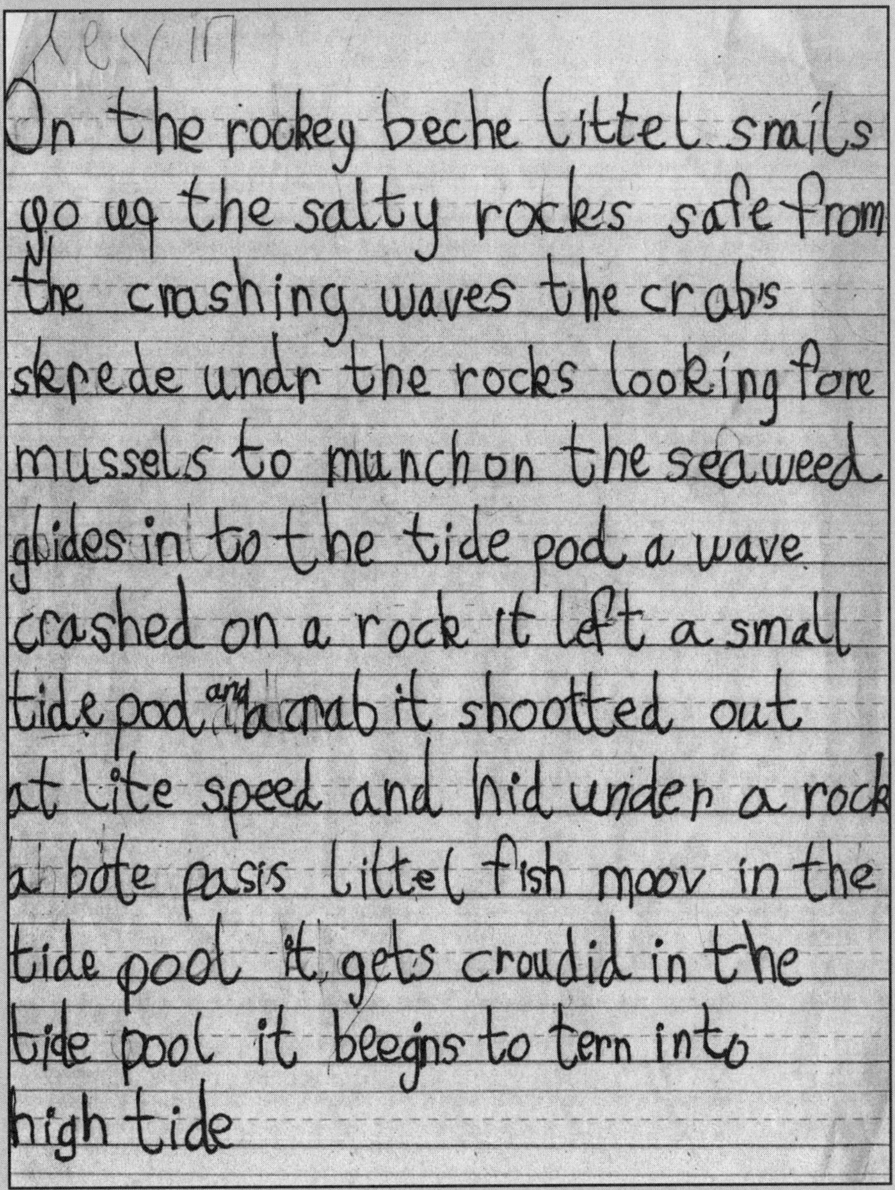

Kevin

On the rockey beche littel smails go up the salty rockes safe from the crashing waves the crabs skpede undr the rocks looking fore mussels to munch on the seaweed glides in to the tide pool a wave crashed on a rock it left a small tide pool and a crab it shootted out at lite speed and hid under a rock a bote pasis littel fish moov in the tide pool it gets croudid in the tide pool it beegins to tern into high tide

Emphasis on Personal/Informational

As both Arlene and Penny (and many other teachers) have discovered, all-about and other informational papers, especially those based on personal experience, are easier for many young students to write than are stories. The notion that storytelling is simple is a myth. To create a true plot with characters who face problems or adventures and come out on top (or not) is exceedingly difficult, and unless the story is based on a real-life event, the writing often dissolves into madcap fantasy or a simple listing of events.

Sometimes, when a student is allowed to write "About My Cat" (see Figure 9.6) rather than forcing information into a *story* of the cat, the writing tends to be more fluid, more authentic, and more detailed. Marcia Freeman suggests that most children "love to tell what they know.... Their natural mode of writing is informational expository: *I love my dog; This is me; I saw a fish.* What they communicate is information that is important to them" (1998, p. x). She goes on to point out that personal informational writing (based on reading, conversation, and firsthand experience) is the "emergent writer's first and natural mode" and "the easiest and best place to begin writing instruction" (1998, p. 94). This is a concrete form of informational writing, quite unlike a more abstract mode, such as persuasive writing, in which the writer must foresee consequences of particular paths of action and compare this path to that. Such writing demands sophisticated predictions,

FIGURE 9.6   *"I have a Cat."*

I have a cat. It is realy cute I think. She is really hairy. She sheds all over the couch. That is why I uashuly sit on the other couch. My cat is a girl. Well it is really the familys cat. She is really lazy. She justs moapes around the house like she is a queen. Are cat is really picky. She only eats some sort of food. She wines alout because she wants to go out side or som thing. In the winter it is really bad. She wants to go out side then she wants to come back in because she dosint want to go in the snow. When I am takeing a bath she come in on th side of the tub and I drip water off of my finger and she licks it up. Sometimes she drinks out of the dogs water bowl. The dog chases the cat all around the house. Oh in case your wondering our cats name is Misty. So, the dog uasly trys to pounce on the cat. My cat jumps on a chair so the dog doesint get her. Misty is a lazy cat. In the summer she chases mice and try's to catch birds. One time she was gone for 7 days. We were worried. Are grandfathe searched for her but he coudint find her. One day she came back. We were so glad to see her. She was holding a mouse in her mouth. I bet she did more than that though. That cat wounders me.

By David, Grade 3

Andy discovers that kittens are more than cuddly: "The claws are poking me! OUCH! One is looking right at me. . . ."

evaluations, and inferences for which primary students may not be ready (Piaget, in Freeman, 1998, p. 94).

Call It What It Is

Marcia Freeman makes the point that it is important to call informational writing (or any writing) by its correct name (1998, p. 95). You can simply call it an informational piece or your piece, your writing, your paper. Do not, however, refer to informational pieces as "stories"—for example, "Bring your story to the author's chair"—unless, of course, the piece *is* a story. This is confusing to students, who often refer to their own writing, regardless of mode, as "my story." Later, this global definition of all writing as stories can prove hard to unteach and can cause student writers to try organizing everything chronologically. It can also make it difficult for many to look at a piece of writing and to state whether it is informational, persuasive, or narrative in form. As one student told me, "If it has the word 'I' in it, it's a story—that's how you know." How confusing and misleading such a definition is. In fact, stories tell what happened from a personal perspective; expository writing gives information. Pronouns have nothing to do with it. The two forms can blend, though, and often do in good writing as students use what they know to

---

FIGURE 9.7

"The Game." Conor (3)

> 3/12/02   The Game ♥
>
> Yells and shouts.
> There are no doubts.
> He shoots he scores.
> The crowd roars.
> The exciting game is tied.
> To win the game, the players tried.
> In the locker room, the coach gives a speech.
> I don't want you day dreaming about being on the beach.
> Five seconds left on the clock.
> It keeps on chanting tick tock tick tock.
> He zips down the court during the fast break.
> He gets to the three point line the shot he takes.
> It glides through the air.
> The buzzer rings, the shot makes it there.
> They shouted, they screamed.
> The coaches gleamed.
> They won the game, and now they have fame.

enrich the telling of an experience. Notice how Conor uses his knowledge of basketball to recount the poetic story of a team's victory (see Figure 9.7). A similar combination occurs in Frances' recollection of her role as the Tin Man in *The Wizard of Oz* (see Figure 9.8). Although much of her writing is narrative, it is not really a story as such. Rather, it is an explanation of how exciting and "nervraking" performing can be, flavored by personal examples. Dylan's paper on Berry

FIGURE 9.8 *"The Wizard Of Oz."* Frances (3)

The Wizard Of Oz

My favorite thing to do is drama. Last summer year 2001 I was in a Play. It was the play of the Wizard Of Oz.. When we did the audions I got picked as the Tin Man. My teacher, Rachel handed out scrips. I had a lot of lines. My brother was the Scarcrow. The Scarcrow, Tin Man, Lion, and Dorathy did scenes together, so I got to know them. But one day I came in with crutches. I had to be the tin man on crutches. I maneged to do it. I was happy because my aunt and uncle came from England. So did my American neigbour. After the show I got a present. Later we went for dinner. It was a good day. I love drama. It is also nervraking because it's a big hall with more the 100 people watching. I love drama. it is my favorite thing to do and I'm good at it!

FIGURE 9.9 *"My favorite gift."* Dylan (2)

Writing Prompt

Think of the best gift you ever received. Tell about receiving that gift. Be sure to include enough detail in your writing so that your reader will understand why the gift was special to you.

My favorite gift I ever got is my teddy bear named Berry. I have had Berry for 6 years. Berry reminds me of when I was a baby. He looks a little funny but I still love him. The color of his fur is brown. I got him from my mom and dad. I put him under the covers of my bed because I have two brothers that might steal him. I also put him in my closet. Sometimes I wrap him around my neck. Berry is very soft and cute. I think Berry is the best bear in the world.

(see Figure 9.9) is mostly description, with hints of narrative. Dylan also uses what he knows, what is close to the heart.

IN MINNIE'S CLASSROOM

Minnie Hutchison teaches writing and art to students in grades 1 through 4. She considers personal experience vital as a foundation for writing or art and also encourages her students to expand what they know through research. Just as Penny Claire has discovered how much art feeds the writing process, so Minnie has discovered how much knowledge influences an artist's response to the world. Art is not just expressiveness, after all (although this is one important element); it is also a way of encouraging thoughtful observation and details that can breathe life into our work.

To this end, Minnie weaves lessons in PE or music into her instruction in art and writing. "We might just watch how bodies move, for example," she explains. When you know what the movement looks like, your pictures capture that detail. When her students were working on a cave unit, they observed animal motions by "stalking an animal" and watching how the legs and body moved in coordination. Minnie is a great believer in integrated lessons, which, she says, make more sense to children because the real world is not divided into separate discrete experiences—art one minute, writing the next, math the next.

To see how much knowledge can influence art, look at the photograph in Figure 9.10. You will see two sets of owl figures done by two different groups of students at Thurgood Marshall School. The groups were given the same amount of modeling clay and asked to construct owl sculptures. The group on the left worked without benefit of any research. The group on the right had completed a WebQuest search on the Internet, looking up information about owls: the size of their eyes, the movement of their heads, the shapes and colors of their feathers, their large wing spread, and so on. As Minnie herself says, "I was truly amazed at the difference in the end products. The work done by the students who worked on the

FIGURE 9.10 *Art without WebQuest search (left) and with WebQuest (right).*

WebQuest shows character, creativity, enthusiasm, and a knowledge of their subject." We can expect to see similar differences any time students have a good foundation of knowledge to feed their writing.

What is the key to magic in Minnie's classroom? Providing a rich knowledge base from which to draw in creating writing or art is certainly part of it. There's more, though. Minnie freely admits, "I'm not neat. I think this helps my students be creative. I want them to love writing, and I'm very honest about that. You don't have to be quiet in my class, either. I like to feed off students' creativity. I'm strict about certain things—no meanness, no taking things, and no being rude to one another. Beyond that, I do everything I can to promote enthusiasm."

IN LOIS'S CLASSROOM

When I first met Lois Burdett (author of the *Shakespeare Can Be Fun* series), I was struck by the apparent modesty of someone so undeniably talented. Lois has rewritten several of William Shakespeare's plays in rhyming couplets and teaches them to her grade 2–3 class; they act out the plays and write in character about the situations in which they find themselves (see the "Sources Cited" at the end of this chapter for references).

Lois's students write with exuberance and detail, and so you have to ask her, "What's your secret? How do you make this happen?" This is what she shared with me, and all these factors (as I have seen for myself in her classroom) are significant:

1. Her students read and write a *lot*. Not all at once, but every day—and for quite a long time (perhaps 2 hours total). Lois reads excerpts from Shakespeare's plays (sometimes her version, sometimes the original) but many other things as well, including journal articles, letters, newspaper articles, and so on.

2. Students write in every subject area. Not all the writings are long. They might list steps for math problem solving or completing a science experiment or just jot down "The most important thing I just learned." They write poetry, observations, and numerous letters, and they write in character as people from Shakespeare's plays.

3. Students share their writing aloud. When one student found this difficult, Lois asked if he might share in a whisper in the corner. He agreed to whisper to himself, then, eventually, to just one other student, and then two. Within a month, he was reading in a subdued but normal tone of voice to a group of three.

4. Lois writes with her students and shares her writing. Writing for her is as natural as reading with her students.

5. Drama is a way of life in Lois's class. Her students have quiet study times, and when she reads, she asks them to listen ("I will listen to *you* when *you* read," she reminds them). But other times they are up on their feet, reciting lines from a play, interacting, moving, dancing, marching, making faces, using body language to give voice to a piece. It is exhilarating to watch.

6. Lois is not afraid to offer her young writers very specific suggestions for improvement, on everything from detail to putting spaces between words. She does so in a very positive way, as if sharing something invaluable she has

learned—a treasure. She calls her tips "writers' secrets." So she will say to one of her writers, "Would you like me to share a writer's secret?" Who can resist? She then offers one—*and only one*—bit of advice at a time: "Did you know that if you. . . ." The writer attempts this new approach (putting in spaces, adding details, using periods or paragraphs, starting sentences differently, finding another word for *very*) next time around.

7. Virtually every outstanding teacher I have known has used questions as a basis for expanding students' thinking and attention to detail. Lois is no exception. In her student conferences (which rarely last more than 2 to 3 minutes), she asks pertinent questions to which she really wants the answer. This is the difference. We can all think up questions, but we are not necessarily interested in the writer's response: "How old were you . . . ," "Where did you live . . . ," "What is your cat's name . . . ," blah, blah. When Lois asks a question, her eyes light up, and her whole face intensifies: "How did you know your hamster was dead?" "What was the most annoying thing your brother did at the party?" "How did you and your dad decide where to bury your cat?" Heartfelt questions produce heartfelt answers—answers with voice.

The real magic, though, I discovered one day as I was watching Lois's children act out the opening scene from Act 4 of *Macbeth*, in which the witches chant "Double, double, toil and trouble; / Fire burn and caldron bubble." Though three "witches" stirred the brew in a huge caldron Lois had brought to class for purposes of this drama, all 22 of her students were participating. They formed two large circles and were weaving their way round the caldron, one circle clockwise, one counterclockwise. "Put on your ugliest witch faces," Lois directed them. "Be fierce." They did, but of course, being second graders, when they looked at one another, they became hysterical and fell in one heap onto the floor, rolling with laughter. I was laughing myself. I couldn't help it. Lois brought us all to attention: "This scene is not supposed to be funny. Let's remember, Macbeth is about to get a message from the witches that spells doom for him. If you laugh, you'll make the audience laugh—and right now we want them a little frightened and full of anticipation, wondering what is going to happen. And by the way, speak up! That man in the last row of the theater can't even hear you." The "witches" shifted their mood. Their faces were more gruesome than ever, but this time, no one laughed. And when they spoke, their voices were clear and audible. These were actors, and they took their work seriously. Later, they wrote with the same intensity.

The magic is in Lois herself. Her love of words, her passion for theater, her uncanny gift to see each child's strength and bring it out, her belief that her students can do what many people would say second graders can't (second graders performing *Macbeth*?), her patience in finding a way for the child who dares do no more than whisper.

MAKING YOUR OWN MAGIC

The magic lies within you, too. "Some teachers are forever attending seminars and reading books and looking for the secret to writing well and loving it. If they could learn to write better, they reason, they would become writers. The secret keeps eluding them, because it isn't found in seminars or books. Even books about writing. Even this book" (Thomason, 1993, p. 5). I love Tommy's words because they remind us that the real magic does not lie in strategies or steps but within ourselves.

For real writing improvement to occur, we must do several things. We must

✔ Share our expectations (criteria for writing success) with students openly.
✔ Invite students to assist in creating classroom criteria so that they have ownership.
✔ Give more weight to performance over time than to individual performances.
✔ Feel good about moving forward in small steps when students are not ready to make giant leaps.
✔ Model good writing.
✔ Model the problems of a struggling writer—and possible solutions.
✔ Invite our students to be writing coaches.
✔ Provide strong and weak examples of writing and discuss them.
✔ Respect our students' opinions about what is or is not good writing.
✔ Ask students to assess and reflect on their own work.
✔ Invite parents to be part of the process by
   ✔ Sharing rubrics with them
   ✔ Showing how they can be good listeners for their students
   ✔ Focusing on growth in conferences
✔ Listen.
✔ Read.
✔ Write.
✔ Look at and value process, not just product.
✔ Teach ourselves to look deeper and closer within our students' work to find the smallest indicators of success.
✔ Offer meaningful concrete and specific suggestions (not "You need a different ending," but "Let me show you some ways I have found to end papers").
✔ Encourage our children to see themselves as writers, right from *day one.*

In the end, though, the greatest gift you can give to your young writers is yourself: Your willingness to "use yourself" as a good actor does when you read—to read with passion and total involvement. Your willingness to write—well or not so well—and to share not only your writing but also the process you are going through to create and your revision or even your hopelessness when the words will not come. Your ability to create a classroom community in which it is OK to fail sometimes as long as you never give up, where writing and reading are always encouraged and risk is applauded even when it does not go hand in hand with perfection. Your ability to listen, really listen, with your ears, eyes, whole body, and mind to every student writer who dares to share his or her work. Your energy when you are almost too tired to move, your continual expression of enthusiasm for your students' work so that they will know that they are not playing to an empty house. Your love of books, of writing, of words, of expression in any form—and do know that when you speak of your favorites, when you read, when you point to the pictures and hold your breath for a moment, your students will know immediately that your enthusiasm is genuine.

The only job I do, the only promise I make, the sole objective that I have is to guarantee safety.

—Nancy Slonim Aronie
Writing From the Heart: Tapping the Power of Your Inner Voice (1998, p. 122)

The traits give you a language—writers' language—for encouraging your students to think and to speak like writers. In the end, though, the traits are only what you make of them. If you are timid in your teaching, you cannot expect much to happen, no matter how many trait charts you post in your room. I observed a second grade teacher one day who wore the most elegant clothes of anyone in her school. Her hair was neatly coifed, and her makeup was impeccable. She stood tall and straight, with rigid and proper posture, every vertebra in line, feet neatly spaced, hands quiet, and voice muted and refined, reading without overtones or expression, turning the pages with silent precision. I couldn't tell you what the book was. The hum of her soft voice was so hypnotic that she might have been reading a bus schedule and I would not have known. Behind her was a poster on voice, neatly pinned to the wall, framed in colored paper, all the margins even. When she closed the book, she asked the students to define voice, and they did, carefully reciting each bulleted phrase from the poster. "The book we just read," she told them, "was an example of voice." They didn't question this. But I wondered—still wonder—if they equate voice with a low hum, a vaguely sleepy feeling, or flat-out monotony.

Do not be timid. To teach voice, write and speak with voice. Read as if your life depended on it. Laugh, cry, respond. Use the words you want to hear from your students. Be fluent yourself. Share your ideas, and speak and write with detail. When you return home at night, you'll feel good—until you look in the mirror. Your hair will be mussed, you may be missing a button or two, your clothes will be wrinkled, your shoes may be untied (or you may have lost one along the way). You may have lost other personal possessions as well (an earring, your favorite pen, loose change, keys, your lunch, your calendar), and it is likely that the only things you have for sure are a headache, tired legs, a favorite book, and the student papers to which you are clinging tightly. Laugh. Rejoice. This day has been a success. You are teaching with voice—which is to say, with your whole self. You are making magic.

Arlene Moore, one of the magic makers: "I love writing with my children—they love it, too. We make up songs about voice. We make up poems about organization. This is the age when little writers absorb words like sponges. They teach me every day."

CHAPTER 9 IN A NUTSHELL

- Our classrooms are extensions of ourselves—and reflect the kind of personal "magic" we put into our teaching.
- Each teacher has a slightly different take on what contributes to the magic—safety, sharing, books,

liveliness, opportunities to try what's new, art and music, or whatever.

- As important as the traits are, they are only a tool. In the end, the real magic comes from you—and from the students who teach you.

EXTENSIONS

1. Think of a teacher who made magic for you—primary grades through college. Who was this person? Write him or her a letter, even if you do not send it. Tell that teacher what he or she did to make the classroom come alive.

2. What is your vision of a successful classroom? Describe it. Make a list of key features. They might be physical features, or curriculum components, or characteristics of the atmosphere. Discuss your vision with those of colleagues.

3. In the final chapter of *Radical Reflections*, Mem Fox lists her "Concluding Ideals." These are the pledges she would make to herself in order to be the "excellent and effective" teacher she wants to be. What would your personal list of ideals look like? Get a copy of Mem's list (1993, pp. 162ff.) and read through it to get your thoughts flowing, but do not feel compelled to see yourself the same way. Make your list as individual as you can; then compare your ideals with those of your colleagues.

4. In teaching, the "magic" that happens in a classroom often lies as much within the teacher's personal approach as within any strategies or techniques that he or she uses. What personal qualities do you bring to your teaching that can strengthen your students' writing/reading skills? List them. How will you make use of them?

5. As depicted in this chapter, Arlene relies on confidence building, Penny on use of art to stimulate imagination, Minnie on integrated curriculum in which art plays a vital role, and Lois on drama combined with a healthy mix of writing and reading in all subject areas. Discuss the ways these various approaches interact with trait-based writing instruction. In other words, how does each teacher, in her own way, make use of the traits in teaching writing?

6. What is your favorite place within your own classroom? Draw a sketch of it or take a photograph. Why is it your favorite? Write a short paragraph or poem to go with your sketch that shows your feelings.

7. What is your favorite time of day in your classroom? What are you and the students doing? Describe it. Read your description aloud to your students.

8. Plan a poster-making project with your class. Remember, writing traits are best owned by any writer when that writer translates them into his or her own words. You do not need to do all the traits. Pick one or two to start with, and think of a way you could encourage your student writers to express their thoughts about that trait in words of their own. Plan to display or otherwise share the posters you create.

SOURCES CITED

Aronie, Nancy Slonim. 1998. *Writing From the Heart: Tapping the Power of Your Inner Voice*. New York: Hyperion.

Benson, Laura. "A Writer's Bill of Rights." *Colorado Reading Council Journal* 13 (Spring 2002):17–25.

Burdett, Lois. *Shakespeare Can Be Fun* (series including *Macbeth, Twelfth Night, Romeo and Juliet, The Tempest, Hamlet,* and others). Willowdale, Ontario,

Canada: Firefly Books (copyright dates vary by edition).

Forney, Melissa. 1996. *Dynamite Writing Ideas*. Gainesville, FL: Maupin House.

Fox, Mem. 1993. *Radical Reflections*. San Diego: Harcourt Brace.

Freeman, Marcia S. 1998. *Teaching the Youngest Writers*. Gainesville, FL: Maupin House.

Hutchison, Minnie. Personal interview with a teacher at Thurgood Marshall Elementary School, April 23, 2002.

Lane, Barry. 1993. *After THE END*. Portsmouth, NH: Heinemann.

Shakespeare, William. 1998. *Macbeth*, Signet Classic Edition. New York: Penguin (first folio edition of the play, 1623).

Spandel, Vicki. 2001. *Creating Writers*, 3d edition. New York: Allyn and Bacon/Longman.

Thomason, Tommy. 1993. *More Than a Writing Teacher: How to Become a Teacher Who Writes*. Commerce, TX: Bridge Press.

Thomason, Tommy, and Carol York. 2000. *Write on Target: Preparing Young Writers to Succeed on State Writing Achievement Tests*. Norwood, MA: Christopher-Gordon Publishers.

Six-Trait Rubric for Grade 3 and Up*

IDEAS

Ideas are the heart of the message: the main thesis, impression, or story line of the piece, together with the documented support, elaboration, anecdotes, images, or carefully selected details that build understanding or hold a reader's attention.

Score of 5. The paper is clear, focused, purposeful, and enhanced by significant detail that captures a reader's interest.

- ✔ The paper creates a vivid impression, makes a point, or tells a whole story without bogging down in trivia.
- ✔ Thoughts are clearly expressed and directly relevant to a key issue, theme, or story line.
- ✔ Information is based on experience or investigation of a topic and goes beyond common knowledge.
- ✔ Carefully selected examples, rich details, and/or anecdotes bring the topic to life and lend the writing authenticity.
- ✔ The reader is *not* left with important unanswered questions.

Score of 3. The writer has made a solid beginning in defining a key issue, making a point, creating an impression, or sketching out a story line. More focus and detail will breathe life into this writing.

- ✔ It is easy to see where the writer is headed, even if some telling details are needed to complete the picture.
- ✔ The reader can grasp the big picture but yearns for elaboration.
- ✔ General observations and common knowledge are as plentiful as insights or close-up details.
- ✔ There may be too much information; it would help if the writer would trim the deadwood.

- ✔ As a whole, the piece hangs together and makes a clear general statement or tells a recountable story.

Score of 1. The writing is sketchy or loosely focused. The reader must make many inferences to grasp the writer's main point. The writing reflects more than one of these problems:

- ✔ The writer still needs to clarify the topic.
- ✔ The writer has assembled a loose collection of factlets that do not, as yet, have any real focus.
- ✔ Everything seems as important as everything else.
- ✔ It is hard to identify the main theme or story: What is this writer's main point or purpose?

ORGANIZATION

Organization is the internal structure of the piece—like a skeleton or the framework of a building. Strong organization begins with an engaging lead and wraps up with a thought-provoking close. In between, the writer links each detail or new development to a larger picture, building to a turning point or key revelation and always including strong transitions that form a kind of safety net for the reader, who never feels lost.

Score of 5. The order, presentation, or internal structure of the piece is compelling and moves the reader purposefully through the text.

- ✔ The organization showcases the central theme or story line.
- ✔ Details seem to fit right where they are placed, even when the writer hits the reader with a surprise.

*Excerpted from Vicki Spandel, *Creating Writers*, 3d ed. Boston: Allyn and Bacon, 2001.

✔ An inviting lead draws the reader in; a satisfying conclusion helps bring the reader's thinking to closure.

✔ Pacing feels natural and effective; the writer knows just when to linger over details and when to get moving.

✔ Organization flows so smoothly that the reader does not need to think about it.

Score of 3. The organizational structure guides the reader through the text without undue confusion. The route may be circuitous, but the reader can see where this writer is headed.

✔ Sequencing seems reasonably appropriate.

✔ Placement of details is workable, although sometimes predictable.

✔ The introduction and conclusion are recognizable and functional.

✔ Transitions are present but may sound formulaic—for example, "My first point . . . ," "My second point. . . ."

✔ Structure may be so dominant that it overshadows both ideas and voice; it's impossible to stop thinking about it!

Score of 1. Ideas, details, or events seem loosely connected—or even unrelated. It is very hard to see where this writer is headed. The writing reflects more than one of these problems:

✔ The writer skips randomly from point to point, leaving the reader scrambling to follow.

✔ No real lead sets up what follows.

✔ No real conclusion wraps things up.

✔ Missing or unclear transitions force the reader to make big leaps.

✔ It is difficult to see any real pattern or structure in this writing.

VOICE

Voice is the presence of the writer on the page. When the writer's passion for the topic and sensitivity to the audience are strong, the text virtually dances with life and energy, and the reader feels a strong connection to both writing and writer.

Score of 5. The writer's energy and passion for the subject drive the writing, making the text lively, expressive, and engaging.

✔ The tone and flavor of the piece fit the topic, purpose, and audience well.

✔ Clearly, the writing belongs to this writer and no other.

✔ The writer "speaks" to the reader in a way that makes him or her feel like an insider.

✔ Narrative text is open and honest.

✔ Expository or persuasive text is provocative, lively, and designed to prompt thinking.

Score of 3. The writer seems sincere and willing to communicate with the reader on a functional, if somewhat distant, level.

✔ The writer has not quite found his or her voice but is experimenting—and the result is pleasant and sincere, if not highly individual.

✔ Moments here and there snag the reader's attention, but the writer holds passion and spontaneity in check.

✔ The writer often seems reluctant to reveal him or herself and is "there" briefly—then gone.

✔ Although clearly aware of an audience, the writer only occasionally speaks right to that audience.

✔ The writer often seems right on the verge of sharing something truly interesting—but then pulls back as if thinking better of it.

Score of 1. The writer seems distanced from topic, audience, or both; as a result, the text may lack life, spirit, or energy. The writing reflects more than one of these problems:

✔ The writer does not seem to reach out to the audience or to anticipate their interests and needs.

✔ Although it may communicate on a functional level, the writing takes no risks and does not involve or move the reader.

✔ The writer does not yet seem sufficiently at home with the topic to personalize it for the reader.

WORD CHOICE

Word choice is precision in the use of words—wordsmithery. It is the love of language, a passion for words, combined with a skill in choosing words to create just the mood, meaning, impression, or word picture the writer wants to instill in the heart and mind of the reader.

Score of 5. Precise, vivid, natural language paints a strong, clear, and complete picture in the reader's mind.

✔ The writer's message is remarkably clear and easy to interpret.

- ✔ Phrasing is original—even memorable—yet the language is never overdone.
- ✔ Lively verbs lend the writing power. Precise nouns and modifiers make it easy to picture what the writer is saying.
- ✔ Striking words or phrases linger in the writer's memory, often prompting connections, memories, reflective thoughts, or insights.

Score of 3. The language communicates in a routine manner; it gets the job done.

- ✔ Most words are correct and adequate, even if not striking.
- ✔ Energetic verbs or memorable phrases occasionally strike a spark, leaving the reader hungry for more.
- ✔ Familiar words and phrases give the text an "old comfortable couch" kind of feel.
- ✔ In one or two places, language may be overdone—but at least it isn't flat.
- ✔ Attempts at colorful language are full of promise, even when they lack restraint or control.

Score of 1. The writer either overwrites, smothering the message, or else struggles with a limited vocabulary, searching for words or phrases to convey the intended meaning. The writing reflects more than one of these problems:

- ✔ Vague words and phrases ("She was nice . . . ," "It was wonderful . . . ," "The new budget had impact") convey only the most general sorts of messages.
- ✔ Redundancy is noticeable—even distracting.
- ✔ Clichés and tired phrases pop up with disappointing frequency.
- ✔ Words are used incorrectly ("The bus *impelled* into the hotel").
- ✔ The writer overloads the text with ponderous, overdone, or jargonistic language that is tough to penetrate.

SENTENCE FLUENCY

Sentence fluency is finely crafted construction combined with a sense of rhythm and grace. It is achieved through logic, creative phrasing, parallel construction, alliteration, absence of redundancy, variety in sentence length and structure, and a true effort to create language that literally cries out to be spoken aloud.

Score of 5. An easy flow and rhythm combined with sentence sense and clarity make this text a delight to read aloud.

- ✔ Sentences are well crafted, with a strong and varied structure that invites expressive oral reading.
- ✔ Purposeful sentence beginnings show how each sentence relates to and builds on the one before it.
- ✔ The writing has cadence, as if the writer hears the beat in his or her head.
- ✔ Sentences vary in both structure and length, making the reading pleasant and natural, never monotonous.
- ✔ Fragments, if used, add to the style.

Score of 3. The text hums along with a steady beat. It is easy enough to read aloud, although somewhat difficult to read with great expression.

- ✔ Sentences are grammatical and fairly easy to get through, given a little rehearsal.
- ✔ Graceful, natural phrasing intermingles with more mechanical structure.
- ✔ Some variation in length and structure enhances fluency.
- ✔ Some purposeful sentence beginnings help the reader make sentence-to-sentence connections.

Score of 1. A fair interpretive oral reading of this text takes practice. The writing reflects more than one of these problems:

- ✔ Irregular or unusual word patterns make sentences hard to decipher or make it hard to tell where one sentence ends and the next begins.
- ✔ Ideas hooked together by numerous connectives (*and, but, so then, because*) create one gangly, endless "sentence."
- ✔ Short, choppy sentences bump the reader through the text.
- ✔ Repetitive sentence patterns grow monotonous.
- ✔ Transitional phrases are so repetitive that they become distracting.
- ✔ The reader must often pause and reread to get the meaning.

CONVENTIONS

Almost anything a copy editor would attend to falls under the heading of conventions. This includes punctuation, spelling, grammar and usage, capitalization, and paragraphing—the spit-and-polish phase of preparing a document for publication.

Score of 5. The writer has excellent control over a wide range of standard writing conventions and uses them with accuracy and (when appropriate) creativity and style to enhance meaning.

✔ Errors are so few and so minor that a reader can easily overlook them unless searching for them specifically. Highly skilled writers may "play" with conventions for special effect.

✔ The text appears clean, edited, and polished.

✔ Older writers (grade 6 and up) create text of sufficient length and complexity to demonstrate control of a range of conventions appropriate for their age and experience.

✔ The text is easy to mentally process; there is nothing to distract or confuse a reader.

✔ Only light touch-ups would be required to polish the text for publication.

Score of 3. The writer shows reasonable control over the most widely used writing conventions and uses them with fair consistency to create text that is adequately readable.

✔ There are enough errors to distract an attentive reader somewhat; however, errors do not seriously impair readability or obscure meaning.

✔ It is easy enough for an experienced reader to get through the text without stumbling, but the writing clearly needs polishing. It is definitely not "ready for press."

✔ Moderate editing would be required to get this text ready for publication.

✔ The paper reads like an "on its way" rough draft.

Score of 1. The writer demonstrates limited control even over widely used writing conventions. The text reflects at least one of the following problems:

✔ Errors are sufficiently frequent and/or serious as to be distracting; it is hard for the reader to focus on ideas, organization, or voice.

✔ Errors in spelling, punctuation, or grammar cause the reader to pause, decode, or reread to make sense of the text.

✔ Extensive editing would be required to prepare this text for publication.

Index